Thorns in the Flesh

DIVINATIONS: REREADING LATE ANCIENT RELIGION

Series Editors: Daniel Boyarin, Virginia Burrus, Derek Krueger

A complete list of books in the series is available from the publisher.

Thorns in the Flesh

Illness and Sanctity in Late Ancient Christianity

Andrew Crislip

Published by
University of Pennsylvania Press
Philadelphia, Pennsylvania 19104-4112
www.upenn.edu/pennpress

Printed in the United States of America on acid-free paper

10 9 8 7 6 5 4 3 2 1

A Cataloging-in-Publication record is available from the Library of Congress
ISBN 978-0-8122-4445-8

For Grace and Renna

Contents

Introduction

The sick saint has long captured the western imagination. Take Anatole France's 1890 novel *Thaïs*. Although France is no longer fashionable (and is hardly in print in English), from the fin de siècle to the 1920s France spoke of the mentality of the times. He was considered by many "the greatest living author" in 1924 (the year he won the Nobel Prize for literature) and praised by such still-revered authors as Edmund Wilson and Henry James.[1] In *Thaïs*, his most popular novel—an international bestseller translated into eighteen languages—France begins his tale of late ancient Egypt with a graphic, pathological image of the early decades of monastic life. Anchorites and coenobites suffer gladly through harsh ascetic behaviors, making themselves sick. This lifestyle transforms the monk into something injured yet aesthetically desirable: "Mindful of original sin, they refused to give to their bodies not only pleasure and satisfaction but even the care that is considered necessary by those who live in the world. They believed that physical affliction purified the soul and that the flesh could receive no more glorious adornment than ulcers and open sores. Thus was the word of the prophets observed: 'The desert shall be covered with flowers.'"[2]

France's adaptation of the prophet Isaiah evokes the image of the desert as body, erupting with the bloom of diseased ascetics, much as each ascetic's body is adorned by the efflorescence of disease. France places the cultivation of illness at the heart of the nascent monastic movement, a distinctive feature of the exotic world of late ancient Egyptian asceticism. While Athanasius of Alexandria in his *Life of Antony* famously characterized the same period of monasticism's birth as a desert transformed into a city of health, led by Antony as a "physician (*iatros*) for Egypt," in Anatole France's version the desert becomes a garden of disease.[3]

A generation later than France in his native Romania, E. M. Cioran too identified illness as central to the Christian ascetic project, drawing on the lives of the saints he had read as a child and the writings of Friedrich Nietzsche, whose *Genealogy of Morals* is suffused with images of disease, sickness, wounds, quack healing, and self-destruction as characteristics of the ascetic. Cioran writes, "All saints are sick, but luckily not all sick people are saints. . . . Through sickness we understand the saints, and through them, the heavens."[4] Sickness—whether of body, soul, or both he does not specify—is endemic among ascetics; it is also, for both the saintly and the not so saintly, a means of transcendence and *gnōsis*. Throughout his 1937 hagiographical meditation *Tears and Saints*, Cioran returns to the role of Christian asceticism ("saintliness" in Cioran's terminology) as the response—but not the cure, strictly speaking—to humanity's endemic illness. Asceticism embraces and transforms humanity's fallen putrescence: "Had there not been any illnesses in the world, there would not have been any saints, for until now there has not been a single healthy one. Saintliness is the cosmic apogee of illness, the transcendental fluorescence of rot. Illnesses have brought the heavens close to earth. Without them, heaven and earth would not have known each other. The need for consolation went further than any illness and, at the point of intersection between heaven and earth, it gave birth to sainthood."[5] For both France and Cioran, ascetics willingly accept—and even court—disease's embrace as a form of ascetic practice and self-transformation.

Such a characterization of early Christian asceticism is echoed among later critics and historians, as it certainly is in numerous early Christian texts. The Syriac poet Jacob of Serug (c. 451–521) turns rot into an object of aesthetic (and ascetic) transcendence, comparing the stylite Simeon's rotting, gangrenous foot to "a tree, beautiful with branches."[6] The literary theorist Geoffrey Halt Harpham characterizes this perspective well, observing, "For the Christian ascetic, pagan beauty was thematized as the demonic, while the disfigured was figured as the desirable."[7]

Such characterizations make meaning of the illness of saints or ascetics by reading it within the symbolic matrix of Christian salvation history and myth. The anthropologist and psychiatrist Arthur Kleinman notes that cultures make meaning out of illness by interpreting the signs of disease not just—or even primarily—on the plane of diagnostic nosology but within the matrix of shared symbols, principally of religious myth and ideology, forming a cultural meaning of illness that can exist independently of any professionalized medical diagnosis.[8] These "cultural meanings," Kleinman says, "mark the sick person." But as he notes, these meanings are contentious, not automatic. They are the result of individuals reconstructing their own illness narratives within the symbolic matrix at hand. They can also be imposed on the sick unwillingly, "stamping him or her with significance often unwanted and neither easily warded off nor coped with," even as far as "stigma or social death."[9] While the work of Kleinman and the field of medical anthropology have recognized and perhaps heightened the overriding concerns of postmodernity with the meaning of illness (both personal and societal), the meaning of illness posed serious interpretive problems in the symbolic world of late ancient Christians as well.[10]

The symbolic world in question is a familiar one, shared in some measure by the modern writers just cited and the ancient ones who will be the focus of this book. In the early Christian tradition illness, bodily decline and decay, and pain, as Elaine Scarry and Teresa Shaw have variously argued, were understood as direct consequences of the first humans' ejection from Eden and god's curse upon the pair and their descendants.[11] While the Genesis account, on which Scarry and Shaw base their readings, touches only indirectly on illness, as opposed to toil, pain, and ultimately death, the popular and widely translated parabiblical *Life of Adam and Eve* makes the causal connection between the fall and illness painfully clear. Probably written in the first century A.D. but widely read, adapted, and interpolated among Christians through the Middle Ages, the *Life* elevates the status of illness as the prime effect of the fall.[12]

At the end of his 930 years Adam announces that he is sick, leaving his children bewildered, as they have never witnessed illness before. Seth then asks one of the most basic existential questions about being human: "What is pain and illness (*ti estin ponos kai nosos*)?"[13] Adam responds by telling the familiar story of primal sin. But in the *Life of Adam and Eve* god's punishment is not mere toil, labor, and return to dust, as in Genesis 3:16–19, but disease. As god tells the couple, "Because you have forsaken my commandment and have not kept my word which I set for you, behold, I will bring upon your body seventy plagues (*plagas*); you shall be racked with various pains (*diversis doloribus*), from the top of the head and the eyes and ears down to the nails of the feet, and in each separate limb." Adam explains that the seventy plagues apply not only to the transgressors Adam and Eve but also "to all our generations."[14]

The popular *Life of Adam and Eve* thus elaborates on the curse implied in the biblical account. Disease and decrepitude are neither "natural" components of the human body nor diabolical ruses by jealous gods unleashed on humanity (as in Hesiod's version of the Pandora's jar myth) but just punishment for humanity's sins, punishment that must be paid out throughout the generations, forever.[15] Illness is the most visceral sign of humanity's fallenness.

The *Life of Adam and Eve* represents a distinctive emphasis on the part of early Christians, who interpreted illness not simply on the plane of physiology or in the common Greco-Roman "care of the self," but more profoundly within the context of a sacred history of decay, disease, and convalescence.[16] Over a century ago Adolf Harnack well described the ideology that resulted from such an orientation: "Christianity never lost hold of its innate principle; it was, and it remained, a religion for the sick. Accordingly it assumed that no one, or at least hardly any one, was in normal health, but that men (Mensch) were always in a state of disability."[17] The remedy for this illness, both psychic and bodily, naturally lay in the saving sacrifice of Jesus, which left for the church the healing sacraments of baptism ("the recovery of life" in Tertullian), the Eucharist ("the potion of immortality" in Ignatius and many after him), and penitence ("the true medicine derived from the atonement" in Cyprian).[18] And while bodily healings could still function in the charismata of the posta-postolic church, Christians were far more focused on awaiting the final cosmic healing promised at Christ's return.[19]

Within the symbolic matrix of a fall into decrepitude and disease followed by the present, anticipatory state of convalescence, illness (and its absence) among ascetics—the focus of this book—could be read in a number of ways. As will be discussed in more detail in Chapters 2 and 3, early observers of Christian monasticism frequently understood the withdrawal to the desert to rectify the primordial lack on the planes of both morality and physiology: asceticism could restore the health enjoyed by Adam and Eve prior to their ejection from Paradise. In monastic narrative the saint frequently functions as an exemplar, as Peter Brown notes.[20] In this capacity the saint (body and soul) symbolically marks the health made possible after the incarnation. H. J. W. Drijvers observes, "Saints' lives and related literature present conceptions of the person with a specific bodily symbolism that stands for a new relation of the individual to his society. The indwelling of Christ's spirit in each individual transforms him into a son of God, makes him return to his original paradisal state, changes his body into the condition it had before the fall."[21] Early monastic literature luxuriates in such restorative rhetoric, as in the *Letters* and *Life of St. Antony*, the *Asceticon* of Abba Isaiah of Scetis, and the *Life of Paul of Thebes*. The very title of the popular aphoristic collections of the late ancient Syriac world, *The Paradise of the Fathers*, reflects this widespread understanding of Christian asceticism as remedy for postlapsarian maladies.[22] Throughout, the saint's status as symbol and moral exemplar renders his or her health or illness especially meaningful within the symbolic matrix of late ancient Christianity.

But clearly the ascetic reclamation of primordial health is not at work in

France's or Cioran's vivid characterizations of ascetic illness. These ascetics do not accept the benefit of Christ's saving intervention. Rather, they emulate him, as well as the other afflicted saints, such as Job and Paul with his thorn and even Jesus on the cross, all righteously suffering the ills of the world. Within this symbolic matrix, the saint—also as symbol—creates a distinctively Christian meaning out of illness that is at odds with the prevalent restorative rhetoric.[23]

Modernists such as Cioran and France and contemporary theorists such as Harpham reflect a notable trend in early Christian approaches to illness in ascetic practice when they point to the embrace of illness and suffering among the saints, their delight in debility, and the desirability of their disfigurement, as do those who note the paradisiacal, restorative rhetoric of late ancient ascetic discourse. But it would be a mistake to take such generalizations as normative, or even typical, of late ancient mentalities. Rather, these two traditions of making meaning out of illness persist in dialectic and tension. Health is the clearest signifier of the reclamation of paradisiacal wholeness, a garden home of the saint. At the same time illness is the great source of glory for the Christian, nothing short of a martyrdom, at the hands not of empire but of nature.

Ascetics and their followers thus made meaning of illness among the saints within the ambiguous territory of early Christian attitudes toward illness. For all the resonance of France's ulcered ascetics or Harpham's disfigured holy men, the sick ascetic did not presage any such stable meaning, whether reflected through saints' lives, rules, treatises, or letters, public or personal. Illness posed special difficulties for late ancient monks in interpretation and regulation; the following chapters will show that monastic writers read illness in a number of ways, denying any special meaning for monastic illness as well as elevating the health or illness of the monk as a most telling signifier of sanctity. Even among those who saw illness among monks as especially meaningful, monastic authors disagreed sharply over how to make meaning out of it. The following chapters contain an exploration of how late ancients used illness in constructing Christian asceticism and ascetic theology. Late ancient Christians presented asceticism as the cure of humanity's endemic illness and illness as asceticism's apogee, the most effective mode self-mortification. Health became one of the most telling features of monastic hagiography, and in return hagiographers resorted to constructing apologia for monastic illness. Illness points to ambiguities of embodiment: it threatens the ascetic's practice, yet could serve as the model and mode of ascetic transcendence and self-fashioning. Through the diverse perspectives from late antiquity discussed here, I hope to demonstrate that the early Christian ascetics understood the experience of illness as a profoundly problematic one, much like other areas of bodily practice, sex and eating most notably. The sustained debate over the practical, ascetical, and theological meaning of the illness experience opened up new ways for Christians to understand the self, the body, and ascetic practice.

Sources and Scope

I draw on a range of monastic and ascetic sources, from the earliest generations of documentary and literary evidence for Christian monasticism through the mid-sixth century. The focus has been primarily on sources from (or relating to) Egypt and to a lesser extent Cappadocia and Palestine. I have not aimed for comprehensiveness. There are, to be sure, relevant texts not treated here, either at all or in the detail that a given reader might prefer. The writings of Shenoute, for example, offer an as-yet-untapped resource for exploring how an ascetic used his own illness to establish his authority and discipline his community. Since the critical edition of the works of Shenoute, of which I am a contributor, is ongoing and Shenoute's *Canons* 6 and 8 (in which he discusses his illness at length) pose particular textual challenges, it seemed prudent to postpone a comprehensive study of Shenoute's illness (and "illness narrative") for a later opportunity. From the *Apophthegmata patrum*, whose complicated transmission and challenges for historical use too frequently go unrecognized, I have drawn sparingly and not systematically, generally when sayings are related intertextually with other literary sources. A more systematic investigation of the *Apophthegmata* in all their complexity might well reward the researcher. Syriac literature too may offer a wealth of other perspectives that might complement this volume's Egyptian focus, and indeed might take the investigations begun here in a different direction. In the Syriac linguistic context we might think of the importance of healing in Ephrem's theology or the ascetic theology of the physician-monk Simon of Taibutheh, to take just two examples.[24] And while the cultural models of the Bible will be persistently present in the chapters that follow, I do not focus in detail on Patristic exegesis.

Nonetheless, my selection of texts has not been arbitrary, but rather based on their interconnectedness, both temporal and generic and intertextual and thematic. My sources include some of the earliest documentation of Christian monasticism, which lies not in the Lives and Rules of great monastic organizers but in quotidian documents from the early monks and their followers, detritus left behind in garbage pits or later reused to bind papyrus leaves into codices of more lasting value.[25] The greatest concentration of early fourth-century monastic papyri is found in several archives identified as from a monastery called Hathor, a community not otherwise documented in literary sources.[26] Much like the more familiar Pachomian monasteries of Upper Egypt, the monastery of Hathor was united with several others in a federation, although it is not clear what kind of leadership role Hathor played, if any.[27] This federation, known only through the publication of documentary papyri in the past century, rivals that of Pachomius for the title of the first union of monastic communities, and apparently belonged to the Melitian church—a schismatic church popular in many parts of Egypt.[28] More details on these documentary sources are included in Chapter 2.

Contemporary with the monks of Hathor are the *Letters* of Pachomius (c. 292–346). Pachomius founded his first monastery sometime after A.D. 323 near the Theban town of Tabenesse.[29] Whether Pachomius influenced the formation of such Melitian monasteries as that of Hathor or was influenced by them (or whether the systems developed independently) remains an open question.[30] The genuine writings of Pachomius comprise eleven *Letters*, along with several fragments of indeterminate genre. None bears a date, but Pachomius is known to have died in 346. The *Letters* are among the earliest literary witnesses to Egyptian monasticism and among the earliest original literature in Coptic. The *Letters* are preserved with various numerations in Coptic (Pachomius's native tongue), Greek, and Jerome's Latin translation.[31] I focus on Pachomius's fifth *Letter*, among the longest and most thematically unified letters and among the few to avoid Pachomius's vexing use of the religiously significant ciphers that dominate most of his letters.[32]

More widely read than Pachomius's frequently opaque *Letters* are the extensive corpus of *Lives* of the coenobitic pioneer. I focus on one important version of the *Life of Pachomius*, what I have called the "Great Coptic *Life*." The textual transmission of the *Lives* of Pachomius is complex and disputed. The principal version discussed here is preserved by manuscripts (some more completely preserved, some quite fragmentary) in the Sahidic and Bohairic dialects of Coptic and in two Arabic versions. Armand Veilleux refers to this version of the *Life* as the Sahidic-Bohairic *Life* (or *SBo*), a designation that is incomplete (since the Arabic manuscripts are an important witness to the tradition, whatever one makes of Veilleux's stemma) as well as a bit awkward. I refer to it as the Great Coptic *Life*, which distinguishes it from the important and ancient Greek tradition and the various extremely fragmentary Sahidic

Lives (such as the First and Second Sahidic *Lives*).[33] My focus is almost exclusively on this *Life*, but whenever it diverges significantly from the First Greek *Life of Pachomius*—which it does frequently and significantly in descriptions of Pachomius's ill health—I refer to the alternative version there as well. While a lengthy discussion of textual stemmatics is avoided, some explanation is needed of the relationship of the Great Coptic *Life* and the Greek *Vita Prima*. Veilleux has convincingly argued that these two primary narratives of the *bios* of Pachomius are independent; neither is the source of the other, but both draw on a common source that gives at least a basic narrative of the life of Pachomius and of his main successors, Petronius, Horsiese, and Theodore.[34] My interest here lies not in reconstructing the life of the "historical Pachomius" but in how one particular collection of stories shaped the memory and memorialization of this important saint in narrative form.[35]

I also look to the seven *Letters* attributed to a contemporary "founder" of Christian asceticism, Antony (c. 251–356), whose *Life*, probably authored by Bishop Athanasius of Alexandria shortly after the monk's death, ranks among the formative cultural productions of late ancient Christianity, and which I also discuss. Much like the other early monastic letters, and unlike Athanasius's influential *Life of Antony*, the *Letters* composed by the famous hermit are relatively little known, even among readers of early Christian ascetic literature. Their lack of familiarity is due in some measure to the complexities of their transmission. The only reliable and complete version of the *Letters* is preserved in Georgian, an obstacle to most scholars of early Christianity, although fragmentary or clearly flawed versions were transmitted in numerous other languages.[36] Furthermore, their frequently abstract and explicitly Origenist contents have not endeared them to a scholarly community more drawn to the stark simplicity of the sayings of the desert fathers or the drama of the lives of holy harlots. Yet after decades of relative neglect, scholars such as Samuel Rubenson and David Brakke have rehabilitated the *Letters* of Antony in recent decades and returned this corpus to its proper place among the earliest witnesses to the intellectual culture of nascent monasticism.[37]

Antony probably wrote his original letters in Coptic, which if so would make Antony one of the earliest original literary writers in the Coptic language, along with Pachomius.[38] Dating the letters is problematic since we know little about the chronology of Antony's life apart from his death in 356.[39] The *Life of Antony*, even if it were considered a reliable witness to Antony's biography, provides little in the way of detail by which we could date the letters. Samuel Rubenson, who has done the most in recent years to bring this epistolary corpus to the attention of historians of late ancient Christianity, argues that Antony's criticism of the Arians, along with the general absence of explicitly Athanasian theology, plausibly points to a date in the 330s or perhaps as late as the 340s.[40] In any case, Antony's death in 356 is a secure *terminus ante quem*.

The *Life of Antony* will also cast a long shadow over the sources explored in this book. The *Life* was probably written between 356 and 360 and is traditionally attributed to Bishop Athanasius of Alexandria. There are numerous good reasons to accept that attribution, although it is still debated.[41] At the very least it concords well with Athanasian theology, and no clear evidence disproves Athanasius's authorship.[42] I take it as generally convincing that Athanasius wrote the *Life* and will refer to him as author below without repeating the previously given caveat. That said, the historical facticity of his authorship is not particularly relevant for my argument. The *Life* will probably be among the most familiar of the sources examined in the volume, and its importance and influence in establishing a popular literature about monasticism hardly need arguing.[43] The *Life of Antony* would come to establish much of the contours of the monastic *bios* as a genre in antiquity.[44]

In addition to the *Lives* of Pachomius and Antony, I draw on other early monastic hagiographies, which in general reflect and adapt the sorts of narrative structures and theological orientations of the *Life of Antony*. Jerome's *Life of Paul of Thebes* is a relatively familiar representative of the literary and theological interests of post-Athanasian hagiographers and offers an important rereading of the Athanasian model of the healthy saint. Jerome's *Letters* too offer an important perspective on the meaning of illness in the life of the ascetic. Perhaps less familiar, but even more interesting for my purposes, is the *Life of Onnophrius*, written by a certain Paphnutius, an Egyptian probably writing around the turn of the fifth century who also composed *Histories of the Monks of Upper Egypt*. Beyond these two books we have no further information about the identity of Paphnutius; it was a common name among monks and monkish writers, and there are a number of possible identities among the known namesakes. Tim Vivian has identified ten possible matches and concludes that the most likely author was a Paphnutius Cephalas of the northern Egyptian community of Scetis. This Paphnutius was known for having traveled widely in the 390s, and the *Life of Onnophrius* has a clear connection to Scetis.[45] Nevertheless the precise identity of the author remains uncertain. Regardless, the text can be placed in the late fourth or early fifth century and would become a popular hagiography in the late ancient Mediterranean and Near East as well as in medieval Europe, preserved in Greek, Latin, Coptic, Arabic, Ethiopic, and other languages.[46] I use the Sahidic Coptic version of the *Life*, as preserved in a British Museum manuscript published by E. A. W. Budge.[47]

I draw on other biographical narratives, such as the *Lausiac History* of Palladius of Helenopolis, dating to around 420; the anonymous *History of the Monks of Egypt*, a hagiographical travelogue written about 400; Theodoret's famous *Religious History* of the monks of Syria, written about 440; and other occasional writings about the lives of ascetics.[48] I also draw on the biographical materials included in the *Life and Regimen of the Blessed and Holy Teacher Syncletica*, pseudonymously attributed to Athanasius of Alexandria but at any rate written in the tradition of the *Life of Antony*.[49] Like the *Life of Antony*, the *Life of Syncletica* includes an extended section of teaching intended especially for the ascetics (primarily women) who looked to her for spiritual and ascetic guidance. These teachings offer a useful counterpoint to the predominantly hagiographical tone of the remainder of her *Life* and the other major hagiographies of the fourth and early fifth centuries.

I look to other contemporary literature focused not on narrative but on moral exhortation and practical advice for the ascetic life, in particular writings of Basil of Caesarea and Evagrius of Pontus. In addition to Basil's own letters and a homily, *That God Is Not the Cause of Evil*, the "rules" of Basil, the *Shorter Rules* and the *Longer Rules*, are examined. The *Shorter* is a collection of 313 questions and relatively brief answers about the ascetic life, the *Longer* a collection of 55 questions answered at much greater length by Basil. These "rules" thus differ significantly in form from the famous and influential regulae of Pachomius, Augustine, and Benedict. Some, such as in Anna Silvas's recent translation, prefer to call them the *Responses*, but with the preceding caveat, I will use their traditional names (*regulae, horoi*).[50]

Evagrius of Pontus (346–99) taught and practiced in the Egyptian monastery of Kellia ("The Cells") in the last two decades of the fourth century. Of his voluminous ascetic and theological writings I draw on two treatises in particular, the *Praktikos* and *On Thoughts*. Evagrius was a mystic and an ascetic theorist, but he was also interested in the practical techniques of monastic life, especially as developed in the semi-eremitical lavras of northern Egypt. He wrote in the generation following Basil and his Cappadocian contemporaries, and in fact was closely connected to them. Ordained a reader by Basil, Evagrius was later ordained archdeacon by Gregory of Nazianzus during his tenure as bishop of Constantinople.[51] Thus it will not be surprising if there are commonalities between them.[52]

Evagrius was to be marginalized as a thinker primarily for his elaboration of a speculative theology based on some controversial elements of Origen's thought. Many of Evagrius's prolific writings were lost. Some treatises were transmitted pseudonymously (especially under the name of Nilus of Ancyra), while others were preserved only in the languages of the eastern churches, especially Armenian and Syriac.[53] Some were preserved under his own name in Greek, so great was his prestige and influence, but these treatises were limited to his more practical writings on the ascetic life. His ascetic and mystical theology forms the basis of much of the Christian mystical tradition—in the West through the influence of his protégé John Cassian and in the East through such writers as Maximus Confessor and John Climacus. Evagrius's influence is still felt, for example, in the tradition of the "eight evil thoughts" (later condensed to seven cardinal—and later deadly—sins), a psychological and spiritual set of theories expounded throughout Evagrius's large corpus of writings (and which we return to in Chapter 6).[54] Elements of his spiritual and compositional technique would have a long history in the Greek ascetic tradition.[55] A generation ago Evagrius's literary corpus and influence were largely unrecognized, even among historians of late antiquity. The situation is very different today.

As a more intimate reflection of the role and strategies of the spiritual director to wrestle with the meaning and function of illness in asceticism I turn to a remarkable body of literature that has been relatively little used as a source for late ancient monasticism: the *Letters* of Barsanuphius and John (active in the first half of the sixth century).[56] The *Letters* (also called the *Correspondence* and *Questions and Responses*) resemble in form the *Rules* or *Responses* of Basil the Great but are far more expansive both in size and in the range of concerns addressed, and are addressed to individuals rather than communities.[57] The correspondence includes some 848 letters from Barsanuphius and John, the "Great Old Men" from the monastery of Thavatha in Gaza, responding to a wide range of queries from other monks and laypeople.[58] Notably the collection also includes the requests that prompted the responses, frequently in summary but often including extracts from the actual letters, sometimes even their entirety. The *Correspondence* as a whole was edited by an anonymous disciple, a contemporary of the Great Old Men (some suggest it was Dorotheus of Gaza, an equally influential writer from Thavatha).[59] The *Correspondence* provides an interesting counterpoint to other, earlier sources. As much as the spiritual and psychagogic practices of the Great Old Men reflect the orientations and arguments of such teachers as Basil, Evagrius, and the desert Abbas and Ammas, the dialogic format of the *Correspondence*, as well as its temporal span, provides a view of the contentiousness and disagreement that were inevitably part of ascetic life. Even in this late collection echoes of the concerns about the meaning and function of illness raised in earlier sources can be heard. Job and Paul and Antony and the desert fathers and mothers are present intertextually in the Gazan correspondence.

*   *   *

The volume is divided into six chapters. Chapter 1 establishes some contextual and methodological base points for the chapters that follow. Illness proved problematic for late ancient writers in two broad aspects: its function and its meaning. Functionally illness aids the ascetic process of self-formation, yet it undermines core ascetic values, especially self-control. Furthermore, when placed in the context of the dominant symbolic world of the time, illness's meaning is equally ambiguous, being the most obvious sign of punishment for transgression against god as well as an affliction borne by the just and holy. Given the fundamental ambiguity in Christianity's unique attitude toward illness and illness's impact (in Christian asceticism and cross-culturally) on ascetic behavior in general, we should not be surprised at the contentious approaches that late ancient Christians took toward making sense of illness in ascetic life.

Chapter 2 looks at three of the earliest collections of monastic literature, including archives of letters written to monks at a Monastery of Hathor in the 340s and 350s, the circular *Letters* of Pachomius written to the communities that made up his monastic federation, and the *Letters* of Antony, written also to other monastic communities.[60] These three letter collections are interesting both for what they say about questions of the meaning and utility of illness among ascetics and for what they do not say. While the silence of sources has limits in what it can tell, at the very least it shows what the authors understood to be most important to present. Of the three early monastic letter collections, the *Letters* of Antony receive the most attention, as we witness in them what may be the earliest elaboration of the paradisiacal, restorative rhetoric of Christian asceticism.

Chapter 3 traces the growth of health and illness as central themes in the hagiographical literature of monasticism. The focus will be on the *Life of Antony* and two later hagiographies that treat similar themes: the *Life of Paul* by Jerome and the *Life of Onnophrius* by Paphnutius. These important hagiographies contrast in important ways with the less reflective letters discussed in Chapter 2. Now the meaning of ascetic healthiness and its utility (or lack thereof) in the ascetic project is a central concern. While Antony in his *Letters* drew on common Christus medicus and Origenist theology to characterize Christian asceticism as healing the cosmic wound of the fall and able to lead to spiritual health for the ascetic, Athanasius in his *Life of Antony* similarly promotes the vision of the ascetic who reclaims bodily health as well. The health of the ascetic thus becomes a signifier of the monk's virtue. While this would be exceptionally influential in later circles, it was not without controversy, even among those who adopted the Antonian *Life* as a basic template for the monastic bios. Jerome's *Life of Paul* and Paphnutius's *Life of Onnophrius* each critique the basic Antonian approach to ascetic illness and health while at the same time work within the same model of ascetic life writing.

Chapter 4 engages other types of late ancient writing that take up these same issues, including letters, rules, didactic treatises, and gnomic sayings. They show that ascetics of a variety of stripes and interests were vexed by the meaning of illness among ascetics and its usefulness for the ascetic project. Through reading ascetic treatises by Basil of Caesarea and Evagrius of Pontus, select *Letters* of Jerome, and the *Life of Syncletica*, we see that illness was a contentious issue that in many ways cut to the heart of the ascetic project in late antiquity. Ascetic writers debated how, in the plane of ascetic practice rather than in the plane of hagiography, the monk should react to illness. As the *Letters* of Jerome suggest, the illness of an ascetic could cause considerable controversy for those around the ascetic, both followers and critics. Within hermitages and coenobia as well, the sick ascetic posed a crisis of interpretation and of communal order. The writings of Basil, Evagrius, and Syncletica reflect three approaches to the challenges to meaning and practice that illness posed for late ancient ascetics.

Chapter 5 looks at the Great Coptic *Life of Pachomius*, which reflects interestingly the hagiographical conventions discussed in Chapter 3 (both the Antonian commonplaces and the subversions of those narrative conventions) and the sort of disciplinary interests on display in Chapter 4. In the Great Coptic *Life of Pachomius* we witness the full development of a different type of saint, a chronically ill and weak saint, set up as a counterpoint to the dominant model of ascetic health promoted by the *Life of Antony*.

Chapter 6 draws on elements from the previous four chapters to show how these controversies over meaning and utility function in the correspondence of spiritual direction between the "Great Old Men" Barsanuphius and John and an elderly sick monk named Andrew. These fifty-two letters are an extraordinary archive of the process of spiritual direction in late antiquity. Written a century or more after most of the other sources discussed in this volume, they show that the interpretation of illness as a component of monastic and ascetic life—and the contentiousness that it provoked—was not something simply limited to the imaginary worlds of hagiography; it really did cut to the heart of the day-to-day concerns of ascetics. Their letters also show that the ambiguities and controversies provoked by illness among ascetics would not be easily solved. The issues continued to cause problems in the monastery of Thavatha in sixth-century Gaza. The correspondence of the Great Old Men and Andrew offers valuable insight into the difficulties of making illness meaningful in an ascetic life and reveals that the answers and interpretations offered by the leading ascetic thinkers of Christian antiquity might not have always convinced the monks they were intended to console. The Conclusion provides a look at an overlooked narrative of ascetic illness and consolation in Theodoret of Cyrrhus's *Historia religiosa*.

It will be clear that certain elements are emphasized. In my previous book, *From Monastery to Hospital*, I focused on more "ordinary" monks (at least as represented in early monastic rules and gnomic literature) and especially focused on healing, largely avoiding issues of theology. Here I am interested in illness rather than healing and furthermore on the pitfalls of interpretation for sickness among saints, leaders, and moral exemplars. I am not the first to note such issues, but the considerable scholarship on illness and healing in early Christianity has tended to focus either on systematic or historical theology (more narrowly construed), or healing and medicine, which are not my primary concern.[61] Some, in more targeted studies, have indeed noted tensions over illness and meaning endemic in late ancient monastic literature. These have been useful touchstones in my evolving thoughts about these issues.[62] This volume explores in some detail a corpus of related texts from late antiquity that point to the persistence of a complicated and complicating discourse about the meaning and role of illness in the life of the ascetic and saint, and the distinct changes in discourse over the course of the late ancient Mediterranean world.

Chapter 1

Illness, Sanctity, and Asceticism in Antiquity: Approaches and Contexts

Preserved in the Nag Hammadi Codices, and thus copied and transmitted roughly contemporarily with many of the Egyptian texts discussed in this book, the *Apocryphon of James* records the risen Jesus saying to the apostles, "Know, then, that [the Son of Man] treated (*afrpahre*) you when you were ill (*šōne*) that you might reign. Woe to those who have recovered (*mtan*) from their illness, for they will relapse into illness. Blessed are they who have not been ill, and have known recovery before falling ill; yours is the kingdom of God."[1] While Jesus's secret words echo the blessings and woes of Luke's Gospel, itself replete with healings by the savior and his disciples (especially the sequel Acts of the Apostles), his talk of sickness and healing points not to the bodily ill; this is no Lucan Gospel of faith healing. Rather, the language of treatment, healing, and recovery points to the process of *gnōsis* and salvation, much like the metaphor of newfound sobriety after a long bender, familiar also from the *Apocryphon of James* and other Valentinian texts.[2] Whether the healing is on the plane of the body or of the soul, the intuitive understanding expected of the reader is quite the same. Health is preferable to illness. Health is a blessing. Health signifies god's favor and marks its possessor as among the elect, the saved.

While the meaning that the *Apocryphon*'s Jesus ascribes to health and illness as blessing and curse is straightforward, illness's meaning for early Christians becomes considerably more slippery and contentious when the ostensibly elect, blessed, and holy themselves fall ill. We can witness the difficulty of making meaning of the illnesses of late ancient ascetics in two related stories from the *Lausiac History*, a hybrid memoir and travelogue by Palladius (c. 365–425, later a bishop in Bithynia) written around A.D. 420. In the last decade of the fourth century, Palladius lived as an itinerant among the monastic communities of northern Egypt (he also included a few stories from Upper Egypt and the Levant). One day as he sat in the cell of his spiritual master Evagrius (to whom I will return in Chapter 4), Dioscorus, the community priest, came by. "Come here," Dioscorus said, "see a new Job who possesses boundless gratitude while in a state of great bodily swelling and incurable sickness (*pathei aniatōi*)."[3] Away they went, says Palladius, to find Apa Benjamin, a respected elder in the community known for his charismatic power to heal others by the holy spirit. Palladius, Dioscorus, and Evagrius found Benjamin grotesquely disfigured with dropsy, the ancient term (and current through the nineteenth century) for severe water retention. He was so swollen "that another person's fingers could not reach around one of his."[4] Eventually the saint was rendered wholly immobile, and his disciples resorted to constructing a wide bench to support his corpulent body. As a final indignity, after his death the monks had to disassemble the door jambs to remove his corpse.

The depiction of the saint hints at the symbolic power of the sick or disfigured ascetic noted by France, Cioran, and Harpham, but also its symbolic instability. Palladius is unwilling to narrate Benjamin's illness in such a straightforward manner, to present the saint as transcendent in his illness, either a diseased flower or a desirable disfigured; he furthermore anticipates that his readers will not be inclined to embrace the paradoxical reading of ascetic illness generalized by Harpham. Rather, he recognizes a disjunction between sanctity and the spectacle of illness.

Palladius's reticence in the face of Benjamin's suffering may be due to the sheer grotesquery of his suffering. Yet I suspect more is at play here. The narrative echoes of such swelling evoke the punishments of sinners, even the very worst of transgressors. In his *Exposition of the Sayings of the Lord*, the second-century writer Papias described the demise of Judas as not from hanging but from dropsy, perhaps elaborating on his curious death by spontaneous disembowelment in Acts 1:18. In Papias's telling, Judas Iscariot swelled so severely from dropsy that he could not squeeze through Jerusalem's narrow alleys, a humiliation much like Benjamin's inability to fit through his cell door. The parallels with the account of Benjamin are striking:

> Judas was a terrible, walking example of ungodliness in this world, his flesh so bloated that he was not able to pass through a place where a wagon passes easily, not even his bloated head by itself. For his eyelids, they say, were so swollen that he could not see the light at all, and his

eyes could not be seen, even by a doctor using an optical instrument, so far had they sunk below the outer surface. . . . . After much agony and punishment, they say, he finally died in his own place, and because of the stench the area is deserted and uninhabitable even now; in fact, to this day no one can pass that place unless they hold one's nose, so great was the discharge from his body and so far did it spread over the ground.[5]

Traditions of Judas swelling and bursting were widespread in antiquity, sometimes assimilated to the familiar Matthean version of his hanging.[6] To an ancient reader familiar with common biblical and extrabiblical stories of Judas's sickness and death, Benjamin's death could evoke a narrative not of transcendent and expiatory suffering but of well-deserved punishment. Whether or not Palladius had such stories of Judas in his mind is unclear. Yet it is clear that it is reflecting these sorts of concerns—if not necessarily Papias's narrative—that Palladius concludes the story with a revealing caveat: "I felt that I must tell about this sickness so that we might not be too puzzled (*xenizōmetha*) when some accident (*peristatikon*) befalls just men (*andrasi dikaiois*)."[7] That is, while France or Cioran might have read this narrative as a customary reflection of the transformation of illness into ascetic transcendence, Palladius betrays no such confidence in the meaning of the saint's decline. At the very least he anticipates that his audience might not know how to make sense of this bloated saint and to find the transcendent meaning in his grotesque end.

Later in his memoir Palladius includes a second story with the same pattern and same curiously dissatisfying conclusion. This time the sick saint, Stephen, suffers a cancer, which Palladius describes with such physiological clarity that at least one modern translator has felt it necessary to censor the passage: "He suffered from the condition called cancer, which produced ulcers all over his testicles and the head of the penis (*kat' autous tous topous tōn didumōn kai tēs balanou*)."[8] In the cultural symbolic codes of illness and suffering in antiquity, like today, venereal disease could evoke moral disapproval, or at least a suspicion of sin. The connection between venereal diseases and sin, not surprisingly, runs deep in Christian tradition. Again according to Papias elsewhere in the fragment quoted previously, even Judas was afflicted with disease of the genitals: "His genitals appeared more loathsome and larger than anyone else's, and when he relieved himself there passed through it pus and worms from every part of his body, much to his shame."[9] More to the point, elsewhere in the *Lausiac History*, Palladius tells of another monk, Heron, who had sex with a prostitute and then developed a "carbuncle (*anthrax*) on the head of his penis (*kat' autēs tēs balanou*)," echoing the very same language of Stephen's case.[10] In both cases venereal ailments are almost inherently symptomatic of sin, and not befitting a holy man.[11]

Stephen's story points not only to the difficulty in making meaning out of the illness of ascetics; it furthermore—unlike Benjamin's sorry tale—points to the potential usefulness of illness in or as ascetic practice. Stephen also reflects the transcendent and transformative potential of illness that Cioran hints at, as he rises above any pain in his treatment: "We found him under the care of a physician. He was working with his hands and weaving palm leaves and he conversed with us while his body was undergoing an operation. He acted as though it were someone else who was undergoing the knife. While his members were being cut away like locks of hair, he showed no sign whatsoever of pain, thanks to the superiority of his spiritual preparation."[12] By juxtaposing Stephen's asceticism (mat weaving, the ascetic enterprise par excellence) with his surgery, Palladius equates the two activities as signifiers of his sanctity: his handiwork interweaving strips of palm fiber and his steadfastness as strips of his flesh are excised.

Yet despite the inspiring image of his self-control and thanksgiving in the face of illness and suffering, Palladius does not offer an unambiguous reading of the events. Witnessing his treatment, the monks Ammonius and Evagrius—who had told the tale to Palladius—note that they "were grieving at this (*hupolupoumenōn*) and were disgusted (*siainomenōn*) that a person who lived a life like his should suffer disease (*pathei*) and such surgical remedies."[13] Here, as in the story of Benjamin, Palladius's narrative gaze betrays no desire for the disfigured or delight in the bloom of disease. He anticipates no desire on the part of his readers either—only confusion and disgust. So Palladius concludes with the same proviso as in the story of Benjamin: "Now I have told this so that we may not be puzzled (*xenizōmetha*) when we see holy people (*hagious*) falling prey to sickness (*pathesin*)."[14]

In one of the more intensive analyses of these episodes, Virginia Burrus interprets these two clearly linked episodes as demonstrations of Palladius's overriding concern with shame and humiliation. She makes much of Benjamin's swelling as a signifier of pride, "powerfully linked" with Benjamin's "excess of fleshly humiliation."[15] To be sure, Palladius elsewhere reflects on shame and humiliation, against their antipode pride, as components of ascetic self-fashioning. Yet it is worth noting that Palladius never mentions shame or humiliation in the stories of Stephen and Benjamin. Burrus notes the lack of pride in the discussion of Benjamin as indicating his status as a "somewhat anomalous figure."[16] The anomalous absence of shame language in the story of these sick saints is important. While one might presume from an essentialist perspective that shame and humiliation must be at play, imputing emotions to historical actors or writers is slippery business, as Barbara Rosenwein argues in her history of early medieval emotions.[17] If we accept that emotions are at least to some extent "constructed" (and not universal, biological features), it is imperative to attend to the words used (a subject I return to in the next chapter). With this in mind, in Palladius's narration of Stephen's cancer, the onlookers do not perceive shame on Stephen's part nor express their own shame at witnessing his humiliation. Rather they are "saddened" and "disgusted," very different emotions indeed. Of course we have no unmediated access to the "real" emotions of the actors in the story, only Palladius's rhetorical telling. Whatever Palladius wishes to impart in these striking tales, a theological meditation on shame and humiliation—or the "instability of bodies" or "excess of flesh" for that matter—is subordinate to other concerns.

More important to Palladius's stories of Benjamin and Stephen is his curious caveat at the close of each, that we should not be puzzled at the sickness of holy people. Burrus insightfully notes that "this justification is not fully satisfying, not least because it sits uneasily within the context of Palladius's strong emphasis on a divine providence that does not usually seem to leave much room for accidents."[18] Such explanations (or failures to explain) would have been unsatisfying to ancient readers as well. These passages betray the contentiousness and ambiguity in the meaning and function of illness among ascetics at the turn of the fifth century. In each case Palladius fails to offer a straightforward attempt to make meaning of the ascetic's illness. Rather, he defers interpretation. Modern literary or philosophical accounts, such as those of France and Cioran, not to mention numerous historical accounts, do not normally acknowledge such ambiguities of the role of bodily illness in ascetic practice. Yet Christian sources from the late Roman Empire are in fact rife with such ambiguities, even outright controversies over the meaning and function of illness within asceticism.

We may compare Palladius's stories with the homilies of John Chrysostom (c. 347–407). Chrysostom—who had been forced to abandon the ascetic life due to his own declining health—devotes two homilies to precisely this question: Why do the saints fall ill?[19] More specifically, what does it mean theologically and ascetically for the saint to fall ill? In the first *Homily on the Statues*, delivered in 387, Chrysostom takes 1 Timothy 5:23 as his prompt, as

Paul encourages Timothy to drink wine for his many infirmities or illnesses (*tas puknas sou astheneias*). Chrysostom's concerns point to the difficulties in making sense of illness among the ostensibly holy, as well as the disruption in social relations between the saints and their clients that ascetic illness causes. Why, Chrysostom asks, voicing his audience's concerns, would God allow such a holy man to fall ill, especially a man whose relics were endowed with healing abilities? Why, furthermore, would he be allowed to suffer such chronic illness? Why did Timothy, if he was in fact so holy a man, not simply heal himself? And how could a man, on whom so many of God's people depended, be allowed to suffer so, thus bringing hardship on the community as a whole?[20]

Chrysostom is at no loss for answers, not all equally compelling. There are eight reasons why the holy fall ill: illness prevents the saints from falling prey to vainglory and arrogance; it proves to others that they are indeed human and not divine; it better reveals god's power when preached through the weak and sick; it proves that ascetics and saints do not live their lives out of hope for earthly rewards; it may convince others of the reality of the resurrection, since even the holiest of men are not rewarded in this lifetime; it consoles those who have also fallen ill; it prevents followers from being dissuaded from imitating the saints, assuming them to partake of a different physiological nature; and it allows Christians to distinguish between the truly blessed and the cursed.[21]

In his *Homily 16 on Timothy*, Chrysostom reflects the same arguments, now contrasting Timothy's illnesses with Paul's "thorn in the flesh" in 2 Corinthians 12:7. Here his response to saintly suffering echoes that of Palladius: "What then was [Paul's] purpose [in not healing Timothy outright]? That even now, if we see great and virtuous men afflicted with infirmities (*asthenountas*), we may not be offended (*mē scandalizōmetha*), for this was a profitable visitation (*sumpherontōs*)."[22] But as for Paul's own thorn, Chrysostom elsewhere denies that it was any such illness—to suggest as much would be impious: "There are some then who have said that [Paul] means [by 'thorn' and 'messenger of Satan'] a kind of pain in the head which was inflicted of the devil; but God forbid! For the body of Paul never could have been given over to the hands of the devil."[23] Ambivalence toward the illnesses of saints runs deep. Chrysostom chides his audience for being offended at the sight of sick holy men yet is himself scandalized at the thought of Paul's "thorn" from Satan as a physical ailment (arguably the easiest reading).

John Cassian (c. 360–430), a foundational writer of the western European monastic tradition and, like Palladius, a disciple of Evagrius of Pontus, addressed a similar morally ambiguous occurrence at some length in his *Conferences*, "On the Slaughter of Some Holy Persons" (*De nece sanctorum*). While Cassian is, like Chrysostom, concerned with meaning, ethics, and theodicy, he is moreover interested in the function of illness in asceticism. Barbarian brigands had swept through a desert monastery in Palestine and slaughtered the holy men with impunity, and Cassian responds to the same interpretive dilemma that Palladius reflects in the stories of the holy Benjamin and Stephen. Some brothers, Cassian writes, were "scandalized" (*scandalizantium*) and "wondered why men of such great worthiness and of so many virtues (*cur tanti meriti ac tantarum virtutum viri*) would be slain by bandits and why the Lord had permitted such a crime to be perpetrated on his servants."[24] This concern is not unique to Cassian; Gregory of Nazianzus reflects in a similar vein on the death of his sister Gorgonia.[25] Whether the saints suffer wounds of violence or the violence of disease, it poses the same moral quandary for Cassian, and he reflects on the illnesses and deaths of saints and sinners—Job, Lazarus, John the Baptist, Judas, the wicked kings of Israel—throughout this *Conference*.[26] The main issue at hand, and the cause of the scandal at the death of the monks, is that some of "little faith and knowledge . . . think that the deserts and rewards of holy persons . . . are given in the short space of this life."[27] In Chapter 3 I explore where such ill-informed people (from Cassian's perspective) might have gotten the idea that saintly monks would receive special rewards in the desert.

Cassian acknowledges the ambiguities of illness and the potential value of illness to asceticism more directly than do Chrysostom and Palladius. Cassian points out that despite all the biblical testimonies of the suffering of the wicked and the bodily reward of the righteous (3.4), illness does not reliably signify the moral decay of the sufferer, nor does health reflect piety (for example, 10.5, 11.1). Cassian draws on the common Stoic triad of good, bad, and indifferent (3.1): illness and untimely death are indifferent, and good and bad exist only in how the sufferer reacts to the circumstances. Illness, in fact, can function as a mode of sanctification and self-improvement. As an example Cassian cites the beggar Lazarus of Luke's Gospel, who, though "full of sores, shows how useful (*commoda*) even bodily sickness (*infirmitas etiam carnis*) can sometimes be."[28] Cassian notes that the scriptures fail to mention any virtues that might distinguish the "blessedness of Lazarus"—kindness, generosity, piety, asceticism, and so on—save one: "he very patiently bore deprivation and bodily sickness." For this alone "he deserved to possess Abraham's bosom as his blessed destiny."[29]

For Cassian, thus, the illness or injury of the ascetic is potentially scandalous: a challenge to meaningfulness, especially since the symbolic world of Christianity offers ambiguous and contradictory models for making sense of illness. Yet illness itself may be of special use as a type of asceticism, a "spiritual exercise" or a "technology of the self," in the terminology of Pierre Hadot or Michel Foucault.[30] Proper behavior in the face of illness facilitates the process of paying attention to oneself to transform the self.[31] In the case of Lazarus, his practice of illness surpasses the value of any other good practices.

The unfolding of the episodes as described by Palladius and the contemporary treatises of Chrysostom and Cassian reflect conflicting elements of Christian experience that are clarified in the crucible of late ancient culture. Arthur Kleinman has noted that "[s]ocial reality is so organized that we do not routinely inquire into the meanings of illness any more than we regularly analyze the structure of our social world."[32] I have no doubt that for many in antiquity the sheer ubiquity of injury and sickness often rendered them unremarkable and without urgent need for much interpretation. In other cases, as we see in some late ancient ascetic literature, illness demanded meaning. In antiquity, however, meaning need not have necessitated any investigation into the soul or moral character of the sufferer. Literary sources as far back as archaic Greece reflect this. The *Iliad* opens with the mysterious plague of the Achaeans, of which a seer is able to determine the divine source. Hesiod interprets all human illness as owing to the primordial envy of the gods, unleashed upon humans from Pandora's opened jar.[33] We might also consider Sophocles's *Philoctetes*, stranded on an island by his companions and suffering from a lingering snake bite as he rails against the injustice of the gods.[34] But in such typical ancient literary reflections on the etiology and meaning of illness, there is little point in examining the soul and character of the sufferer; the authors do not focus on the sufferer's morality as much as on the gods' capriciousness (and in Philoctetes's case the trickery of his rivals). After all, it is not Agamemnon who suffers plague from the wrath of Apollo for his crime but other soldiers uninvolved in the intrigue. In Hesiod's poem the roving diseases are mute: they no longer attack humans for any reasons that can speak to us.[35]

The intent here is not to draw a strict contrast between Christian and non-Christian sources. Nonetheless, unlike early Greek texts (which would continue to be influential through late antiquity), late ancient ascetic literature focuses overwhelmingly on the moral and religious interpretation of illness. Especially for the exceptional, the ascetic, or the holy, illness and health were laden with meaning, signifiers of both sin and sainthood, of god's guiding presence and his wrath. Late ancient Christians—ascetics and their observers—needed to make sense of illness as part of the ascetic or self-forming practice of Christianity. In the development and spread of the nascent monastic movements, Christians debated what sickness or health could reveal about the inner soul and ascetic merit of the Christian. A number of writers—such as Palladius, Chrysostom, and Cassian—were so immersed in this debate over meaning that they felt the need to justify the sickness (or health) of a holy man. In the eyes of some, illness came to be regarded as a useful component of Christian asceticism, even the highest form of asceticism. Others presented health as the surest signifier of ascetic sanctity. Still others withheld judgment. This volume investigates how such debates took hold of the late ancient imagination about monasticism.

Some Notes on Method and Approach

The reflections of Palladius, John Chrysostom, and John Cassian on the illnesses and misfortunes that befell the saints of either the Bible or the desert each in its own way highlights two broad and interrelated concerns among late ancient Christians about illness: its function and its meaning. Both of these elements play significant parts in the chapters to come (though not necessarily in equal measure). Here some preliminary methodological orientation for approaching each of these problems of interpretation is set out. The approach in this study is intentionally eclectic, informed by cultural anthropology, social psychology, and phenomenology of religion.[36] I turn first to the methodological perspectives on the function or role of illness in or as an ascetic practice and then to the ways of making meaning out of illness.

The Function of Illness

The location of the ascetic in antiquity was by default a liminal one, posed at the fault lines of contradictory social expectations and values. Aviad Kleinberg has described this tug of war as the "ascetic pendulum." Ascetics are expected—in his example—"to adopt two contradictory modes of behavior," to withdraw from the dominant society (the process of *anakhōrēsis*, becoming an anchorite) as well as "to be close enough to edify and serve the community and its often rather worldly needs."[37] The passages just discussed from Palladius,

Chrysostom, and Cassian show that the late ancient ascetic did not dwell merely between the conflicting imperatives for withdrawal and engagement, but in the midst of contradictory expectations about ascetic health. Does the ascetic partake of the reclamation of prelapsarian health, the paradisiacal bliss of the primordial humans? Or does the ascetic gain transcendence through the abasement and suffering of illness as a process of ascetic self-fashioning?[38] This pendulum, this contradictory tug between expectations of illness and health among ascetics, will be a recurrent theme in this book. As we could hardly expect the contradictory expectations of withdrawal and engagement ever to be definitively resolved, so too we will see that despite the proliferating discourse devoted to the topic in late antiquity, the contradictory pull of health and illness would be difficult to reconcile.

As the *Life of Adam and Eve*'s narrative of the origins of illness suggests, Christians frequently frame discussion of ascetic illness and health within the context of specifically Christian views of anthropology and salvation history. I therefore do not wish to undervalue how historically bounded early Christian views could be. Yet Christian attitudes are not formed exclusively by theology. We hardly need resort to an essentialist or universalist view of human nature to note that the contested interpretations of the function and meaning of illness within the life and practice of early Christians are neither uniquely Christian nor specifically ancient but are rooted in a fault line at the junction of illness and ascetic practice found across many cultures.

How then does illness impinge upon the self-fashioning project of asceticism? In short, the relationship between illness and asceticism is dialectical. On the one hand, illness functions as a component of asceticism: it accomplishes many of the same goals as other practices that are more commonly classified as "ascetic." On the other hand, illness undermines asceticism.

Illness in/as Ascetic Practice

Social psychologists have noted that a primary function of ascetic behaviors—including both the types of asceticism documented in early Christianity and a range of more broadly ascetical "technologies of the self"—is to "shrink" the self, to condense and constrain the self into the bounds of the body, its regulation, and its functions.[39] Social psychologists and phenomenologically minded scholars of religion have identified a host of ascetic behaviors, from prayer to exercise to self-mutilation, that achieve this same goal.[40] Illness too has this function of altering, narrowing, and intensifying the sufferer's experience, even necessitating a withdrawal from the normal life-world of the sufferer. Susan Sontag may have been reflecting this withdrawal when she wrote, "Illness is the night-side of life, a more onerous citizenship. Everyone who is born holds dual citizenship, in the kingdom of the well and in the kingdom of the sick. Although we all prefer to use only the good passport, sooner or later each of us is obliged, at least for a spell, to identify ourselves as citizens of that other place."[41] The movement from the kingdom of the well to the kingdom of the sick is a withdrawal (or *anakhōrēsis*), at times social, experiential, and spatial. It forces the abandonment of the old self and the fashioning of a new "citizenship," or *politeia*, as ancient monks called it. We need not conflate the modern with the ancient self (in all its variety) to follow this line of analysis, and certainly ancients did possess a different "self" than that in the industrialized west.[42] An advantage of viewing illness and asceticism from this perspective is that it does not presuppose a modern self or meaning of illness.

The anthropologist Byron Good has provided a compelling explanation for how illness brings about experiential change for the sick. Serious illness entails an immediate and visceral change in the self, since "for the sufferer, the body is not simply a physical object or physiological state but an essential part of the self. . . . The diseased body is therefore not simply the object of cognition and knowledge, of representation in mental states and the works of medical science. It is at the same time a disordered agent of experience."[43] The potential for this disordered embodiment to effect change in religious experience and ascetic practice—particularly in a late ancient context—is enormous, since early Christian religious practice embraces embodiment as a mode of performance and cognition. Susan Ashbrook Harvey, for example, notes that late ancient Christian practice is "strikingly dependent on the direct engagement of bodily experience as its context." She observes, "Bodily experience and bodily expression become primary epistemological tools in both realms of existence, as we seek relation to God; the knowledge they convey is a knowledge that cannot be gained in any other way."[44] While Harvey focuses on Syrian Christianity, her point applies to late ancient Christianity as a whole. To disorder one's bodily experience—as illness does—is to disorder one's devotional practice, as well as to alter the ways one comes to "know" oneself and the divine.

While this may be in some sense intuitive, Good usefully draws on the phenomenology of Alfred Schutz to lay out the process by which illness, especially "chronic or life-threatening illness," transforms or even deforms the life-world of the sufferer. [45] Good highlights three of Schutz's six "features of common-sense reality" that speak to how illness alters or deforms the life-world of the sufferer: the relationship between embodiment and selfhood; a shared sense of sociality and shared experience; and a shared, conventional sense of time.

First, in the "everyday world" two very different aspects of embodiment and selfhood coexist, of which one may hardly be aware: the self, the "I," both has a body and is a body. Illness ruptures the normally unproblematized coexistence of the two understandings of the body/self relationship. Good explains, "In the everyday world, the self is experienced as the 'author' of its activities, as the 'originator' of on-going actions, and thus as an 'undivided total self.' We act in the world through our bodies; our bodies are the subject of our actions, that through which we experience, comprehend and act upon the world."[46] Yet sufferers of illness commonly conceive of the body as something other than the self, as Good puts it, "an object, distinct from or even alien to the experiencing and acting self."[47] How this alienation of self from body plays out depends on the culture's view of the self, mind, and body. In a culture that values a holistic integration of body and mind (or soul) into one unitary self, as is common in modernity, this self-alienation is indeed disconcerting and even demoralizing for the sufferer. Yet in a culture that values or encourages such a dissociation of self and body (for example, the famous maxim of the monk Dorotheus: "[My body] kills me, I will kill it") illness may function as a positive aid toward asceticism.[48]

The second feature of everyday reality, which illness disrupts, is its "form of sociality."[49] That is, "[o]ne of the most fundamental assumptions of everyday life . . . is that we live in the same world as persons around us, that the world we experience and inhabit is shared by others." For the sick, however, "[t]heir world is experienced as different, as a realm which others cannot fully fathom. They feel alienated from others, separated from the everyday world of work and accomplishment."[50] Illness is "self-absorbing" and "isolating," as Kleinman describes it.[51] Good sees this alienation from ordinary social relations as negative, as his informants—typical of modernity—perceive this alienation, withdrawal, and isolation as painful. In another context—such as late antiquity, in which both social and geographical withdrawal (*anakhōrēsis*) were prized ideals—this could be perceived as a benefit to the sufferer.

The third feature of Schutz's everyday world "is the experience of having a 'common time perspective,' one we share with others. This is far more subtle than we often imagine, as becomes clear when persons discover they have life-threatening illness and begin to reassess time. Such persons often report experiencing time differently than those around them." The sick's altered perception of time is not limited to the cognitive changes that may follow from forthrightly facing one's impending mortality, an aid to spiritual and ascetic development well recognized in antiquity, as Antony famously advises: "As we rise daily, let us suppose that we shall not survive till evening."[52] Illness moreover may alter the sufferer's perception of the flow of time. Those who have suffered a serious illness might commiserate with Good's characterization of the different time perception of the ill: "Time caves in. Past and present lose their order. Pain slows personal time, while outer time speeds by and is lost."[53] The disturbance of time is a common feature in the phenomenology of sickness.[54] Yet such a disturbance of time, especially the collapse of time into a continuous present, is a core element of spiritual exercises well known in antiquity, as Pierre Hadot has discussed.[55]

Good's presupposition throughout his analysis is that the changes to the life-world that illness—particularly chronic illness—brings about are negative; and certainly most sufferers of chronic illness in a modern context take this view. The philosopher Samuel Gorovitz too understands illness to be a negative experience and points out some features of the illness experience that coincide with Good's analysis. Illness, Gorovitz notes, "results in an undesirable egocentricity that shrinks the sick person's view of the world."[56] Yet what if the goal is to "shrink the self," as Bruce Malina and others have characterized the process of asceticism? In the context of cultivating religious transcendence, the alienation of self from body, the withdrawal from ordinary sociality, and the collapse of time into a continual "present" may take on a very different meaning and function indeed.

From the perspectives of medical anthropology and social psychology the process of "unmaking" the ordinary life-world and creating a new "primary form of reality" (we might say a new subjectivity) could achieve something useful or favorable, as Cassian and Chrysostom claimed, although not in the same way that an anthropologist would. Through these transformations illness contributes to asceticism; the new reality of illness may overlap considerably with or help inaugurate another significant "reality" (in the terms of phenomenology), "the world of religious experience."[57]

The complementarity of illness and asceticism, and religious experience more generally, may be clarified in the light of recent theoretical work on asceticism. Richard Valantasis has suggested that, in contrast to the manifold definitions of asceticism as constituted by some or other specific practices, at its root asceticism creates a new subjectivity on the part of the ascetic.[58] In his words, "Asceticism may be defined as performances within a dominant social environment intended to inaugurate a new subjectivity, different social relations, and an alternative symbolic universe."[59] Even in solitude ascetics perform in the gaze of an implied audience, be that god, demons, or even—as Valantasis puts it—"the 'other self,' the deconstructed person, the thoroughly socialized being who is being rejected."[60] All of the aspects of the illness experience described above may heighten or enable this sort of "new subjectivity." Illness alienates the sufferer from the body and alienates the sufferer from the common "sociality" of ordinary life. Illness is a forced withdrawal, to recall Sontag's phrase, to a separate kingdom from that of the well. Illness changes the sufferer's bodily practices as well, his or her proclivities and abilities to eat, sleep, work, and pray, even altering the sufferer's perception of time. We may return to Harvey's observation of the epistemological centrality of the body in late ancient religious practice: it is through the body that the religious comes to know god and self. Thus the radically altered subjectivity of illness may also lead to its own epistemological shifts, such as religious transcendence and visionary experiences.

Illness's ascetic utility evokes Pierre Hadot's category of spiritual exercises. A possible distinguishing feature between Hadot's exercises and the experience of illness is that, in Hadot's definition, spiritual exercises are voluntary.[61] One cannot call being hit with a falling brick a spiritual exercise. Yet even within the contours of Hadot's definition, illness opens up for the sufferer new modes of spiritual exercise unattainable in the kingdom of the healthy. We will not be surprised to find late ancient monastic sources replete with praise about the utility and merit of illness as an ascetic practice in and of itself. Not infrequently late ancient monastic writers, such as Joseph of Thebes (in the *Sayings of the Desert Fathers*), Amma Syncletica, and Barsanuphius of Gaza, praise the proper suffering of illness as among the highest forms—even the highest form—of asceticism. In this way illness, like fasting, prayer, vigils, and even intentional self-hurt, functions as a primary means of spiritual development. Late ancient authors, however, do not always adhere to Hadot's delimitation of spiritual exercises as voluntary. Chapters 4 and 6 especially show that ancient authors hold that illness functions as asceticism in itself by effecting spiritual exercises (such as fasting, vigils, and chastity) apart from the will of the sufferer. Illness both opens up space for new modes of *askēsis* and may function as asceticism in itself.

Illness as Threat to Asceticism

Yet the relation between illness and asceticism is not so straightforward. While the complementarity of illness and *askēsis* has been noted by both the ill and the ascetic (in antiquity and modernity), the same sources recognize that illness threatens the very core of asceticism: control of the body and self-control, *enkrateia*, a common term for asceticism among ancient Christians.[62] This reflects the obverse of a core element of Good's analysis of the illness experience: the alienation of the self from the body. Very simply, illness is the body rebelling against itself, a metaphor that still lends much to popular and professional talk about disease. One of the universal problems of illness is "the problem of control," as the sociologist Arthur Frank describes it.[63] E. M. Cioran puts it well in his essay "On Sickness": "Flesh freeing itself, rebelling, no longer willing to serve, sickness is the *apostasy of the organs*; each insists on going its own way, each, suddenly or gradually, refusing to play the game, to collaborate with the rest, hurls itself into adventure and caprice. . . . As our infirmities accumulate, we fall victim to our body, whose whims are equivalent to so many decrees. It is our body that commands and controls us, . . . spies on us, keep us under its thumb."[64] For the ascetic, who should be constantly surveilling the body, this is threatening. While the ascetic should be performing for god, now he or she performs under the watchful surveillance of the body. Furthermore to lose control of one's body invites moral disapproval. If losing control over the self (*enkrateia*) is normally a source of stigma and shame, it is all the more the case for the ascetic.[65]

From other perspectives, both modern and premodern, the situation facing the sick self may be even more disturbing. Illness represents not only the body rebelling against the self, or the self's alienation from the body, but the insurgency of myriad "others," independently motivated—if not sentient—organisms that the human body carries within it, normally unbeknownst to the human self. From the perspective of modern biology, the largely unperceived bacteria and parasites acting within our bodies for their own purposes (frequently at odds with those of the host) destabilize the modernist ideal of a unitary and autonomous self, as the psychologist David Barash has argued.[66] Ancients could be even more aware than moderns of the unsettling otherness of illness; while Galen or Oribasius would surely disapprove, for many ancient people disease could signify demonic invasion, the parasitic inhabitation of another being within one's own flesh.[67] Illness (or its various malign bacterial, viral, or—in antiquity—demonic insurgents) fundamentally undermines any attempt to control the body or mind and renders the self subservient, dominated, and—as the saying goes—at the will of the body.

Illness's threat to ascetic self-control is in large measure intuitive, surely more intuitive than sickness's aid to asceticism. A serious illness impedes all the core components of ascetic life. The sick maintain mental discipline only with great difficulty, and very likely not at all. They require a special diet rather than the usual fasting. The sick cannot work and cannot participate in the normal rigors of liturgical life. In addition the sick become painfully aware of their dependence on others, an extremely hard shortcoming to accept in a society that idealizes anchoritic solitude and self-sufficiency. Awareness of illness's threat to asceticism permeates late ancient ascetic literature on illness.

Making Meaning of Illness

Of course, while it is of special interest to the arguments in this book, the utility of illness, whether it hinders or helps the ascetic project, is often not the issue of most immediate concern to ancients faced with the sight of the sick (or healthy) ascetic. Illness most fundamentally is interpreted in moral and religious terms across cultures, and no less in the Christian tradition.[68] I suspect that in most cultures, the "symbolic worlds" in question do not provide any mechanistic, unreflective, or consistent way of making sense of illness. The case is no different in late ancient Christianity. The meaning of illness is polysemic and ambiguous, and thus frequently contested.

The medical anthropologist Arthur Kleinman writes of illness's multiple significations, "Illness has meaning . . . in several distinctive senses. . . . From an anthropological perspective and also a clinical one, illness is polysemic or multivocal; illness experiences and events usually radiate (or conceal) more than one meaning. . . . As in so many areas of life, their very ambiguity often supplies illness meanings with relevance, inasmuch as they can be applied now this way, now that way to the problem at hand."[69] Sufferers and those around them, as Kleinman observes, make sense of their suffering and navigate the ambiguity of illness by "narrativization," by "making experience into a story."[70] Such illness narratives are frequently incomplete, halting, inconsistent, and constantly revised. And of course the attempts at making meaning out of suffering do not emerge de novo from the individual's consciousness. Rather, turning again to Kleinman, "Illness takes on meaning as suffering because of the way this relationship between body and self is mediated by cultural symbols of a religious, moral, or spiritual kind."[71] Whether we call them "explanatory models," as per Kleinman, "cognitive" or "cultural models," or "master narratives," the models for rendering illness meaningful can be temporary, evolving, inconsistent, and even contradictory, and they depend on the social context in which the sufferer is embedded.[72] If the illnesses of the ordinary are so deeply laden with moral and religious meaning, then so much more the afflictions of the saintly, society's moral exemplars.

Such an approach, maintaining an awareness of the models available for making meaning and narrativization, may fruitfully illuminate ancient Christian "illness narratives," as it has elucidated illness conceptions in a modern anthropological setting.[73] Susan Garrett, for example, takes such an approach in reading Paul's comments in his Corinthian correspondence about his thorn in flesh (*skolops tēi sarki*, 2 Cor. 12:7), most likely an illness or bodily affliction, pace John Chrystostom's offense at the idea.[74] Chrysostom's interpretation, in fact, was in contradistinction with that of many other early Christian exegetes, who understood the thorn most commonly as a bodily ailment, frequently described as headaches. Modern biblical scholars have been inclined to see Paul's thorn as epilepsy, or the Sacred Disease in common ancient terminology.[75] It gives me pause, however plausible this may be, that no ancient author seems to have drawn the connection between Paul's affliction and what is among the more widely discussed ailments in antiquity, the subject of one of the most famous and celebrated Hippocratic treatises.[76]

Setting aside questions of paleopathology, Paul's thorn (though the topic of only a few lines in Paul's letter) offers an instructive and early example of the conflicts that surrounded the holy, conflicts over meaning, practice, and authority; for like Apa Benjamin or Stephen, Paul's endurance of his thorn scandalized followers at the suffering of a moral exemplar. To unpack Paul's brief and elusive apologia for his suffering, Garrett employs the concept of "cultural models" to show the process of making meaning. These cultural models, in Garrett's words, are "socially transmitted, taken-for-granted mental representations of different aspects of the world. . . . Such models shape human experience by imposing culturally distinct patterns of order on the world. They supply interpretations of events and inferences about them, and provide a framework for remembering, reconstructing, and describing experiences."[77] Garrett identifies three dominant cultural models in early Christianity that make sense of the experience of suffering: the Job model; the paideia model; and the cross/resurrection model. All of these are implicit in Paul's discourse. The Job model draws more from extrabiblical depictions (especially the *Testament of Job*) than the biblical depiction of Job the Just, afflicted as a test from Satan and yet patiently suffering and refusing to complain or blaspheme. The paideia model identifies god as the source of illness, which is sent as a trial to chastise the sufferer for his or her own sins (or the sins of others). The cross/

resurrection model frames illness as a means of vicariously participating in the weakness and suffering of Jesus, to be followed by vicarious participation in his postresurrection exaltation. In Garrett's reading, Paul makes meaning out of his affliction and defends his own reputation against those who apparently were taken aback at the sick apostle by adapting and drawing on these various models at his disposal in necessarily original and creative ways.[78] The models of affliction provide a set of potential interpretations of his illness that he can draw from selectively and recombine to describe and frame his own experience. Even in Paul's brief remarks consistency was not the priority in making sense out of suffering (certainly not a feature unique to Paul). As Garrett notes, "Christians could alternate among different cultural models, without perceiving what may strike us as 'logical contradictions' in thought."[79] Such flexibility to the point of contradiction is to be expected in the face of the world-destroying power of pain and disease.

We need not adopt the specific list or taxonomy of cultural models that Garrett proposes nor apply the anthropological terminology too rigorously to recognize that such models are a significant component in how illness is understood. The dominant "master narratives" or cultural models that were available to early Christians—primarily biblical, but also traditional Hellenistic models—offered no consistent or reliable means for explaining illness. As always, the models or master narratives are not a straitjacket; they merely provide the symbolic morphemes out of which the cultural observer creates a narrative or creates meaning. And certainly they go far beyond the three cultural models of affliction that Garrett observes in Paul's letter.

The ancient Mediterranean culture presented in literary sources traditionally interpreted illness or disability as divine punishment.[80] This need not mean that this is the only attitude toward the sick in antiquity. The chronically ill, injured, and disabled (and ancients would not have distinguished neatly between these modern categories) must have figured prominently in the overwhelmingly public life of antiquity to a degree not expected in the modern industrialized world. Certainly ancient sources display a diversity of approaches to illness and disability.[81] Yet influential ancient literary sources frequently speak of the seriously ill or disabled in harshly judgmental terms.[82] Health was among the highest ideals in ancient Mediterranean culture, a feature not unique to antiquity by any means; to judge by literary culture at least, illness was most easily explained as a punishment, whether of a moral wrong on the part of the sufferer, a mere accidental trespass (as in the case of Philoctetes), or something entirely unknown (as in the case of Hesiod's mute, roaming illnesses). This is not to say that this was a universal characteristic or even normative. It is probably not too much to presume that ancients, like many today, were inclined to view the illnesses and injuries of friends sympathetically and yet to see the misfortunes of enemies or strangers as their just deserts, or simply to decline to make any interpretation. But this is precisely the point, especially in narrating the lives of saints or regulating the practices of ascetics; such familiar models were powerful tools in conflicts over authority and prestige.[83] It is thus not particularly surprising when the morally wretched meet their end in misery, while sages and moral exemplars are frequently described by later followers as extraordinarily healthy.[84]

For a late ancient Christian making meaning out of illness, the symbolic world of the Old Testament offered an interpretative schema that shares much with early Greek culture. Illness is largely seen as a just punishment from god. Of course within the context of a literary corpus inclined to promote a strict, even radical monotheism, the field of possible disease etiologies is narrowed considerably.[85] In much of the Old Testament illness and healing both come from Yahweh. So the Deuteronomist has god declare, "But if you will not obey the Lord your God by diligently observing all his commandments and decrees, which I am commanding you today, then all these curses shall come upon you and overtake you. . . . The Lord will make the pestilence cling to you until it has consumed you off the land that you are entering to possess. The Lord will afflict you with consumption, fever, inflammation, with fiery heat and drought, and with blight and mildew; they shall pursue you until you perish (Deut. 28:15, 21–22, NRSV)." God afflicts any number of sinners in the Old Testament with disease.[86] Unlike in the contemporary Greek and Mesopotamian cultures, Hector Avalos argues, Israelite culture normally insisted that god punishes the wicked only for violation of the covenants; this violation should be knowable to the punished, and its punishment is inherently just.[87] The horrors of disease, like the violent punishments that preoccupy so much of the Israelite covenantal relationship, have a preeminently pedagogical role.

Yet this is not the only model for making sense of illness in the Old Testament. Amundsen and Ferngren note that the Old Testament tells a number of stories of the righteous afflicted with illness.[88] Certainly Job offers a compelling model—if itself ambiguous—for interpreting illness among the righteous.[89] In the Old Testament sickness may be both a mechanistic sign of god's anger and the sufferer's sins (or that of a relative or the nation), and a test of the just, allowed but not ordered by god.

The texts included in the New Testament too are ambiguous toward the meaning of illness and suffering, differing considerably in their approach to illness, both among themselves and with the Old Testament. Modern scholars tend to characterize Jesus as a critic of those who impute sin to the sick and suffering, and a number of Gospel stories may be read to support this view.[90] Yet at the same time some passages are sufficiently ambiguous, such as the Johannine Jesus's command to the healed paralytic to sin no more (John 5:14), that their interpretation is still debated to this day. Illness is sometimes traced to demonic invasion, but interestingly the Gospels writers do not ever specifically claim that demonic possession is caused by any moral fault of the sufferer. Furthermore, such demonic etiology is not normative among New Testament writers, despite widespread assumption of the contrary among scholars.[91] Amundsen and Ferngren note that in most cases in the New Testament, especially outside the Gospels, illness is not "theologized." With the exception of Paul's thorn, the epistolary authors do not normally treat illness as a sign for spiritual interpretation or as a problem of theodicy.[92] This is an important reminder that early Christians were not compelled to make meaning of illness within the symbolic matrix of Christian salvation history and did not necessarily narrativize it in the terms of biblical or Greco-Roman cultural models.[93] It remained an option not to make any meaning on this level.

That said, the New Testament does provide compelling cultural models and master narratives for making sense of illness. In short, the transcendent value of suffering is encouraged through the mimetic performance of the death and resurrection of Christ and is positively accepted as a trial by god. At the same time any transcendent value of suffering illness may be undermined by interpreting illness as a sign of demonic possession, and even denied altogether as an evil that will be eliminated in the imminent coming of the kingdom of god. This does not even take into consideration other non-Christian models, professional and folk (cultural elements that might not register in the long view of history with the clarity of the New Testament), on which Christians could draw. For Christians attempting to make sense of their illnesses and those of others through the conceptual "toolbox" at their disposal, there was no "Christian" meaning, only contradictory and contested narrative models. Such models, in antiquity as today, could have very real effects on the experience of illness and classification of the diseases of others.[94]

Conclusion

Illness poses problems of meaning and function in early Christian asceticism, where questions of practice and meaning common to late ancient Christians were intensified. Illness paradoxically both hampers and encourages asceticism and holiness. Illness may render bodily self-control impossible and culminate in the annihilation of the body and the self. But this may have a transcendental and salutary effect as well, a phenomenon that Cioran describes as "the double aspect of sickness: *annihilation* and *revelation*; sickness cuts us off from our appearances and destroys them only the better to open us to our ultimate reality, and sometimes to the invisible."[95] Also ambiguously Christianity's authoritative texts promote illness behavior as a signifier of God's favor and the sufferer's mimesis of Christ's suffering. At the same time illness is also the clearest possible signifier of God's wrath. The ambiguous function and multivalent meaning of illness in asceticism, both fostering and undermining ascetic behavior, signifying and undermining holiness, give rise to a crisis in interpretation in the ascetic literatures of late antiquity. That is to say, ascetic writers and theorists made meaning out of illness with a moral urgency and interest, even if in some cases only to decline meaning. The confluence of the experience of illness and the religious experience is an enduring theme in Christian and religious literature. The following chapters expose the interweaving of illness, asceticism, and sanctity in the formative period of early Christian thought and practice.

Chapter 2

Asceticism, Health, and Christian Salvation History: Perspectives from the Earliest Monastic Sources

Around A.D. 394 a group of seven joined the pilgrimage network that had emerged in the recently Christianized eastern Mediterranean. This trade in people and mementos not only spanned the "holy" lands of Jerusalem and greater Palestine but also incorporated Syria, Asia Minor, and Egypt, extra-Israelite lands that preserved the memories of biblical figures and events. They also were the homes of martyr shrines and, especially in fourth-century Egypt, host to now well-established communities of saintly ascetics. Although they declined to record their names, these anonymous pilgrims left behind a detailed record of their travels, narrated by one of their company, that came to bear the title *History of the Monks in Egypt* (*Historia Monachorum in Aegypto*).

In the region of Thebes, whose tombs and temples, especially on the west side of the Nile, had been fertile ground for the efflorescence of organized asceticism, the narrator describes a monastery under the leadership of a certain Isidore. Isidore was a common name among monks, and the precise location of this monastery has not been identified to my knowledge, presuming, of course, that he refers to a real monastery rather than a literary construct.[1] As is so often the case, the "reality" of the monastery—whatever that may have been—matters less than what the pilgrim narrator makes of it.

The pilgrim describes Isidore's monastery as expansive, housing a thousand monks. Since he describes it as "fortified with a high brick wall," the monastery was likely a coenobium, rather than a lavra or semi-eremitical monastery, a type of residence also widespread at an early date in the Thebaid.[2] Beyond what the pilgrims could see from the exterior, just the wall more or less, their knowledge of monastic life in Isidore's monastery was limited to what the elder in charge of the gatehouse told them, since the pilgrims were restricted to the guest quarters in the gatehouse and the monks were forbidden to leave. So constricted by these limitations for observation, the pilgrim describes the cloister: "Within the walls were wells and gardens and all that was necessary to supply the needs of the monks, for none of them ever went out. The gate-keeper was an elder, and he never allowed anyone to go out or to come in unless he wished to stay there for the rest of his life without ever leaving the enclosure. This gate-keeper had a small guest house near the gate where he put up visitors for the night. In the morning he would give them gifts and send them on their way in peace."[3] So far this is a fairly typical description of a late fourth-century coenobium, if a bit extreme in describing the ban on monastic travel. It is not too much to hear echoes of Eden in the description, a forbidden sanctum of gardens and flowing water. The account reflects a common occurrence in these early decades of monastic pilgrimage: an encounter with monastic guest-master, which is then filtered through a pilgrim's interpretation in comparison with other accounts.[4] Similar mediated interactions between pilgrim outsiders and monastic wardens occurred at countless gatehouses in antiquity, as they still do.

In this vignette, as throughout the *History of the Monks in Egypt*, the narrative tells more about popular (and idealized) perceptions of monastic life than monastic life itself.[5] In particular the *History* shows how deeply rooted in early popular perceptions of monasticism was the expectation that monks would enjoy a certain measure of preternatural health. According to the author of the *History*, the elder provided a remarkable account of the marvelous health of the monks inside: "The elder who was permanently employed at the gate told us that the monks within the walls were such saints that all could work miracles and none of them ever fell ill before he died (*mēdena . . . empesein eis noson pro tēs teleutēs*). On the contrary, when the time came for each to depart, he announced it beforehand to all the others and then lay down and fell asleep."[6] While the *History* does not make it explicit, the monks of Isidore's community had achieved in some measure a reclamation of paradise before the fall, including—as reflected in the *Life of Adam and Eve*—a level of health unheard of in the fallen world. For the veteran reader of monastic hagiography, such an account of superhuman health among the holy might not raise an eyebrow, so common is the motif of monastic health in the literature of late antiquity. But did the narrators expect this account to be believed? Or was this a simple part of the commonplace narrative of outlandish marvels and monsters in ancient travel literature?[7]

It is not uncommon for writers who describe the fantastic and exotic to affect a posture of skepticism, or at least agnosticism, an affectation that allows the narrator to include entertaining and fantastic stories without sacrificing reliability as narrator, a rhetorical posture as ancient as Herodotus's *Histories*. In late antiquity Palladius of Helenopolis, author of a collection of monastic reminiscences published some two decades after the *History* (around A.D. 420), regularly takes such a narrative posture when recounting wondrous tales at secondhand. Jerome in his *Life of Paul of Thebes* reflects such an expectation when he speaks of a marvel of the desert, a Christian satyr: "No doubt should move anyone to disbelief in this event."[8] For Jerome, not to acknowledge the implausibility of Antony's encounter with the satyr would make himself less credible as a narrator. Athanasius too in his *Life of Antony* affects this tone (as we will see in the next chapter).

But the author of the *History* shows no sign of incredulity (either his own or that of his presumed audience) in passing on the guest-master's account of monastic health.[9] We can compare this with the *History*'s epilogue. Engaging the topos of explaining that he has included but a few of the many possible wonders he has seen (as seen also in the *Life of Antony* in the next chapter), the narrator concedes of the monks of far Upper Egypt that "[o]ne would not believe their ascetic practices, which surpass human capabilities."[10] Yet the narrator refers not to what he has described, such as the remarkable health of Isidore's monks, but to the wonders that he has not described, for he does not narrate any visits beyond the Thebaid toward Syene (Aswan).[11] In contrast, without any incredulity the pilgrim presents the exploits of the monks of Egypt as pushing the limits of human capabilities, and at times surpassing them.

In this fashion extraordinary and even preternatural health features prominently in the *History*'s presentation of Egyptian monasticism. John of Lycopolis survived at least until 90, when the pilgrims visited him, and still never lessened his ascetic regimen, surviving on fruit alone.[12] Abba Or too was "about ninety years old," and Elias near Antinoe was approaching 100 when the company visited him.[13] Apollo was over 80 years of age, while the priest Copres, despite his seemingly inauspicious name, was nearly 90.[14] Father Chronides, with his more temporally auspicious name, lived at least 110 years.[15]

The author of the *History* makes it sufficiently clear that the monks' longevity did not come from maintaining any sort of "rationally" healthful regimen in the Hippocratic-Galenic tradition. Rather, monastic longevity came from a brutal asceticism that was transformed into health through the intercessions of Christ or the angels. The narrator demonstrates this process in a story told to the pilgrims by a monk named Apelles about his neighbor John, whose asceticism comprised standing under a rock for three years or more and eating only the communion host on Sundays. As for John, says Apelles, "When his feet had swollen and split from his standing motionless for so long, and the discharge had caused putrefaction, an angel appeared and touched his mouth, saying, 'Christ is meat indeed for you and the Holy Spirit is drink indeed (cf. John 6:55). For the time being this spiritual food is sufficient; otherwise your stomach will become too heavy and you will vomit.' And having healed (*therapeusas*) him, the angel made him leave that place. From that day he spent his time in the desert wandering about and eating plants. But on Sundays he was always at the same place to receive Communion."[16] In narratives such as this (and a similar healing of Piammonas), as the angel explains to John, the monk's physiology is such that he apparently reacts to nutriment differently from ordinary folk. Should the ascetic partake of carnal food rather than spiritual, it would make him sick.[17] In fact the general trend of the *History* is not to dwell on the illness and suffering of the ascetic. Patricia Cox Miller characterizes this trend in the *History* as traces of the tension in the monk's position—we might recall Kleinberg's notion of the "ascetic pendulum"—between sordid embodiment and spiritual transformation: "By aligning images of mutilation and disfigurement with images of light, hagiographers of desert ascetics maintained their subjects in a tensive perch between transcendence and materiality."[18] Yet I sense something quite different at play in stories such as that of Apelles. In Apelles's story as in others, transcendence and putrescence are not in synchronic tension but are linked sequentially and causally. Here in the *History* the monk's transcendent health is the culmination of material (ascetic) struggle, not its antipode.

Throughout the *History of the Monks in Egypt* the desert is presented as a realm of health, just as it is the realm of asceticism. Much like the obverse of Susan Sontag's reflection on the dual realms of the sick and the healthy, and quite in contrast to the imaginative reconstructions of the desert as awash in disease, the *History* presents the desert as the daytime kingdom of health, in contrast to the endemic illness (and sin) of the secular world. Thus the few stories of sickness in the *History* function more properly as stories of health, as monks heal their suppliants or their fellow ascetics.[19] Such healings—reflecting the desert as the realm of health—are presented as so ubiquitous that Father Copres is portrayed as nearly yawning at their sheer banality when compared to other wonders to be found among the desert monks.[20] Furthermore stories of death, inescapable even for preternaturally healthy monks, also follow the pattern found in Isidore's monastery in the Thebaid. Death is controlled, foreknown, and a sign of the monk's power and control. Death pleasantly translates the monk to paradise, except in the rare case of some sinning monks, whose untimely deaths clearly signify the worldly sickness of their souls.[21]

I have focused on this passage from the *History of the Monks of Egypt* for two reasons. First, far from being exceptional, the story shows just how common by the turn of the fifth century was the expectation of the monastic life—especially in the Egyptian desert—as a realm of health. In fact stories such as these are quite typical of the protological interests of late ancient monastic hagiography, as Peter Brown has shown; the ascetics of the end times return to their prelapsarian beginnings.[22] As Gillian Clark has argued, such expectations of exceptional health among ascetics would have been quite at home in a variety of Greco-Roman philosophical viewpoints, although the specifically Christian protological explanation for this ascetic health would not likely have held sway.[23]

Yet more important here, the *History*'s description of Isidore's monastery presents very different representations of monastic health from those found in the earliest sources that survive, which predate the *History* by fifty to seventy years. As ubiquitous as such representations as that of the anonymous pilgrim would become in late ancient monastic literature, they were not always or universally so. Rather they developed in a specific historical context and would be contested and controversial in late ancient monasticism (as shown in Chapters 3 and 4).

In this chapter I will discuss the representation of illness and health among ascetics in the earliest strata of written sources for monastic life in Egypt, sources which predate the well-developed popular presentations of monastic "realities" in the *History* by two generations. In particular I will engage three corpora of letters from the earliest period of monastic writing: (1) the archives of private letters addressed to the monks Nepheros and Paphnutius of the monastery of Hathor; (2) the *Letters* of Pachomius, who founded an influential federation of coenobitic monasteries in Upper Egypt (and whose later *Lives* I will discuss in detail in a later chapter); and (3) the *Letters* of Antony, famed hermit of the eastern desert and protagonist of Athanasius's *Life of Antony* (discussed in the next chapter). Each of these letter collections ranks among the earliest written sources for Egyptian monasticism: the archives of the monks Paphnutius and Nepheros from the 340s and 350s respectively; the *Letters* of Pachomius from no later than his death in 346; and the *Letters* of

Antony probably from the 330s but certainly no later than his death in 356. Apart from these letter collections, we have precious little from this early period in Egyptian monasticism.[24]

Like the later travelogues of the *Lausaic History* and the *History of the Monks in Egypt*, each of these collections reflects a concern with the meaning of health and illness as a component of monastic life. Yet the three early letter collections differ considerably from one another in their particular concerns, and they differ quite dramatically in presentation from that of the *History of the Monks in Egypt*. These letters show that at the very start of writing about monasticism, nonmonks and monks alike saw the monk's health and illness as important components of understanding the meaning of asceticism and sanctity. But the particular interpretations of health and illness in monasticism that we see reflected in the late fourth-century *History* are not reflected in most of the earliest sources and are only very partially reflected in the *Letters* of Antony. Specifically it is in Antony's *Letters* that a theology of ascetic health (and illness) is presented. By ascetic practices the monk may reverse the sickening aftereffects of humanity's primordial fall from Edenic wholeness.

Documentary Papryi: Archives from the Monastery of Hathor

Documentation for the monastery of Hathor is preserved in three collections of papyri (or archives), each of which preserves documents related to a single monastic personage: Paieous (330s); Paphnutius (340s); and Nepheros (350s).[25] Each of the archives is dominated not by the letters of the monks but by letters written to the monks—usually by their nonmonastic followers or *clientes*.

The letters represent the early decades of Egyptian monasticism only fleetingly. We can glimpse only fragments of correspondence, sometimes in a context that is not clear, between people we know poorly. In using such papyri we see, to use James Goehring's adaptation of Paul, through a glass darkly. Yet it is all too rare to have any such mirror at all.[26] The letters to Paieous, Paphnutius, and Nepheros number some thirty-five, representing at least fifteen authors. While papyri may never be used as a "random sample" of Egyptian society, these letters constitute as much of a cross-section of Egyptian society as one might reasonably hope to extract from the papyri.[27] They represent the viewpoints of women and men, monks and seculars, Greek and Coptic, the politically elite and the downtrodden. These followers, clients, admirers, and supplicants depended on the monks as spiritual patrons in all the ways now familiar from the last several decades of scholarship on late ancient piety.[28] They beseech intervention in financial and legal hardships, rely on miraculous healing through the monks' intercessory prayer, and are consoled by the assurance that they will find a place in heaven through the good offices of the monks. The archive of Paieous (330s) reflects more the economic and political negotiations of the monks, while the latter two archives of Paphnutius (340s) and Nepheros (350s) reflect most extensively the monks' perceived abilities as healers obtaining divine aid for their followers through prayer and the application of blessed oil, both of which remedies were believed to be efficacious even at long distances. The letters to Hathor also offer a rare glimpse at how the meaning of monastic health and illness was interpreted by some of the earliest witnesses to the Christian monastic movement.

In fact the topic of monastic sickness and health is one on which the letters frequently touch. And yet with all their diversity of social, economic, and geographic location, the correspondents concur with unanimity on the significance of monastic health and sickness, a meaning that would be quite out of place in the later *History*. The letter writers evince concern for the health of their monastic patrons: sixteen of the thirty-five letters explicitly mention the authors' hopes for the monks' continued health and/or anxieties at their potential sickness. Expressions of concern take a variety of forms. Common is the basic closing "I pray you are healthy" (*errōsthai se euchomai*),[29] often expanded to "I pray you are healthy in soul and body" (*psychēi kai sōmati*) or "I pray that you may be healthy for a long time" (*epi megiston chronon*).[30] Frequently the writers invoke either god or providence as the protector of the monk's health. A certain Athanasius (not the bishop of Alexandria) writes, "May divine Providence keep you healthy for the longest time, always remembering us, O beloved, most honored." Others offer similar wishes of good health to the monk Nepheros.[31]

Their concern is no idle one; the writers depend on the monk's continued health for the perceived benefits that he provides. A certain Heraclides writes to Paphnutius, "I pray that you may be healthy in the Lord for a long time, praying on my behalf continuously, most pious father."[32] Indeed without the monk's aid there might be no hope. Heraclides continues,

> You always have the chance to pray on my behalf and I need help from you who are stronger (*kreittonos*) on account of prayer. Both because of my name and because of the sickness that has seized and oppressed me (*pros tēn katalabousan me noson epigousan me*), I now beg you to do this

additional thing: send me the oil. . . . For I do not believe that I will be helped otherwise. May you hold up Christ as long as you have health (*heōs hugeiian ekheis*). [second hand] . . . The prophet also shouted, "In affliction I called out and he heard me." Now truly it is an affliction in which I live, where help can be received neither from a brother nor from any other, except for the hope through our Lord Christ expected on account of your prayers.[33]

Very simply, the followers of the monks of Hathor depended on them for benefits, foremost among which were bodily healing and the assurance of salvation. These benefits could be bestowed only—or most reliably—by a living monastic. Thus it is no surprise that the correspondents of Paphnutius and Nepheros exhibit anxiety and concern for the health of their monastic patrons.

The well-wishes and anxieties of monks' correspondents are distinguishable from the epistolary conventions of contemporary nonmonastic letters only by the increased insistence of their worry. Ancient letter writers, Christian and pagan alike, prominently displayed their concerns with the health or sickness of their correspondents—and for good reason.[34] In a society with little in the way of practical hygiene and with virtually no concept of preventative medicine, antisepsis, or bacteriology, the mortality rate was frighteningly high; over 40 percent died before the age of five, and those who survived childhood would be fortunate indeed to see fifty.[35] For inhabitants of the late ancient world, the notion of sickness and that of death were inextricable. A sudden death following any disruption of the body (by wound, humoral imbalance, or demonic invasion) was neither uncommon nor unexpected. As Roger Bagnall well states the case, "Death came soon, and it came quickly; sometimes also without any explanation. . . . Unlike the modern belief (reasonable enough today) that most infections are either self-limiting or curable, the ancient expectation was that any illness might end in death without much warning. Probably for this reason ancient letter writers are obsessed with wishes for health, reports on the sender's health, and inquiries after the health of the recipient."[36]

The ubiquity of wishes for good health in monastic and nonmonastic, Christian and non-Christian letters alike might seem a mere formality, a meaningless topos. To the contrary, recent work in the history of emotions has argued that we must take seriously such seemingly (and perhaps frustratingly) formal expressions of emotion, whether they are in letters, tombstones, diaries, or any other text. While it is not possible to evaluate the "feeling" or "authenticity" of emotions as represented in the Hathor archives, this is extraordinarily difficult to achieve even in face-to-face conversation or a laboratory, for that matter. Rather, the very fact that they survive and are used denotes their shared cultural meaning, as Barbara Rosenwein notes in her study of early medieval emotion.[37] The epistolary convention, formalized greeting, expression of concern, or term of endearment such as in the Hathor archives is a valuable historical artifact, as Rosenwein notes, for it "tells us about prevailing emotional norms. For the historian, this is precious enough."[38] When ancient letter writers express their concern over their correspondents' health, they do so because it reflects shared cultural meanings and values.[39]

The point of all this is to suggest that monastic health and sickness were indeed significant in the view of the nonmonastic followers of Paieous, Paphnutius, and Nepheros: they communicated something important to the suppliants. Monastic sickness communicated the worldly Christians' tenuous link to the power of the monk. The fragility of monastic health and the inescapable imminence of death signified the potential loss of monastic patronage and its many benefits, both tangible and intangible. For these early monastic followers, the health and sickness of a monk signified a simple and practical concern: their privileged access to the divine was only as secure as the monk's own unexceptional health.

The *Letters* of Pachomius

Contemporary with the community of Hathor, Pachomius founded his first monastery sometime after A.D. 323 near the Theban town of Tabenesse and gradually expanded his authority over a federation of monasteries across Upper Egypt and beyond.[40] At a minimum, Pachomius—or at least his biographer— was certainly familiar with the Melitian communities.[41] Like the archives of the Melitian monks, Pachomius's writings reflect accepted interpretations of the significance of monastic health and sickness. Chapter 5 discusses the hagiographical traditions about Pachomius, but for now the focus is on his own writings.

Illness, health, and their meaning in Christian asceticism, to be sure, do not constitute the dominant themes in the *Letters* of Pachomius, in contrast with the overweening interest in the illnesses of Pachomian ascetics (especially the Father himself) in the Great Coptic *Life of Pachomius*, as I will argue in Chapter 5. Pachomius's own interests lie elsewhere. Apart from a brief allusion to illness in *Letter* 3, the topic of monastic health and sickness is raised only in his *Letter* 5. Nonetheless in *Letter* 5 Pachomius's concern with monastic health—or more properly monastic illness—is an important component in this festal letter and is thus worth discussing in some detail. It is all the more valuable considering the paucity of sources from these early decades of Egyptian monasticism.

Generically the archives of Paieous, Paphnutius, and Nepheros are private documents, while the *Letters* of Pachomius were self-consciously literary, intended as encyclicals for the several monasteries in his federation. Politically the archives from Hathor represent the Melitian church, while Pachomius—at least in the memory of his biographers—fell firmly behind Athanasian orthodoxy.[42] Socially the letters to the monks of Hathor represent the attitudes and views, the desires and fears of lay followers; the *Letters* of Pachomius reflect monastic self-understanding and presentation. The differences between the documents from Hathor and the literature of Pachomius are reflected in the significance attributed to monastic sickness and health therein. Pachomius presents the presence of sick ascetics in his monasteries not as a reflection on the sanctity of the sick or as a reflection of their own ascetic practice but as a risk and opportunity for the proper enactment of ascetic ideals by the healthy.

The occasion for Pachomius's *Letter* 5, addressed as an encyclical to the monks, is the annual Easter celebration at Pachomius's home monastery of Pbow. The Easter gathering posed a significant organizational challenge for the Pachomians: all monks were to travel to Pbow—a journey of over one hundred kilometers for some. Travel outside the coenobium was always problematic due to the need to remain withdrawn from the world while traveling through it. It therefore entailed special arrangements for transportation, food, and accommodation, as well as special behavioral guidelines for reentering the coenobium.[43] The celebration of Easter, highlighted by sermons from the Father—not to mention a break from the routines of monastic life—was greatly anticipated by the coenobites. The Easter celebration was also one of the biannual occasions on which Pachomius assigned leadership positions throughout the federated monasteries.[44] It is in this occasional and preparatory context that Pachomius raises the issue of monastic sickness and health.

The letter constitutes a series of instructions to his spiritual children for the celebration to come. The instructions are quintessentially Pachomian. He avoids the specific formulation of rules and instead limits himself to a recitation of scriptural passages and a call to emulate the saints of Christian memory, primarily the patriarchs of the Old Testament. Thus, Pachomius offers general moral guidance, providing few specific instructions for the feast. Pachomius exhorts his children to the virtues of obedience to superiors, kindness to others, and mutual aid, the foundational monastic precepts of Pachomius's system.[45] As Noah obeyed God's commands, Pachomius says, so too should they. Remembering the examples of the disobedient Canaan and Esau, monks should obey their spiritual fathers. And as the Apostle commands, the brethren should "[bear] one anothers' burdens."[46]

In this rhetorical line Pachomius urges his children to care for the sick monks among them: "When you come to us [for the Easter feast], take care to make the bed of the sick and not to be short of bread, and also, if possible, to find a pillow or a head-cushion, so that those who are weak may rest."[47] Pachomius justifies caring for the sick as a necessary fulfillment of the scriptures, at least as Pachomius interprets them. He explains: "This [care for the sick] is in order to fulfill the warning left to us in writing: 'Anyone who does not look after his own relations, especially if they are living with him, is worse than an unbeliever.'"[48]

Pachomius's discussion of the sickness and health of monks may be understood in the context of his overriding interest in forming "a community built upon mutual respect and mutual support."[49] More specifically, Pachomius intended the monastery to act as a surrogate for the biological family or household, the only reliable source for the necessities of life in antiquity. Although they lived among virtual strangers, monks were expected to live as a family, providing all the supports that biological kin normally would: food, shelter, clothing, emotional support, and health care.[50] A call to mutual aid undergirds all of Pachomius's writings and indeed characterizes the memory of him as preserved in his *Lives*. In the other passages in which Pachomius draws attention to the sickness and health of monks, it is likewise in the broader context of the exhortation to mutual assistance (*Letters* 5.11, 3.3).

The context of Pachomius's correspondence—the obedient provision of mutual aid to fellow monks—indicates the significance of monastic sickness, and indeed it was significant. In fact the exhortation to care for the sick is the only specific administrative instruction in the fifth *Letter*. Why does Pachomius foreground the care of the sick? Very simply, caring for the sick posed an exceptional risk for monks to fail in their obligations to care for their fellow monks, especially in the context of the Easter celebration that is the focus of *Letter* 5. All the monks were to leave en masse for Pbow for at least three days, including travel time and the proceedings—at least, that is to say, all the healthy monks. In accordance with what would become standard practice in

Pachomian monasteries, the sick were excused from requirements of worship, diet, and manual labor and were left to rest and recuperate. In the preparations for travel and during the feast, Pachomius assumed that those left behind were at risk of neglect. That this was indeed a risk during occasions of collective travel is reflected by the later *Rules*, attributed to the Father but actually a later accretion, which mandate that an officer—here identified as a *minister* [*aegrotatum*], a "nurse"—remain behind with any sick monk during funerals, the most common occasion for all monks to travel outside the monastery en masse.[51] Certainly in Pachomius's time—as in the later *Rules*—the sick would not have been marched up to one hundred kilometers for the Easter celebration. But in the absence of such a formal regulation, Pachomius's admonition serves as a simple reminder to provide for those left behind.[52]

Monastic sickness thus poses both an opportunity for monks to perform acts of mutual aid and a threat to that obligation, a chance for monks—intentionally or not—to ignore the needs of their brethren. Monastic sickness also bears an eschatological significance for Pachomius, as he contemplates the potential negligence of his spiritual children: in neglecting the sick the monks risk their immortal souls. But by caring for the afflicted they may yet share in their reward in the cosmic reversal of fortunes to come. He writes, "Let us toil, 'carrying each other's burden,' as Christ 'carried our diseases in his body' without flinching. If Christ is our master, then let us imitate him and bear his injuries, lest in the age to come we be separated from our brothers who suffered afflictions."[53] For Pachomius, the model of Christ typifies the practices of the healthy, unlike Cassian's and Paul's evocations of Christ as the model for the sick.[54] The presence of sick monks in the koinonia thus served as their cross to bear, or to switch metaphors, as a crucible to separate the worthy monks from the unworthy; it provided an opportunity for monks to enact the highest ideal of Pachomian monasticism: the Christ-inspired provision of mutual support. It also represented a dangerous opportunity for monks to fail in that duty.

It is not surprising that the *Letters* of Pachomius reflect different concerns from those of the letters to the monks of Hathor. While we might characterize the correspondents of Hathor's attitude as nontheologized, Pachomius certainly saw the presence of sick monks as an issue of theological and moral import. Yet it is a different theological concern from those of Palladius, Cassian, Chrysostom, or the *History of the Monks in Egypt*, who in their own ways read health and its deficiency as signifying the moral status of the monk. We do not know what else Pachomius might have argued elsewhere, especially orally, and we do not know the views of his fellow monks about these issues and how they might have compared with the later sources just mentioned. At least, however, we can see what Pachomius chose to emphasize in his monastic communication. In the surviving *Letters*, the sickness of a monk is not presented as controversial, puzzling, or inappropriate to asceticism. Pachomius's interest in monastic sickness lies not in the behavior of the sick or in the interpretation of the moral significance of sickness, but in the specific difficulties posed for the provision of mutual aid among the monks. Monastic sickness warns of the moral precariousness of the healthy, rather than signifying the ascetic merits or failures of the sufferer.

The *Letters* of Antony

As detailed in the Introduction to this book, Antony's (c. 251–356) seven *Letters* are contemporary with the letters of Hathor and by Pachomius and may even predate them to the 330s. In Antony's *Letters* are found the core elements that would come to characterize so much later theological, hagiographical, and disciplinary reflections on the meaning and function of illness within ascetic practice. Antony envisioned asceticism as a process of convalescence and recovery, not from mere bodily illness and disability but from the great cosmic wound inflicted on humanity as a result of Adam and Eve's disobedience, elements of which we have already seen in the *Life of Adam and Eve* and the *History of the Monks in Egypt*. Yet Antony presents a vision of monastic healing and health that differs in important ways from the influential narrative elaborations of this understanding of monastic sickness and health that will be the subject of the next chapter.

Antony's theology in general, and of monastic health in particular, reflects the influence of third-century Alexandrian and particularly Origenist thought. But Antony presents a moderate Origenism—if I may be excused for such a term—drawing on the Origenist *koinē* that suffused the theological cultures of the late ancient empire. His letters do not cite the Alexandrian scholar explicitly; nor do they betray the elements of his speculative theology that would cause so much controversy at the turn of the fifth century, many of which were arguably more products of Evagrius of Pontus's reception of Origen.[55] Put simply, Antony's Origenism is rooted in a salvation history that begins with a loss of primordial unity of minds (*nous*) with god, minds who then grow forgetful and fall away, growing cold as they recede from god. This first fall produced a diversity of creatures, one of the definitive features of reality as we know it. Some fell only slightly and are now angels; others fell further into the abyss, becoming fully ensouled, and are humans; others fell yet further into the cold abyss and became demons.

For Origen and Antony, the creation of the natural or material world in which humanity now dwells is effectively pedagogic. Through ethical action and theological contemplation in the material world individuals come to gain authentic knowledge (*gnōsis*) of natural and divine matters and may come to repent of their sinful ways, shed their wicked passions (*pathē*), and thus anticipate the second coming of Christ. Demons play an important role in this pedagogy, reflecting Christian logos theology going back to Justin Martyr, as adversaries of humanity, envious fallen beings who cleverly attempt to distract humanity from their calling to the divine. It is his demonology that is probably the most familiar aspect of Antony's theology to students of late ancient monasticism.[56] Demons, as in Origen before him and Evagrius after him, primarily attack the Christian through evil thoughts (*logismoi*); it is thus through a recognition of one's demonically induced thoughts and their eradication that the individual Christian may come to free himself from sin.[57]

Before Antony's treatment of health and illness and their meaning in asceticism are discussed, some detail on the nature of these letters is in order. The *Letters* of Antony are not epistolary treatises but "real" letters written for spiritual direction to various communities in response to their pastoral needs. Thus the more controversial theological speculations of Origen, whatever Antony might have thought of them, would probably not be at home in the seven *Letters*. In this respect his extant letters are quite like the other letters that Antony is described by other late ancient sources as sending.[58]

The *Letters* of Antony may be divided into two groups: *Letters* 2–7 and *Letter* 1.[59] *Letters* 2–7 are thematically closely connected, so closely, in fact, that the letters frequently overlap word for word. Given their shared wording and thematic connection, Rubenson suggests that they were written close to the same time, all by Antony, and sent to different communities.[60] They are addressed variously and vaguely to the "[b]eloved and honored brothers," "members and joint heirs with the saints," "beloved children, holy Israelite children, in their spiritual essence," and "all his dear brothers, who are at Arsinoë and its neighborhood."[61] In *Letters* 2–7 Antony returns repeatedly to the turning points of Christian salvation history, from the fall, to the teachings of the patriarchs and prophets, to the incarnation and future return of Christ. Within this general framework of historical themes, Antony acts as spiritual guide, providing consolation and moral exhortation. He variously urges his correspondents not to neglect their salvation (2.34), to distinguish between good and evil (3.43–44), to oppose the teachings of Arius (4.17–18), to understand the original unity of creation (5.40), and to put off irrationality (2.4–5, 6.22–23, and others). *Letter* 1 stands apart from the rest of the corpus. While it does not share the explicit interest in Christian salvation history that *Letters* 2–7 show, it presupposes their generally Origenist framework while providing spiritual direction for monks of a more specific and practical nature than the general exhortations of the other *Letters*.

For all their differences, these two parts of the epistolary corpus complement each other thematically. This is certainly the case when we consider Antony's reflection on health and illness. In contrast with the two contemporary letter collections discussed previously, health and illness, both on a macrocosmic and historical level and in the microcosmic body of the monk, take their place as important themes in Antony's *Letters*; these are also themes that have not received the attention that other elements of his thought have.[62] *Letters* 2–7 establish the centrality of fallen existence as disordered, demon-afflicted, and sickly and the role of Jesus Christ and the saints as the physicians of the cosmic wound. *Letter* 1 lays out the practical disciplines by which the Christian—particularly the ascetic—may reclaim a spiritual health that prefigures the future reunion with the divine.

Among the unifying themes of Antony's *Letters* is his adaptation of the ancient and widespread "physician" motif of early Christology. As early as Ignatius of Antioch (c. 35–c. 107), theologians had conceptualized Christ's salvific activity through medical or quasi-medical metaphors. The image of Christ the physician logically proceeds from New Testament Christology and the Gospels' familiar stories of Jesus as healer of physical ailments. Yet for all the emphasis on the cure of the lame, withered, bleeding, and possessed at the hands of Jesus and his apostles, ancient theological reflection on Christ the divine physician develops the son's role more as healer of the soul and bringer of eternal life in the kingdom to come. In early Christian reflection, such psychic healing is brought about most powerfully through the life-giving sacrament of his body and blood.[63] Many in the diverse theological cultures of the ancient Mediterranean world put the image of Christ the physician to use in establishing and elaborating their theological and disciplinary programs.[64] Within the context of the early Egyptian Christianity under discussion in this chapter, Clement of Alexandria and especially Origen are influential proponents of medical Christology.[65] Since it is Origen who is more responsible than anyone for the wide spread of this Christological motif in the third century, it is hardly surprising to see Antony making prominent use of the specifically Origenist elaboration of Christus medicus theology in his *Letters*.[66]

Antony places Christian monasticism within the long narrative arc of the providential economy of salvation. In focusing on the broad sweep of Christian salvation history, Antony draws thematically more from such expansive works as Origen's *Peri archōn* than, for example, the sapiential traditions of the desert fathers as reflected in the later compilations of *Apophthegmata*.[67] Drawing on common Origenist theology, the cosmos as we know it began with the fall of "rational beings" (2.4) or "minds" (6.5–13) from their original unity in "spiritual essence" (4.10) with God. These spiritual essences, minds, or rational beings "descended into the abyss" and became "completely dead." As a result of this fall, the "law of promise" that dwelled in the rational beings "had grown cold" (5.16–17), which echoes Origen's theory that minds cooled down and became gradually "en-souled," drawing on the folk etymology of *psykhē* (soul) from *psykhomai* or *psykhros* (to cool, cold).[68] This "first movement" (6.102), the cooling off of the mind, engendered the created order's present and confused diversity: angels, in all their multiplicity; demons, with all their subcategories; and humans.

For humans, apparently unlike the angels and demons, the cooling off that followed the first movement caused the death of the "faculties of the mind" and the loss of *gnōsis*, "so that they [humans] can no longer know themselves after their first formation," and "they have all become irrational and serve the creatures instead of the Creator."[69]

The Great Wound

It is in this context—humanity's fallen and degraded irrationality and ignorance, immured in the created world of matter—that Antony elaborates his ascetic theology of illness and healing. In contrast to the correspondences of Pachomius and the monks of Hathor, the endemic illness of the world—and asceticism's role as its cure—is central to Antony's ascetic theology in the *Letters*. Antony is particularly fond of medical imagery to characterize the condition of humanity and the world. Antony generally refers to the dissolution of the primal unity of the creator and the created into a multitude of irrational and beastly forms as a "great wound" (3.20, 6.11).[70] In Antony's ascetic theology, the cosmos is universally wounded or disabled, cut off from health and salvation, which in Antony's native Coptic were expressed by the same word, *oujai.* Not only is humanity severed from its primal unity with god, but also humans, irrational and sinful, are dismembered from one another (2.23, 3.25). For Antony, humanity's wounded dismemberment is both the primary symptom of the fall and the cause of further sin. Wounded, cut off from their original unity with god and with one another, and so trapped in irrationality that they are effectively dead (2.4–5, 7.6–8), humans are buffeted by animalistic urges under the influence of demons (3.36, 6.22–23).

Demons, who fell the furthest among the primal minds at the time of the first movement, oppose humanity out of envy (*phthonos*), preferring to destroy humanity rather than witness them gain what the demons will not, "since their part is in the hell to come. Therefore they want us to be lost with them, so that we shall be with the multitude" (6.20). It is from the suggestions of these demons—the passions, Greek *pathē*—that human evils become manifest (for example, 7.7).[71] While Antony's ascription of the passions to demons would not find many adherents among pagan philosophers, it shares a core perspective of many an ancient philosopher or poet on the passions: passions, or emotions, are forces that come from beyond the self and are thus mysterious and especially dangerous.[72] Antony includes a lengthy catalog of demonic evils: envy, resentment, slander, self-importance, to name but a few.[73] It is, thus, thoughts and desires, the passions, rather than demonic possession or apparitions familiar from so many monastic hagiographies, that Antony identifies as the primary mode of affliction by demons. The woundedness of the cosmos, like the demons, reveals itself most readily in the quotidian—if painful—passions of fallen humankind.

Curing the Great Wound

Some, Antony admits, have tried to live righteously on their own and to achieve *gnōsis* through natural contemplation but have failed in their attempts. "[F]rom the creation of the world," writes Antony, "some have prepared themselves to come to the Creator through the law of his promise, learning from that how to worship their Creator as is proper."[74] But on their own such attempts at true worship always failed: "But through much weakness, the heaviness of the body and the concern for evil the law of promise has grown cold and the faculties of the mind have been worn out. Thus they have not been able to discover themselves as they were created, namely as an eternal substance, which is not dissolved with the body but still cannot be freed through its own righteousness."[75] In the economy of Christian salvation history such endemic putrescence could not go untreated. In response to this incurable wound (*ouplēgē nattalco*) afflicting all of creation, god and his son, Jesus Christ, sent a series of visitations to humanity to cure it of its wound in the form of the prophets, at whose head is Moses, whose role as legislator Antony mentions in a number of *Letters*: "But the Creator saw that their wound was great and needed care. He, who is himself their Creator and healer, Jesus, thus sent forerunners before himself."[76] But significant for Antony is Moses's failure: "Moses built the house, yet did not finish it, but left and died." He could not heal the wound. Neither could the "council of the prophets" who came after and "built upon the foundation left by Moses, but could not complete it and likewise they left and died."[77] In their failure prophets called for the only-begotten, lord Jesus Christ, the savior, a great and true physician to heal the wound that the prophets had left festering.[78] According to Antony it is of this seemingly terminal wound that Jeremiah laments, "Is there no balm in Gilead? Is there no physician there? Why then is not the health of the daughter of my people recovered? We would have healed her, but she is not healed: now therefore let us forsake her."[79]

The response to Jeremiah's lament is found in the incarnation. The incarnation not only brought knowledge (*gnōsis*) of humanity's spiritual essence to creation;[80] it also healed the formerly incurable wound that had disabled humanity, cutting them off from god and from one another, leaving them to the afflictions of demonic passions. Antony echoes Origen's distinctive description of Christ as the chief physician, or *archiatros*, over the many physicians (*iatroi*) who had preceded him in the guise of the prophets.[81] Christ, for Antony, is the physician par excellence, "He, who is himself their Creator and Healer, Jesus," "the great healer who is able to heal this great wound," and "He, who is the great and true high priest and true physician, who is able to heal the great wound."[82]

Yet in Antony's theology Christ the great physician bears little resemblance to the healing messiah of the Gospels. Antony does not present Jesus Christ as a healer of specifically bodily ailments, bringing sight to the blind and mobility to the lame. Antony's physician Christ is not the biblical exorcist, and Antony does not refer to Christian faith healing in any way, unlike the contemporary followers of Paphnutius and Nepheros.[83] Rather, Christ is physician of the mind and heart (the same word in Antony's Coptic, *hēt*) who "resurrect[ed] our minds" and "resurrect[ed] our hearts from the earth."[84] The incarnation thus healed humanity of a primarily cognitive wound. It also reassembled the dismembered body politic in Christ, "teaching us that we are members of one another."[85]

Further in contrast to the healing ministry of Christ in the Gospels, which portrays bodily healing as a clear sign of the immanence of god's eschatological kingdom, in Antony's *Letters* the therapy wrought by Christ's incarnation has produced not an instantaneously healed humanity but rather only a humanity with the potential for health. Antony laments those who have willfully turned away from Christ and descended back into irrationality and the continuing threat that heresy, specifically that of Arius, poses to wound humanity again.[86]

Ascetic Health

Antony's soteriological health is gained through supplication to the saints and emulation of their ascetic practices, just as the saints bear witness to the pitiful and wounded state of humanity and rejoice at humanity's journey to soundness, testifying on its behalf: "Truly, my children, this affliction and humiliation of ours gives distress to all the saints. For our sake they weep and moan before the Creator of all. Thus, because of the moaning of the saints, the God of all is angry with all our evil deeds. But our progress and justification stirs up the assembly of the saints, and they pray devoutly and make joyful exultation before our Creator, and he himself, the Creator of all, rejoices in our good deeds on the testimony of his saints and so he grants us great gifts of grace."[87] The model of the saints is critical to Antony's medicalized soteriology. The movement from illness and woundedness to healing and salvation lies not just in acquiring knowledge of humanity's true spiritual essence but also in emulating the practices of the saints. While he clearly refers to the ranks of heavenly saints in *Letter* 5, elsewhere—if with trepidation at the potential for vainglory it poses—Antony acknowledges that "the saints" include living ascetics, people like himself who "[wear] the habit" and "[have] the name of saints."[88] Specifically it is through the saints and through asceticism that humanity reclaims the primordial health that characterized existence before the fall into irrationality.

As *Letters* 2–7 set up the context, *Letter* 1 lays out the practical results of the healing operation of Christ now made possible in the world, especially through the ascetic program advocated by Antony. The new age allows the Christian—and given the audience of Antony's *Letters* we can understand this to refer principally to Christian ascetics—to regain Adam's original, prelapsarian state through controlling the passions and thoughts. Echoing the parable of the sower, Antony claims that there are three kinds of souls who have received the word of god. Some receive it by the "law of promise." They are of the class of Abraham and "easily attain the virtues, since their hearts are ready to be guided by the Spirit of God." Others respond to the threats of punishment in the next life and thus "try to enter into their calling." Still others come to their senses only through "afflictions and chastisement" that "God the merciful sends" "until through their afflictions they are made aware and repent and return." Once they do so, they "attain the virtues, like the others." "These," Antony says, "are the three gates for the souls who come to repent."[89]

How to repent? For Antony, repentance is achieved through asceticism, by which the Christian learns to control the body and soul together and thus may return to God. He writes, "He [Christ] sets for them a rule for how to repent in their bodies and souls until he has taught them the way to return to God, their own Creator. He also gives them control over their souls and bodies in order that both may be sanctified and inherit together."[90] The "rule" includes all the familiar exercises of Christian asceticism, "fasts and vigils" and "the exertion and the exercises of the body, cutting of[f] all the fruits of the flesh."[91] Thereby mercy may be received: "If the soul endures and obeys what the Spirit has taught it about repentance, then the Creator has mercy on the weariness of its repentance through the labours of the body, such as prolonged fasts, vigils, much study of the Word of God and many prayers, as well as the renunciation of the world and human things, humility, and contrition. And if it endures in all this, then God the merciful sees its patience in the temptation and has mercy and helps it."[92] Through this rule the mind then learns to purify the body and the soul through discernment of "what is natural to the body."[93] This returns the body to its prelapsarian condition, just as the mind is resurrected through the healing activity of Jesus Christ, as Antony describes in *Letters* 2–7. The mind then "leads each member of the body back to its original condition, free from everything alien that belongs to the spirit of the enemy," and "[t]he body is thus brought under the authority of the mind and is taught by the Spirit, as the words of Paul testify: *I castigate my body and bring it into subjection*."[94]

This discernment works by distinguishing the three kinds of movements in the body: (1) "natural, inherent movements," which operate with the soul's consent; (2) movements from gluttony, that is, caused by excessive or improper consumption of food and drink; and (3) movements from evil spirits, "tempting us out of envy and seeking to divert those who attempt to sanctify themselves," such as the long litany of ills that Antony gives in *Letter 6*. With proper training the soul may purify itself of these three movements.[95]

Antony frames this purification, again, in quasi-medical terms of healing of afflictions and returning the body and soul to their proper state: "[W]hen the mind accepts this struggle, then it prays in the Spirit and begins to expel the afflictions of the soul which have come upon it through its own greed. The soul is then in communion with the Spirit, since it keeps the commandments it has received. And the Spirit teaches it how to heal all its afflictions, and how to expel them one by one, from head to foot, those mingled with what is natural to the body as well as those which are independent of the body, but have been mingled with it through the will."[96] This process of healing is not limited to the mind's receiving *gnōsis* about its true nature and the nature of the created world; rather it is actualized through ascetic practices of bodily renunciation. The ascetic reclamation of humanity's prelapsarian purity comprises renunciations that include movements or "afflictions of the soul which have become mingled with what is natural to the body" and movements of the soul alone.[97] Regarding the psychic movements that impinge on the body, Antony runs down the body, from the eyes to the feet, explaining how the renunciant, with teaching by the holy spirit and Christ the physician, may "heal all its afflictions." The bodily members are sometimes described as "sick" (eyes, ears, tongue) and other times as disordered or unsound (hands, feet) or simply insatiable or unquenched (belly, genitals). Regardless, through adherence to the ascetic rule they may be "purified" of their afflictions and unnatural movements. The ascetic may also repent of the afflictions "proper to [the soul] alone," the passions or emotions, which include pride, self-glorification, insolence, hatred, envy, wrath, pusillanimity, impatience, and other unnamed passions.[98]

A brief comparison of the role of health and illness in Antony's *Letters* with their role in the letters previously discussed is in order here. It is first important to note the differing character of the authors' interests. While the health or illness of ascetics is certainly worthy of note in the archives of Hathor's monks and the *Letters* of Pachomius, the concerns of those authors are quite different. The correspondents of the monks of Hathor evince the same concern for the monks' health found in late ancient letter writing in general; and it is clear that the correspondents would have a very real motive for hoping for the continuing earthly presence of the monks, as they served as patrons to their lay *clientes*. In the case of Pachomius's *Letters*, concern with health and sickness, and here specifically those of monks, was both of a practical nature, assuring the adequate care of invalid monks during the Easter travel, and of a theological and moral nature: the monks' attitude toward their sick brethren and their care for them impinge on their future salvation.

In the context, then, of contemporary monastic reflection on the meaning of health and illness in monastic life, Antony's reflections in the *Letters* are striking. Health and sickness, both of humanity as a whole and of the ascetic in particular, are among the predominant motifs in the seven *Letters*. Health and sickness in Antony's thought are central ways of describing the arc of salvation history, from the fall and dissolution of initial unity, to the wounded state of fallen existence, to the dispensation of various prophets over the centuries who attempted—and failed—to heal the great wound of humanity's fall, to the penultimate visitation by the great physician Jesus Christ, whose teachings enabled the "great wound" to be healed, to the anticipated eschatological return of the savior. In Antony's stage of salvation history, humanity possessed the cure, but some still refused it, preferring to immerse themselves lasciviously in irrationality.[99] Heretics too, such as Arius, continued to threaten humanity's health, by wounding them with false teachings. All of the preceding is very much in the tradition of Origen's medical Christology.

What is new and extremely important in Antony's reflections on health and illness is the role of the ascetic, the saint. Specifically, Antony does not highlight the sacraments as the saving medicine of the soul, as is so common in early medical Christology. Rather, Antony locates Christ's saving medicine in ascetic practice. Through the range of self-fashioning spiritual exercises that characterized early Christian monastic *askēsis*, the monk may regain the state of prelapsarian health, purifying the movements of the bodily members from head to toe and purifying the thoughts and passions from the envious attacks of the demons, themselves incurable and destined for eternal torments.

The symbolic echoes of protological health through asceticism may be unmistakably heard in the *History of the Monks in Egypt*'s description of Isidore's garden of health. Yet Antony does not explicitly or implicitly portray the life of the monk as one of perfect bodily health, at least as might be manifested in long-lived freedom from disease. The health of the monk's body is not an issue of great concern to Antony in his surviving *Letters*. Antony's concern lies in the much more important and lasting health of the eternal mind, the essence of humanity that will outlast the body. In his discussion of the purification of bodily members, he focuses on the interplay between the soul and the body parts, not the body itself. Antony writes of health and sickness on the levels of soul, mind, and cosmos, and his ascetic theology espouses the healthiness of the mind and soul, looking forward to the eventual reunification of human minds with god, rather than to the earthly manifestation of prelapsarian health in the monk's body.

Underlying these distinctions between Antony's espousal of ascetic healthiness and that of the *History of the Monks in Egypt* is, of course, an important connection, not reflected in the letters to the monks of Hathor and the *Letters* of Pachomius. In both the *History* and Antony's *Letters*, the monk is expected to reclaim through ascetic practices a healthiness that had been impossible since the expulsion from paradise, healthiness made possible through the incarnation of god's son. How, one might ask, do we get from Antony's presentation of monastic health to that of the *History of the Monks in Egypt*, some fifty to seventy years later? Certainly such a question cannot be answered definitively, but one could do worse than to look at the biography of Antony, which would overshadow his own *Letters* in presenting an ideology of Christian monasticism and of the monk's health to the late ancient world and beyond. In the next chapter I turn to the hagiographical elaboration of ascetic health, which narrativizes and complicates the psychic and bodily transformations that Antony describes in his *Letters*.

Chapter 3

Paradise, Health, and the Hagiographical Imagination

The *Life of Antony* (probably written between 356 and 360) marks a watershed in the history of monasticism: the birth of a popular literature of monasticism. The *Life* marks the first (surviving) literary work intended to inform the nonmonastic public about monasticism, an educative process also intended to entertain and edify.[1] The *Life of Antony* would enjoy a fast rise to popularity, which it still enjoys. Furthermore the monastic *bios* as genre would become one of the most popular forms of literature in late antiquity.[2] Whether penned by Athanasius or not, the *Life*—and its ideology of ascetic health—bore a remarkable influence over the late ancient hagiographical imagination, which in turn would impinge on the behaviors of "real" monks (to be discussed in Chapter 4). In short order Athanasius's Antony would assume the role of exemplar in monastic mythology, and his *Life* would become a template for later hagiography.

Despite the attention that the *Life* has drawn, studies have not sufficiently appreciated the role that ascetic health (and its obverse, illness) plays in the *Life of Antony*, not to mention the contention it evoked in other late ancient sources. When set alongside the epistolary documentation for monasticism in the 330s through the 350s presented in the previous chapter, the *Life of Antony* provides a strikingly coherent model for making meaning out of the health and illness of ascetics. The *Life of Antony* echoes any number of elements of Antony's *Letters*, not least its emphasis on the monk's reclamation of primordial, Edenic health through ascetic practice.[3] In sharp contrast with texts that will be the subjects of later chapters, which argue that illness functions as an aid—even the most effective tool—for asceticism, Athanasius promotes a model of Christian sanctity in which proper ascetic practice leads to the elimination of illness. While this model would provide the narrative template for many later hagiographies, the *Life*'s conceptualization of ascetic health would provoke no shortage of criticism from later writers, especially monastic authors. Writers in the wake of *Life of Antony*, for all its influence, did not adopt its hagiographic model without anxiety. Later writers, even those writing in the familiar Antonian mode, modify, critique, or subvert the model of monastic health promoted by the *Life*. Sometimes these critiques are subtle, as is the case in the other Lives discussed in the present chapter, Jerome's *Life of Paul of Thebes* and Paphnutius's *Life of Onnophrius*. Both Jerome and Paphnutius work within and elaborate (sometimes fancifully) the narrative and theological structures established by the *Life of Antony*, both in making meaning out of the relative health of the ascetic and by assessing the function of health and illness in establishing the sanctity and authority of the monk. Yet each critiques the Antonian model. Jerome uses the standards set by the *Life of Antony* to displace Antony's originary status, while Paphnutius creates an even more paradisiacal garden of health in the desert, at the same time closing off the gates to that garden as a practical goal and model for his monastic readership. In Chapters 4 and 5 I show that other writers would be more open in their criticism of the *Life of Antony*'s ideology of monastic health.

Antony's Asceticism and Health

The *Life* is familiar enough that there is little need for a detailed summary. Suffice it to say that Athanasius presents Antony as enduring a harsh and unrelenting *askēsis*. Throughout Athanasius's description of Antony's ascetic career he is depicted as pushing himself to the point of death. Antony's first experiments in monastic asceticism were severe, at least by the standards of popular asceticism; he slept on a rush mat, refused to bathe, and survived on water, bread, and salt, eaten at most once a day but more typically every other or every fourth day.[4] He undertook such regimens to "accustom [his body] to pains [or toils (*ponois*)]." Taking to heart Paul's admonition of 2 Corinthians 12:10, "When I am weak (*astheneō*), then I am strong (*dunatos*)," Athanasius has Antony claim that by rendering the bodily pleasures sick or weak (*astheneō*) the "force" (*tonos*) of the soul is intensified (*ischuō*).[5] The use of *tonos* ("force," "intensity," or "tension") to describe the soul evokes the image of the soul as a sort of muscle or tendon to be conditioned and exercised by *askēsis*. This may reflect the influence of Stoic natural science, which characteristically described the *psykhē* in muscular terms, with a tension that may be slack or tight.[6] The "force" of his soul thus allows Antony to push his body to limits that would kill any ordinary mortal yet could leave the heroic monk—at worst—only mostly dead, as he is once mistaken for dead by his servant.[7]

Asceticism could be painful indeed and injurious to the body. The *Life* characterizes his early attempts at solitary asceticism in the tombs as dominated by pain (*ponos*), though it is important to note that the pain and wounds are caused by demonic tests and are neither the results of specific ascetic exercises nor the indication of any sin on Antony's part.[8] Athanasius insists that, in the face of such enormous pain, Antony's regimen did not harm the body irreparably. Quite to the contrary, his strengthened (*ischuō*) soul in turn strengthened his body. Thus after undergoing torment and pain from Satan and his theriomorphic demons, Antony is rewarded with renewed health: "The pain (*ponos*) of his body ceased," and once again he breathed "more easily" and was "relieved of the sufferings."[9] The ascetic regimen did not merely return Antony to his formerly healthy state; it left him transformed, physically enhanced: "[H]e was so strengthened that he felt that his body contained more might than before."[10] His health, in the bishop's description, manifests the internal state of his soul. It bears witness to his ascetic merit: he has endured tortures that would have broken a lesser man. And it signifies him as one of god's protected, for whom god interceded and whom god imbued with exceptional power and strength, in both body and soul.

Athanasius betrays some concern in the *Life* that his claims about the special signification of monastic health—not to mention the other wonders of Antony's career—might be difficult to accept as anything other than a tall tale, a phenomenon noted in Chapter 2. Athanasius responds by downplaying the exceptionality of Antony's exploits. In fact he claims that the ascetic feats described therein represent only a small sampling of his virtues. He urges his readers, "Do not be incredulous about what you hear of him from those who make reports [that is, Athanasius]. Consider, rather, that from them only a few of his feats have been learned, for these hardly gave full description of so much."[11] The events described in the *Life*, Athanasius swears, are true.[12] Any possible incredulity notwithstanding, Athanasius encourages his readers to emulate Antony.[13] Athanasius writes, "Antony's way of life provides monks with a sufficient picture for ascetic practice."[14] He furthermore urges, "[R]ead these things now to the other brothers so that they may learn what the life of the monks ought to be."[15] At least one of Athanasius's contemporaries understood the *Life* to be a rule, no less than any coenobitic *regula*, a habit of hagiographic reading that could cause problems, however (as we will see in the next chapter).[16]

There is little question that readers of Athanasius could have reasonably interpreted Antony's ascetic health to be a true model for the ascetic life. According to the influential treatise *On Virginity*, which had circulated under Athanasius's name at least since late antiquity, ascetic fasting induces and maintains health. (Probably Pseudo-) Athanasius draws on ethical and medical commonplaces to explain the healthful effects of asceticism (discipline of both the soul and the body): "Humility is a great remedy (*pharmakon*)"; "Fasting, prayer, and pity are a great safeguard (or amulet, *phylaktērion*)"; and most tellingly, "Look at what fasting does: it cures diseases (*nosous therapeuei*), dries up the bodily humors (*rheumata sōmatika*), expels demons, chases away evil thoughts, makes the mind brighter, the heart pure, and the body sanctified, and raises the human to the throne of God."[17] Athanasius's ancient readers would have been justified in seeing the healthful effects of Antony's asceticism in just such terms.

While the *Life* does not reflect medical imagery with the same specificity as the pseudonymous treatise *On Virginity*, Athanasius's insistence on the dialectical influence of body and soul reflects ancient physiological and medical theory on a general level. The use of *tonos* as a psychic attribute, with its semantics of stretching, tensing, bracing, and strengthening, reflects the fact that the ancient Greeks, Romans, and Egyptians had none of the modern Cartesian duality of material body and immaterial soul.[18] Rather the soul was "material" (*physikē*) too, just of a finer sort of "stuff."[19] Body and soul impinged upon each other: psychic illness could lead to bodily dysfunction, just as bodily illness necessarily affected the health of the soul, as, for example, a superfluity of yellow bile could lead to delirium, black bile to melancholy, or phlegm to lethargy in Galen's *The Soul's Dependence on the Body*.[20]

Athanasius's portrait of an ideal asceticism shares some superficial commonalities with medical and philosophical literature of the Roman Empire. These commonplaces are well enough documented that they need not be detailed here except to say that the educated class commonly assumed that health could be maintained and many ailments could be avoided by ascetic regimen: a light diet of vegetables, bread, water, and wine in moderation.[21] Meat was ideally to be avoided. Other forms of physically stimulating activities—bathing, sex, drinking with friends—were also recognized to be injurious. Furthermore ascetical care for the soul—that is, ongoing moral self-examination—was also encouraged to better the health of the body. Illness of soul—that is, any passion (*pathos*), such as lovesickness—could lead to dysfunction in the body; likewise illness of the body, such as that caused by neglect or overindulgence, necessarily affected the soul's health.[22] Thus it is not surprising that the moral figures of the empire (Socrates, Pythagoras, Diogenes, certain Egyptian priests, for example) were regarded as unusually healthy, even "radiant" in their appearance, much like the Antony of the *Life*.[23] For those readers familiar with the philosophical-medical-ethical *koinē* characterized by such wide-ranging authors as Plutarch, Galen, and Porphyry, Athanasius's representation of monastic health as directly signifying the monk's ascetic merit would hold a certain commonsensical attraction.

Beyond such superficial similarities, the regimen encouraged as a model and rule in the *Life of Antony* is much harsher than those recommended by physicians and moral philosophers of the late empire. In the words of the medical historian Owsei Temkin, "Antony's mode of life broke all the rules of Hippocratic hygiene," even while he appeared the model of health.[24] While medical and moral writers encouraged sexual abstinence and moderate diet, avoidance of meat, for example, is one thing, while fasting for two (let alone four) days at a time is quite another. While such moralists as Plutarch recommended restricted bathing, they hardly intended their readers to go their entire lives without hygienic care.[25] Indeed classical Greek medicine could look at such asceticism with great suspicion. The influential Hippocratic work *Aphorisms* thus advises against ascetic diet, even for those of robust constitution: "Sick people (*hoi noseontes*) are in error when they take a light diet which only increases their distress. Then, whatever be wrong, they only become more ill on a light diet than they would on a slightly more substantial one. For this reason, light and frugal diets, when persisted in, are dangerous even for the healthy, because the undernourished do not bear an illness so well as the well nourished. Therefore, on the whole, light and frugal diets are more dangerous than those which are a little more substantial."[26] Physicians could be similarly suspicious about excessive abstinence from wine and sex, not to mention bathing—a staple of ancient medical treatment.[27] Indeed, Antony's *askēsis* was not that of the medically sophisticated class and did not promote a middle way of moderate self-control.

Rather, Athanasius characterizes "health" in Antony's asceticism in the *Life* as less medical than protological. Echoing Antony's characterization of the potential for renewed health through asceticism in the *Letters*, the ascetic regains the psychic and somatic unity that characterized prelapsarian health. Reflecting this unity, soul and body were locked in dialectical influence, which may be observed in both directions, as Athanasius explains in the fragmentary treatise "On Sickness and Health." Here Athanasius emphasizes the soul as a signifier of bodily virtues. In a manner evocative of Antony's discussion of purifying the self of the passions, member by bodily member (discussed in Chapter 2) Athanasius writes,

> In short, lest I linger making clear the particulars, one must know that the body is composed of members, but the inner person is not composed of bodily members, but rather possesses the significance (*tēn sēmasian ekhei*) of the members' actions. Thus, the soul's progress toward virtue is the feet, and the accuracy of its reflections is the hands, and the clearsighted mind is the eye, and the discrimination of thoughts is the tongue itself. And it is said to have even a womb, so that the productive capacity of thought itself might be made manifest, as it is written, "From fear of you, we have conceived, and been in labour, and given birth to a spirit of salvation, which we have wrought upon the earth."[28]

But it is the body's signification of the monk's ascetic merit (rather than the soul's signification of bodily purity) that occupies the central role in Athanasius's *Life of Antony*. In fact Antony's physical appearance, viz. his remarkable health, is a central component of Athanasius's ascetic theology. Antony, whose soul is guided by the divine logos, brings his flesh under control, subjugating it to the soul.[29] The primary sign of this is that Antony has transcended the mundane susceptibility to illness and is himself a *corpus incorruptum*.

Such extraordinary health is emphasized in Antony's emergence from his desert tomb after twenty years of solitude, as well as at his death. This public debut, as the *Life* presents it, was quite against Antony's will. In the previous twenty years Antony's reputation had grown steadily, fed by the reports of the visitors who had occasionally glimpsed the hermit through the cracks in the doorjamb and heard the sounds of wild animals and corporeal struggle. His followers, burning with desire to imitate the anchorite, "came and tore down and forcefully removed the fortress door" to behold fully Antony for the first time in two decades. Antony's appearance leaves them stunned: "Antony came forth as though from some shrine, having been led into divine mysteries and inspired by God. . . . And when they beheld him, they were amazed to see that his body had maintained its former condition, neither fat from lack of exercise, nor emaciated from fasting and combat with demons, but was just as they had known him prior to his withdrawal."[30] It has been well established that the presentation of Antony's health in this passage concords nicely with Athanasius's theology. It may also reflect the influence of Porphyry's *Life of Pythagoras* and Iamblichus's *On the Pythagorean Way of Life*.[31] Antony's bodily and psychic equilibrium is an expression of his guidance by the word of god. As David Brakke argues, "Antony's soul has recovered its likeness to the Word and, as a result, has regained proper control over the body."[32] The "proper control over the body" is signified in both Antony's exceptional health and his ability to help others, through healing, exorcism, and instruction. His equilibrium endows him with control of the passions, perhaps reflecting the influence of Iamblichus's *On the Pythagorean Way of Life*, and an exceptionally long life.

The remarkable health witnessed at his emergence from the tomb held throughout his life, because of his steadfast adherence to strict asceticism, which, according to Athanasius, he kept unabated until his death. Athanasius delineates the precise external signs of the healthful soul, signs that point to the endurance of severe ascetic practices. He claims that

you can deduce . . . what kind of person the man of God, Antony, was, who kept his fervent commitment to the discipline (*tēs askēseōs*) from youth to such an advanced age. He never succumbed, due to old age, to extravagance in food, nor did he change his mode of dress because of frailty of the body, nor even bathe his feet with water, and yet in every way he remained free of injury (*ablabēs*). For he possessed eyes undimmed and sound, and saw clearly. He lost none of his teeth—they simply had been worn to the gums because of the old man's great age. He also retained health in his feet and hands, and generally he seemed brighter and of more energetic strength than those who make use of baths and a variety of foods and clothing.[33]

Athanasius not only echoes the prelapsarian health of Adam and the stories about Pythagoras but also follows the biblical exemplar of Moses for his model of Christian sanctity: at the age of 120 "his sight was unimpaired and his vigor had not abated."[34] Athanasius's portrait of the ascetic as possessor of preternatural health thus draws on (or at least reflects) a number of elements: the protological characterization of asceticism by Antony in his *Letters*; the motif of the health of the spiritual athlete in Greek philosophical Lives; and the biblical model of Moses.

A brief comparison to the significant corpora of monastic evidence from the two generations before the *Life of Antony* sets Athanasius's vision of monastic health and illness in sharp relief. Absent are the mundane references to monastic sickness and health that characterize the attitudes of Pachomius and the followers of the Melitian monks. Absent is any notion of monastic sickness as an unquestioned, everyday occurrence, even if one that could pose (in the case of Pachomius's writings) special administrative challenges or (in the Hathor archives) a loss of the monk's patronal aid. And despite the shared protological imagery in both the *Letters* and the *Life*, the *Life* draws very different practical implications for the lifestyle of the monk. The healing of the "great wound" through ascetic discipline in Antony's *Letters* occurs on the level of the soul and spirit. Antony the letter writer betrays no belief that the ascetic will achieve any freedom from bodily decrepitude and illness. Athanasius clearly has a different vision in mind. This may partly reflect the conventions of the different, nascent genre of monastic biography, but it will be clear in later chapters that even within a given genre (intramonastic letters, saints' Lives) authors had great leeway to negotiate and redefine (contentiously so) the meaning of the relationship between sanctity and health.

In the stead of these early representations of the significance of monastic sickness and health, Athanasius transforms the health of the monastic into one of the clearest signifiers of monastic virtue. Through the endurance of extreme asceticism Antony is endowed with strength and bodily health that exceed those he enjoyed before entering the ascetic contest. Antony's health is one of the primary signs to his followers of the state of his soul. Consequently his fame and the marvel of his extraordinary health provide indisputable "[p]roof of his virtue" (*tēs aretēs . . . gnōrisma*).[35]

In Antony's model the suffering of pain, wounds, and illness is not an inherent fact of human existence but the effect of a discrete and passable stage in ascetic progress. Such wounds and pains are caused not by ascetic practice in itself. They are attacks from the devil. If the monk, such as Antony, succeeds in his ascetic exercises, the devil may be vanquished, which will leave the monk's soul as toned as an athlete's muscles—neither tight nor relaxed but at an ideal state of control and flexibility. The monastic's success in conditioning the soul will then be reflected externally in the state of the body, which naturally will be healthy due to the perfect balance or equilibrium. The health of the monastic thus offers the observer a window into the monk's soul and an indication of his or her ascetic merit.

Illness and Ascetic Merit after Athanasius

There is little need to argue the influence of Athanasius's *Life of Antony* on the worldview of late ancient Christians. The *Life* circulated widely and was quickly translated into Latin and the languages of the Christian Near East. It established the primary template for later monastic biographies.[36] The ascetic whose sanctity manifests in extraordinary health would become in short order the model on which later hagiographers developed their own pious fictions. In this tradition the *History of the Monks in Egypt* presents the longevity of the saint as a near necessity in "collective biography," as even coenobitic monks en masse may live without illness or injury until their peaceful, orderly death in old age.[37]

But later elaboration of this theme was not limited to unthinking imitation. Writing in the *Life of Antony*'s wake, hagiographers adapted the theme, modifying, twisting, and critiquing it. Two such texts adopt the basic model of ascetic health promoted in the *Life of Antony* while simultaneously reshaping it: Jerome's *Life of Paul the Hermit* and Paphnutius's *Life of Onnophrius*. These narratives show how attractive—even inescapable—Antony's *Life* was as a narrative template; they also reflect the potentials and difficulties of using it as a model for understanding monastic health and illness. (In the following two chapters I discuss other texts, both hagiographical and nonhagiographical, that are much more critical of the *Life of Antony* as a model for ascetic life in saintly narrative.) In Jerome's composition Jerome uses the health of his protagonist Paul and the relative health of Antony as a fulcrum in his attempt to displace Antony's centrality in the ancient historiography of monasticism and at the same time to highlight that of Paul. In the *Life of Onnophrius*, Paphnutius elaborates the paradisiacal elements of desert asceticism that Athanasius introduces into the *Life of Antony* and which Jerome in turn augments. The health of the ascetic and the health-giving properties of the desert are given a centrality in Paphnutius's narrative that far surpasses that in the *Life of Antony*. At the same time Paphnutius shifts focus considerably from that of Athanasius, who intended his description of Antony's asceticism to serve as a model for emulation. Paphnutius argues quite the opposite. Paphnutius's narrative removes the Edenic health in the "inner desert" from the potential lived experience of his readers; it is distant, fantastic, and—perhaps with a hint of melancholy—no longer accessible to the monks of his generation, who must content themselves with the more mundane comforts and hardships of Nile monasticism.

The Life of Paul of Thebes, the First Hermit

Jerome's *Life of Paul of Thebes* stands out as an early example of discomfort at the normative and nearly canonical status of the *Life of Antony*. Unlike some later critiques, however, Jerome's *Life of Paul* stands out both in its explicit dependence on the *Life of Antony* and in its own popularity.

Everyone knows the story of Antony, says Jerome, writing in 377, some twenty years after the publication of the *Life of Antony*. Many think that Antony was the "first monk to dwell in the desert," or at least "this is the common opinion of the uninformed."[38] Of course Jerome intends to claim that honor for his own hero, Paul. Jerome adopts Antony's *Life*—and its particular ideology of monastic health—as the very model of the virtuous ascetic (in contrast to the competitive narration that we will see in the Great Coptic *Life of Pachomius* in Chapter 5). Yet all the while he draws on this same motif to undermine Antony's primacy as the founder of desert monasticism.[39]

Jerome's one-upmanship runs throughout the *Life*. Paul precedes Antony by two decades. Unlike the unlearned Antony, Paul is "highly educated in Greek and Coptic." In addition Paul's invention of desert asceticism makes the Edenic imagery of the *Life of Antony* seem positively subtle. Journeying without aim in the desert in flight from the emperor Decius's persecution, he comes upon "a great cave closed off by a stone," a sight that echoes the discovery of a lost Eden as well as the discovery of Christ's promised resurrection. Inside this cave of treasures, which Paul finds to be a centuries-abandoned "clandestine mint," "he came upon a large room open to the sky," a speluncar microcosm in which "an ancient palm tree formed with its spreading branches a ceiling" and a "crystal-clear spring" flowed.[40] Here Paul lives for nearly a century in a paradisiacal existence, with all his needs supplied by god via the date palm and a bird who brings him a half loaf of bread each day.[41] He lives in concord with the animals, apparently sharing the cave with a she wolf. In the *Life*'s perhaps most iconic image, mourning lions appear at his death to dig his grave and pay their respects to his new disciple Antony.[42] The *Life of Paul* presents a paradigmatic picture of the monk's return to paradise.

Perhaps the most significant aspect of Paul's recovery of paradise, however, is his extraordinary health. While Paul's healthy longevity is well known, the significance of the theme of prelapsarian health has not been as properly noted. For example, in Alison Goddard Eliot's study of the paradise theme in early Christian hagiography, *Roads to Paradise*, the motif goes unmentioned, unlike diet, chastity, and concord with animals.[43] In fact it is this aspect of the saint's life that Jerome highlights as of special significance, as Jerome writes to another Paul, of Concordia (in Aquileia), to announce the completion of his *Life of Paul of Thebes*. Paul of Concordia had just passed his one hundredth year, and in this short letter Jerome identifies longevity as a sure signifier of sanctity and highlights the longevity of Paul of Thebes as a core component of the narrative.[44] In the following passage, Jerome praises the longevity of his correspondent as a sign of his holiness and emphasizes that his seniority has not seen any decline in health. It can be no coincidence that his language echoes the description of Antony's health at the end of his days, though reflecting Jerome's reliance on more medical terminology than in the *Life of Antony*.[45] While Jerome acknowledges that one's health is not always reliable as a signifier of virtue, in the case of Paul of Concordia (and of course Paul of Thebes as well) it is reliable and prefigures the resurrection:

> For see, the hundredth circling year is already passing over you, and yet, always keeping the commandments of the Lord, amid the circumstances of your present life you think over the blessedness of that which is to come. Your eyes are bright and keen, your steps steady, your hearing good, your teeth are white, your voice musical, your flesh firm and full of sap; your ruddy cheeks belie your white hairs, your strength is not that of your age. Advancing years have not, as we too often see them do, impaired the tenacity of your memory; the coldness of your blood has not blunted an intellect at once warm and wary. Your face is not wrinkled nor your brow furrowed. Lastly, no tremors palsy your hand or cause it to travel in crooked pathways over the wax on which you write. The Lord shows us in you the bloom of the resurrection that is to be ours; so that whereas in others who die by inches while yet living, we recognize the results of sin, in your case we ascribe it to righteousness (*iustitiae*) that you still simulate youth (*adulescentiam*) at an age to which it is foreign. And although we see the like haleness of body (*corporis sanitatem*) in many even of those who are sinners, in their case it is a grant of the devil to lead them into sin, while in yours it is a gift of God to make you rejoice.[46]

Thus in this short letter announcing the publication of the *Life of Paul,* Jerome presents one aspect of Paul's character as signifying his sanctity: his healthy longevity. This is in sharp contrast to the shortness of human life, a direct consequence of human sin and the expulsion from Eden.[47] The individual's illness and decrepitude—Jerome implies—too indicate the individual's sin. It is further important to underscore that Jerome describes the health and age of his correspondent as reflecting the health of the great saint Antony, health and longevity that Paul of Thebes surpassed, a detail that Jerome notes in the close of his letter.[48]

Likewise in the *Life of Paul*, Jerome emphasizes that Paul lives to 113, a point that Jerome foregrounds in Paul's *Life* rather than mentioning it at his death.[49] The contrast is clear, as Antony's sanctity allowed him to live merely to 105, a biographical detail that Jerome hardly needs to mention. While Antony's strength of soul allows him to live in full health until his very end, this is hardly as remarkable as Antony's *Life* would make it seem, since Jerome's correspondent Paul of Concordia possesses the same longevity and health. Paul's healthy appearance, in contrast, endures even further than Antony's. Even in death he was so strong as to be virtually indistinguishable from the living Paul: "[W]hen [Antony] entered the cave, he saw Paul kneeling, with his head held high and his arms extended to the sky. But the body was lifeless. At first, Antony believed Paul still to be alive and so knelt beside him to join in prayer. But when he heard not even a breath of normal sound from his partner in prayer, Antony embraced and kissed him, wept, and understood that even the corpse of the holy man was praying in appropriate posture to the God for whom all things live."[50]

The undecaying corpse of the holy man would become a standard feature in later hagiography, in Jerome's as well, such as the *Life of Hilarion*, whose corpse exudes sweet perfume when disinterred by eager relic hunters.[51] But the imagery in the *Life of Paul* is especially important, since Paul is not simply a *corpus incorruptum*; his body continues the ascetic practice of unceasing prayer (and one would expect also fasting and chastity) well after his death. Unlike Paul of Thebes, however, Antony is weak. Jerome describes Antony as "[e]xhausted and panting" (*fatigatus* [ms. variant *defatigatus*] *et anhelus*), "his body weak with fasting" (*corpus inane jejuniis*), though no doubt exceptional and holy.[52] He does not go as far as the Great Coptic *Life of Pachomius* will in subverting the *Life of Antony*'s narrative of ascetic health (see Chapter 5) but adapts it to advocate for the priority of his Paul over Athanasius's Antony. Jerome accepts the basic definition of ascetic sanctity that the *Life of Antony* advocates. Saintliness is most centrally signified by a healthy longevity, the single aspect of Paul of Thebes's lifestyle that he notes in his letter announcing the publication of the *Life*. Yet Paul knocks Antony down a peg, so to speak.

His endurance fails in comparison to Paul's, and his lifespan is shorter. Antony is no doubt holy, but if only by a hair, Paul bests him.

The Life of Onnophrius

The *Lives* of Antony and Paul would exercise wide influence over the Christian cultures of the late ancient Mediterranean and Near East, but as Jerome's *Life of Paul* demonstrates, the cultural presence of a master text such as the *Life of Antony* does not necessarily inspire slavish imitation, for all of Athanasius's insistence that the lifestyle be emulated. Later writers, even those working in the hagiographic mode, would find ways to expand upon the templates and narrative models established in the foundational lives, elaborating the lives in ways that could in fact undermine or counteract some of the core arguments or suppositions of early hagiographies.

The *Life of Onnophrius* stands out as an early hagiography that adopts the master narrative of the *Life of Antony* and the *Life of Paul*, showing the pervasive influence of the texts but at the same time complicating the received traditions about the meaning and function of health and illness in asceticism.

While the text describes itself as a *Life* and shares some features with the genre, the form of the text, as others have observed, is closer to that of the travel narrative or *peregrinatio*, such as the *Lausiac History* and the *History of the Monks of Egypt*.[53] Yet the narrative shares many elements and motifs with that of the *Lives* of Antony and Paul, the latter in particular. The connections between the *Life of Paul* and the *Life of Onnophrius* are so close that it is tempting to posit a direct influence.[54] Regardless it is clear that Paphnutius composed his *Life of Onnophrius*, like his *Histories of the Monks of Upper Egypt*, within the shared, burgeoning culture of monastic hagiographical and travel writing.

As such, Paphnutius begins the tale in the first person and sets off into the inner desert in search of any brother monks, thereby following the general itinerary ascribed to Antony in the *Life of Paul*. He leaves far behind any familiar territory, traveling for four days and nights. Echoing Antony's discovery of Paul after his return to the inner desert, Paphnutius comes upon an unnamed monk kneeling in prayer in a cave. Paphnutius's version of the story turns toward the grotesque: when he reaches for the monk's arm, it comes off in his hand and "disintegrate[s] into dust" (*afbōl ebol afrkah*).[55] Onnophrius then digs a grave for the rest of the monk's body and heads further into the desert. Already the *Life of Onnophrius* establishes that the journey into the desert will present marvels of travel and the lives of ascetics whose asceticism can transcend death.

Paphnutius wanders on to find another cave, this one inhabited by a living monk, Timothy, who resembles Paul's unclothed, Edenic state: "he was naked and his hair covered his shame and served as clothing over him."[56] While Paphnutius's text bears the title *Life of Onnophrius*, Timothy's story makes up much of the early portions of the text; and Timothy's narrative of his withdrawal to the desert establishes perhaps most clearly in late ancient monastic literature the close connection between monasticism, the reclamation of paradise, and a new, monastic state of health. Timothy begins as no hero, in contrast with the *Lives* of Antony and Paul. Timothy's narrative is set in a later generation than the Athanasian and Hieronymean ur-Lives. His career began as a coenobitic monk in the Thebaid, from which in search of greater solitude and holiness he withdrew to a hermit's cell. This attracted the envy (*kōh*) of the devil, who sent a female monk to him (*shime mmonakhē*), and over time through the devil's envy, evoking the language of Wisdom of Solomon 24:2, they "gave birth to death and brought forth wickedness."[57] After living in sin for six months, Timothy repented and withdrew further into the desert, where he discovered, like Paul before him, a cave with a flowing spring and a date palm. The date palm providentially, Timothy tells Paphnutius, sprouts one bunch of dates each month, which still provides him with sufficient food. All his other needs are provided for as well, since his hair grows to provide clothing, and the climate is somehow different from the rest of Egypt and the desert, temperate.[58] The explicitness of the paradisiacal imagery surpasses even that of the *Life of Paul*.

However, the dialogue between Paphnutius and Timothy in the *Life of Onnophrius* takes up a topic left only implicit in the *Life of Paul*: How does the desert monk stay healthy? Was Timothy's state of Edenic equilibrium instantaneous or the result of a process? In Paphnutius's words, "When you came here did you suffer a great deal (*akhise tōnou*)?" Timothy concedes that indeed he suffered greatly when he started in the desert. But as Antony underwent suffering at the hands of the devil when he first began his *askēsis* in the tomb only to be strengthened (permanently) by Christ, so Timothy had to suffer a similar process, although the sufferings in the *Life of Onnophrius* are presented as the consequences of bodily *askēsis* rather than diabolical. Timothy explains, "Yes, I suffered (*aihise*) a great deal, my son, so much that I threw myself to the ground on account of my grief (*p⟨e⟩mkah nhēt*), crying out to the Lord on account of my many sins. I also suffered great pain (*ounoc mmokhs*) from an infirmity (*petkas*) laid upon me."[59] While his ordeal echoes that of Antony, left "struck and wounded" by the demons, "groan[ing] because of the pain felt in his body," Timothy's illness is not clearly caused by demons.[60] His suffering is furthermore only ambiguously connected to his previous sins. While he suffers emotionally for his past behavior, it is not explicit that his infirmity is a result of sin. Yet the later appeal to Jesus's words to the cripple of John 5:14 (itself a notoriously ambiguous passage) suggests some connection, however ambiguous. Notwithstanding any ambiguity of the meaning of Timothy's illness, it is only temporary. As Antony was aided by "a certain beam of light" (*aktina tina phōtos*) that descended toward him and took away "the pain of his body" and left Antony "both breathing more easily and relieved from the sufferings," Timothy is aided by "a man radiant with glory" (*efhaeoou emate*).[61] But unlike in the *Life of Antony*, in which the monk is simply "strengthened" by the light, Timothy in the *Life of Onnophrius* describes the healing process with great specificity. The problem is clearly not the beating and battering of the demons; it is disease that the ascetic must overcome:[62]

He [the glorious man] said to me, "Where are you sick (*šōne*)?" And my strength (*tacom*) returned to me a little and I said to him, "Lord, it is in my liver that I am sick (*eišōne epahēpar*)." He said to me, "Show me where you are sick (*pma etkšōne erof*)." So I pointed him to my diseased liver (*pahēpar etšōne*). He stretched out his hand over me, with his fingers joined together, and he cut open my side as with a knife. He brought out my liver and showed me the wounds (*neplugē*, for *neplēgē*) in it. He bound them and applied a bandage to their lesions (*afhokou afti nneuouamome eutoeis*) and returned my liver to its place again. He wiped my body with his hands, and joined together the place that he had divided. He said to me, "Behold, you are healed (*akoujai*). Do not sin again that no worse evil happen to you (John 5:14). But be a servant of the Lord now and forever." Since that day all of my insides have been healthy (*anetmpasa nhoun tērou oujai*) and I have ceased suffering illness in my liver (*ailo eišōne epahēpar*). I live here in the desert without suffering (*khōris hise*). And he taught me about the bandage that the lesions are under.[63]

In Timothy's vividly detailed story we have moved far beyond the nonspecific and disembodied imagery of the *Life of Antony*. The beam of light is replaced by a man, that is, Jesus Christ, and the remedy is specific and bodily. Jesus here acts quite literally as a physician not just of the soul but also of the body, who heals not just by word but also with his hands, as a surgeon. After Timothy has undergone his suffering, he recovers from surgery without pain and from that day has lived in the desert without suffering. And Christ, it appears, has trained the monk Timothy as an apprentice in some sense, teaching him about the details of the surgery. In contrast with the *Life of Antony*, the *Life of Onnophrius* does not explain the good health of the monk as a result of the monk yoking the body and soul in concord, guided by the rational faculty (*logos*) of God, nor is it a result of a healthy diet or any other ascetic practice. The ascetic's good health results from the movement from sin to confession and penance, and ultimately from Christ's intervention as surgeon of the desert.

Paphnutius's journey through the rest of the *Life of Onnophrius* follows the basic contours of desert asceticism that Timothy has narrated. The life of the monk is to suffer; but if he bears the suffering, then through a miraculous intervention the monk becomes "strengthened" (variously expressed, for example, *atacom ei eroi; afticom nai*).[64] In the case of Paphnutius, it is the monk Timothy rather than Christ who "strengthens" him so that he may continue his journey into the inner desert.

After another four days of travel, Paphnutius at last comes upon Onnophrius. The general scheme of Onnophrius's narrative is the same as Timothy's: by enduring suffering (*hise*) through ascetic practices, the monk attracts the mercy of Christ or the angels, who strengthen the monk and provide all the necessities of life for him. Yet unlike Timothy's, Onnophrius's sufferings are not connected with any specific sins on his part. Furthermore, while in the case of Timothy this renewed health and strength were apparently permanent, as he had not suffered since the glorious man performed surgery on his liver, in Onnophrius's case health and strength are merely long-lasting. While Paphnutius encounters Onnophrius, looking quite like Timothy or Paul of Thebes, garbed in his own hair, Onnophrius does not radiate health: "Now when [Onnophrius] came closer he threw himself down for a while under the shadow of the mountain ledge; he was in great distress on account of the hunger and thirst he was suffering (*nfthlibe emate etbenhise etfšoop nhētou pekho mnpeibe*). He was in grave danger (*nfkunduneue* [for *nfkinduneue*] *emate*)."[65]

When Onnophrius notices Paphnutius observing him, he calls him over and tells his story. The story is by now a familiar one for the desert traveler. Like Timothy, Onnophrius had lived in a monastery in the Thebaid but longed for the more challenging life of the desert anchorite. The anchorites, it seemed to Onnophrius, were the more accomplished ascetics, since they did not have companions to care for and comfort them when they were hungry, thirsty, or in trouble (*ršan outhlipsis tahoou*, for example, when they were sick).[66] When he asked his brethren about the anchoritic lifestyle, they informed him that the anchorites were not as alone as they might seem; as long as they endure sufferings, "the mercies of God support them (*tahoou*). He causes the angels to serve them with food and he brings them water from a rock. . . . If trouble (*thlipsis*) overtakes them or danger (*oukindunos*) rises up against them, they immediately stretch out their hands and pray to Jesus the King until his help quickly comes to them. . . . God gives to each person according to what he has suffered (*erepnoute ti mpoua poua kataphise*)."[67] Onnophrius describes the comfort and help provided to him and other suffering monks slightly differently than does Timothy. First, comfort and strength are not indefinite but at least last for "a long time" (*oumēēše nouoeiš*).[68] Second, Onnophrius describes the aid not as divine surgery but as a heavenly journey.

Paphnutius begins his interview with Onnophrius with the same question he had asked Timothy: "[W]hen you first came to this place, did you suffer from the weather?"[69] As before, the suffering of the saint is ascribed not to the demons, as in the *Life of Antony*, but to natural phenomena, weather or ascetic practice. Like Timothy before him, Onnophrius assures Paphnutius that he indeed suffered greatly from the weather and from hunger and thirst due to his ascetic practices. But, he adds, "When God saw that I endured (*aihupomeine*) in the good contest of fasting (*hmpagōn etnanouf*) and that I devoted myself completely to ascetic practices (*aiti mpahēt etaskēsis*), he had his holy angels serve me with my daily food; he gave it to me at night and strengthened my body (*eftaho eratf mpasōma*)."[70] And again for Onnophrius, god provided a palm to provide his food and also made the desert plants taste sweet to him.

Moreover, Onnophrius explains, this is typical for all who live in the desert. If they are in need of comfort or "desire to see someone, they are taken up into the heavenly places where they see all the saints and greet them, and their hearts are filled with light; they rejoice and are glad with God in these good things. Now when they see them they are comforted and they completely forget that they have suffered (*šausolsl nserpōbš jeaušphise eptērf*). Afterwards, they return to their bodies and continue to feel comforted for a long time."[71] As in his interview with Timothy, after hearing Onnophrius's words Paphnutius is strengthened from his journey. Meeting the desert saint has the same effect on him that the heavenly journeys have on the saints: "I forgot all the sufferings I had undergone. . . . The strength returned to my body and youthful vigor returned to my body and soul (*aucom ei epasōma auō aumntbrre ei epasōma mntapsykhē*)."[72]

While there are differences between the narratives of Onnophrius and Timothy, the core depiction of the desert and the life of anchoritic asceticism is coherent. The desert is the realm of divinely assisted health. While they may suffer for their sins, ascetics more generally suffer from the elements and their ascetic practices during their early days in the desert, wearying from the climate and their hunger and thirst, suffering from illness. The devil, however, unlike in the *Life of Antony*, is hardly to be found. Timothy's encounter with the devil, who causes his affair with a nun, occurs in Egypt (that is, the Nile Valley) and inspires him to make the long journey into the desert, where the devil is not heard from again. For desert ascetics, the cure for such natural sufferings and illnesses is simple: to endure in their ascetic practices.[73] But for the monk who endures, help is on the way, for Christ, god, or his angels come to care for the sufferer, either sweeping him up to heaven to see the saints, which makes him forget his suffering, or performing surgery on the monk's body. In either procedure the monk recovers—strong, healthy, and comforted—"for a long time," which in the case of Timothy is the whole of his ascetic life.

Here, as in the *Life of Antony*, the monastic *Life* adapts Paul's reflection on the duality and ambiguity of suffering, "For when I am weak (*asthenō*, which could just as easily mean 'sick'), then I am strong" (2 Cor. 12:10). In the monastic context of Paphnutius's tale (as with that of Antony), weakness and strength, sickness and health are sequential, not synchronic: by enduring weakness and suffering, the monk becomes healthy and strong. The recovery of health looks both forward to the Parousia and back to Genesis. As Tim Vivian has noted, the *Life of Onnophrius* presents the life of the desert ascetic as "Paradise regained"; and at the core of this paradisiacal lifestyle is the recovery of prelapsarian health.[74]

In many ways the *Life of Onnophrius* seems a natural progression from the Edenic-tinged master narrative of Antony and the more explicitly paradisiacal *Life of Paul*. In the *Life of Onnophrius*, the recovery of paradise forms the dominant motif of the narrative, not just of the book's namesake but also of the monk Timothy, of his companions whom Paphnutius meets after his interview with Onnophrius, and—as Onnophrius reports—of all the monks who live in the desert. The *Life of Onnophrius* thus expands and elaborates the earlier portrait of the healthful monk and depicts the paradisiacal health of

Antony or Paul not merely as the exceptional feature of a trailblazer but as a defining feature of all desert anchorites.

Yet Paphnutius betrays an ambivalence toward the expected health of the desert ascetic and the possibility for himself, or his readers, to attain the Edenic existence of Onnophrius or Timothy. As Anton Voytenko has noted, the *Life of Onnophrius* frames the reclamation of paradise by the desert ascetics within the loss or closing of that paradise to Paphnutius and his readers.[75] Paphnutius, though repeatedly strengthened by the stories and consolations of the monks he encounters in the desert, cannot stay in the desert Eden. When Onnophrius dies, appropriately with full knowledge of death's imminence and at the conclusion of his prayers, Paphnutius buries the body amidst the chorus of angels singing "Alleluia." After his prayers the date palm—the source of his food, as for Timothy and Paul of Thebes—falls over. Onnophrius's Eden, the cave with the running stream and palm tree, is closed, and Paphnutius must leave.[76]

The process continues, as Paphnutius is twice more sent away from the desert back to Egypt. Paphnutius moves on and again encounters Timothy, this time along with his three companions. After their meal of loaves delivered by a bird (evoking the meal of Paul and Antony in the *Life of Paul*), Paphnutius begs the monks to allow him to stay with them for the rest of his life and is denied: "Our fellow-laborer, it has not been determined that you should stay here. Rather, rise and go to Egypt and tell those whom you see that the brethren here keep them in their thoughts, and it will profit those who listen."[77] They hold out no possibility of Paphnutius's return, nor do they encourage his Egyptian brethren to make the journey. After Paphnutius sets off again, he encounters another group of ascetics. Paphnutius asks these monks as well that he be allowed to stay, and again he is denied: "The Lord does not assign to us the work that we want to do, but God gives to each person what he can bear. Now, then, rise and go, for that is what the Lord has determined for you."[78] So Paphnutius leaves the desert, and thus the hope of a this-worldly paradise, with mixed emotions: extremely sad (*eilupē emate*) at his forced departure and yet happy (*neiraše pe*) at the blessing he had received.[79]

Thus, as much as it has internalized and expanded on the basic model of monastic health promoted in such foundational works as the *Life of Antony* and the *Life of Paul*, the *Life of Onnophrius* undermines the Athanasian goal of encouraging readers to "emulate" or "surpass" the exploits of the hermit, or the conceit that the ideal *Life* should provide "monks with a sufficient picture for ascetic practice," or a sense of "what the life of the monks ought to be."[80] Paphnutius does not portray the ascetic practices as a rule for his intended audience at all or hold out hope that they might achieve a measure of Antonian or Onnophrian health and vigor throughout their lives. Rather, the preternatural health of the desert ascetics is the function of another place, a place effectively as distant and inaccessible as paradise. Even if one were to reach it, as in the spiritual journeys of Paul of Tarsus centuries before and the saints whom Paphnutius visited, one cannot stay for long. Ultimately the sojourner must return to the mundane world, in Paphnutius's case Egypt. The most that the monk can hope for is not the health of Timothy, Onnophrius, and the desert anchorites but their prayers.

Conclusion

For all the one-upmanship of Paul or the ambivalence of Paphnutius regarding the expected health of the ascetic, neither would displace the near-canonicity of the *Life of Antony*'s master narrative of ascetic and saintly health. Just as the *Life of Antony* became a template for later hagiography, the Life (as genre) provided a primary means for disseminating knowledge about the ascetic life. The urbane laity who were interested in adopting the monastic lifestyle could read the Lives as both inspiration and preparation for the drastic changes in lifestyle that joining a cloister entailed. So just as Antony was called to the ascetic life by the word of the Gospels, others in turn—such as Augustine of Hippo—became enamored with the ascetic life through the fantastic tales of Antony. In fact it is through the *Life of Antony* that Augustine claims to have first glimpsed the monastic lifestyle. This is in spite of the fact that flesh-and-blood monks lived in Milan at the very same time, under the organization of Bishop Ambrose, no less.[81] Augustine describes the role of the *Life of Antony* as monastic pedagogue, leading the secular to their first contact with Christian asceticism: some civil servants, associates of his friend Ponticianus, chanced upon a copy of the *Life* in a nearby house of "men poor in spirit." "One of them began to read it and was so fascinated and thrilled by the story that even before he had finished reading he conceived the idea of taking upon himself the same kind of life."[82] Notably the civil servant does not learn of monasticism directly from the "men poor in spirit" themselves, urban ascetics, but by the tales of Antony they found in the men's house. Many others, no doubt, were driven to similar worldly renunciations by the *Life*, regardless of the frequent proximity of flesh-and-blood monks. The fantastic, exotic exploits of Antony proved much more attractive to the late ancient Christian than the mundane world of village and urban ascetics.

There is every indication that the attributes of Antony—such as the moral signification of sickness and health—were widely accepted to be normative, at least in the eyes of those outside the monastery. It is surely in the wake of such ur-hagiographies as Antony's that the pilgrim narrator of the *History of the Monks in Egypt* describes the monks of Isidore's monastery in Thebes, not to mention the many other long-lived, healthy saints. The pilgrims thus describe their experiences in the terms of Athanasian hagiography and its elaboration in such texts as the *Life of Onnophrius*: whole communities may be found where illness no longer exists, and virtuous monastics live until the hours of their deaths without suffering or weakness. Their deaths, like those of Antony and Paul, are orderly, painless, and appropriately timed. The model of making meaning out of ascetic health and illness that Athanasius promoted provided an attractive template for later writers and readers of saints' lives, and for later reflections on the role of asceticism in Christian life. There is no shortage of good reasons for the popularity and influence of the *Life of Antony*, not least of which is that it is a very good book. The *Life of Antony* provided a consistent and beautiful model for the health of the ascetic.

Doubtless some monks did endure harsh asceticism to achieve long lives relatively free from illness. It is tempting to cite comparative descriptions of ascetic health from the phenomenology of religion to claim that asceticism in general promotes exceptional longevity and health, but sources in other religious traditions are too subject to their own ideological biases, such as are clear in the *Life of Antony*.[83] But we should be wary of taking the states of preternatural health at face value. It will be clear from later chapters that late ancient Christians did not. As we have already touched on in the discussion of Palladius, Cassian, and Chrysostom in Chapter 1, ancient sources are rife with the sometimes troubling observations that the ascetic lifestyle did not reliably produce the bodily manifestations of prelapsarian health in longevity and healthfulness. Monks, even those who followed the example of Antony, could fall ill and die at any point.

For my purposes such monks who fail to achieve Antonian or Mosaic health are far more interesting. To make meaning out of the bodily constitu-tion of the healthy ascetic is straightforward; health provides a sure index of the sanctity of the soul. I know of no ancient text in which bodily health and radiant visage are read as signs of spiritual decay. In this sense ascetic health is less interesting. Far more interesting, because explanations are so elusive, is the illness of ascetics. Further compounding the contentious interpretation of ascetic illness is the widespread influence of the *Life of Antony* and its imitators. While illness might not always demand explanation and meaning, texts such as the Lives discussed in this chapter make the meaning of ascetic illness much more necessary and much more fraught.

Chapter 4

Choosing Illness: Illness as Ascetic Practice

A concern with illness within the life and practice of the monk was not limited to the world of hagiographic imagination. Rather, the problem of how to interpret illness as a marker of moral and theological meaning within the life of the monk and the ways that illness might or might not be useful in the monk's asceticism were topics of sustained debate in the later Roman world in letters, rules, homilies, didactic and practical treatises, and gnomic sayings.[1] The debate was grounded in the widespread influence of the types of ascetic models promoted by monastic hagiography, as well as the complementarities and tensions between illness and asceticism discussed in some detail in Chapter 1.

Choosing Illness

Jerome's *Letters* provide a case in point of how such competing approaches to making meaning out of ascetic illness could dwell in dialectical tension even in the writings of a single author. They also reflect the lingering presence of hagiographical models in evaluating the lifestyles of "flesh-and-blood" ascetics. Jerome's descriptions of (even apologies for) the ascetic practices of two Roman women, Asella and Blesilla, exemplify the difficulty of adopting the asceticism of Antony or Paul of Thebes, to take Jerome's own creation, as a model for asceticism among monks whose lives transcend the textual boundaries of hagiography.

Writing in 384, a decade after he had published the *Life of Paul*, Jerome wrote of the ascetic lifestyle of the virgin Asella to her sister Marcella (325–410), the influential Roman ascetic matron. Though living as a monk in Rome rather than in a desert cave, Asella had created for herself a sort of Pauline Edenic existence: "in her narrow cell she roamed through paradise."[2] She practiced a constant renunciation. Even her limited food was another means of affliction, for "the bread and salt and cold water to which she restricted herself sharpened her appetite more than they appeased."[3] She fasted for two to three days at a stretch throughout the year and during Lent would go a whole week without eating. Incredibly—Jerome makes a point of noting how exceptional it might seem—she suffered from no ill health: "[S]he lived this life until her fiftieth year without weakening her digestion (*non doloret stomachus*) or bringing on herself the pain of colic (*non viscerum cruciaretur incuria*). Lying on the dry ground did not affect her limbs, and the rough sackcloth that she wore failed to make her skin either foul or rough. With a sound body (*sana corpore*) and a still sounder soul (*animo sanior*) she sought all her delight in solitude, and found for herself a monkish hermitage in this centre of busy Rome."[4] The echoes of the *Lives* of Antony and Paul are unmistakable. Here in a letter written to someone who knows Asella well we see the portrait of an ascetic whose life fulfills the hagiographical promise of these earlier *Lives*: that the monk may reach a sort of paradisiacal existence in this world, manifested perhaps most emblematically by a nearly incredible health. Asella did not even have to journey to the desert to achieve it.

Yet Jerome's own letters betray an obvious problem with this assurance of ascetic health. A harsh regimen of self-mortification does not reliably result in superhuman longevity and health. The demise of another of Rome's elite, Blesilla, daughter of Paula, shows the controversy that could arise when ascetic practice ends badly. Blesilla had turned to the ascetic life after she was widowed as a young woman. But unlike Asella, who roamed through paradise in her cell and never suffered from ill health, Blesilla was plagued by fever. In contrast to the Job-like suffering of monks such as Benjamin and Stephen in Palladius's *Lausiac History*, Jerome reads Blesilla's illness as pedagogic.[5] Jerome assures her mother that her suffering is indeed meaningful: it has been sent by Jesus "to teach her to renounce her over-great attention to that body which the worms must shortly devour," which I suspect was of little consolation.[6] Prior to her conversion Blesilla was preoccupied with her appearance. Even though now, according to Jerome, Blesilla had exchanged all vain adornment and bodily comfort for rough clothes and poor hygiene, apparently she still needed discipline (Jerome does not explain why the lord continued to afflict her with illness when she had already changed her ways). Whatever the pedagogical function of Blesilla's fever might have been, she died within a few months of taking up the ascetic life. In contrast to his response in *Letter* 38, in which he so facilely explains the meaning of Blesilla's illness, in *Letter*

39 Jerome acknowledges that her quick decline and death after her conversion to asceticism raise difficult questions and doubts. Why should such an
innocent as Blesilla suffer an early and painful death? "Do not great waves of
doubt surge up over my soul as over yours? How comes it, I ask, that godless
men live to old age in the enjoyment of this world's riches? How comes it that
untutored youth and innocent childhood are cut down while still in the bud?
Why is it that children three years old or two, and even unweaned infants, are
possessed with devils, covered with leprosy, and eaten up with jaundice, while
godless men and profane, adulterers and murderers, have health and strength
to blaspheme God?"[7] Difficult questions indeed. Jerome answers these questions by deferring the search for meaning: whether in sickness or in health,
our constitutions are up to the will of god, for which we should give thanks
in either case. The lord will do with us as he wills, as even in the case of Paul
of Tarsus he afflicted him three times and declined to heal him. Jerome quotes
the ubiquitous words of Paul "when I am weak, then I am strong."[8]

But others in Rome did not defer the search for meaning simply to leave
it up to god's inscrutable will. Others saw the cause of Blesilla's suffering all
too plainly: excessive asceticism. Jerome had already become a controversial
figure in Rome, both for his biblical translations and for his suspicious sym-
pathies toward the theology of Origen.[9] Blesilla's death pointed to yet another controversy over his ascetic teachings. Jerome writes of the whispering
attendants at her funeral, who blamed her death on her ascetic lifestyle (and
not on her previous vanity, as Jerome had claimed): "When you [Paula] were
carried fainting out of the funeral procession, whispers such as these were
audible in the crowd. 'Is not this what we have often said. She weeps for her
daughter, killed with fasting. She wanted her to marry again, that she might
have grandchildren. How long must we refrain from driving these detestable
monks out of Rome? Why do we not stone them or hurl them into the Tiber?
They have misled this unhappy lady; that she is not a nun from choice (*quam
monacha esse noluerit*) is clear. No heathen mother ever wept for her children
as she does for Blesilla.'"[10] The issue of choice is important. In Jerome's telling
the crowd blamed the monks for Blesilla's illness and death. It (along with her
subsequent illness) was their choice; she was too weak to resist their influence.
It would not be surprising for her (and his) alleged critics to discount Blesilla's
agency. But what if her asceticism and her illness were her choice?

The diverging cases of Asella and Blesilla demonstrate the contentious
place of health as a characteristic of asceticism in the later Roman Empire.
In the wake of hagiography's explosive popularity, including Jerome's own

contributions, readers and observers were inclined to see in the ascetic's health or sickness a reflection of their ascetic life. The saint's sickness demanded explanation; it demanded meaning. Is it an enactment of Job-like endurance, a tool of god's paideia, or the sign of a misguided, extreme asceticism? In the case of the healthy monk Asella, the meaning was clear; she had attained a foothold of paradise in her cell, and her piety and asceticism resulted in incredible health. In the case of the sick Blesilla, however, the meaning of illness was contentious. In Jerome's view it was pedagogical but still—like the deaths of infants—difficult to explain. It rather called for the suspension of judgment: it was up to god in his inscrutable providence. Yet for other observers, her illness was due to human fault. Those who had chosen a life of *askēsis* for her had chosen a life of illness too; if one were to consider her an active agent in her own right, then Blesilla chose this sorry end for herself.

Illness, thus, for some or many in the decades following monasticism's rapid rise in popularity pointed to an *askēsis* gone awry. It raised a number of fundamental questions. Did the illness of the ascetic indicate the obverse of Antony's or Paul's health, a failure of asceticism? Did illness come from the devil or from god? How much responsibility should the individual ascetic, or her peers, bear for illness? Should one be allowed to choose such an injurious lifestyle? This is especially problematic given that illness, as Jerome's letter to Paula reflects, is rarely individual: it also affects the family and significant others around the sick.

Jerome concerns himself primarily with the ambiguous meaning of ascetic illness. As discussed in Chapter 1, illness also functions ambiguously in the practice of asceticism: it can both undermine and aid the ascetic fashioning of the self. Reflecting such concerns, we may look at a saying attributed to a certain Joseph of Thebes, one of the ascetics known as the "Desert Fathers," comprising mostly fourth- and fifth-century monastics who lived for the most part in the loosely organized lavra monasteries of Lower Egypt, the Nile Delta, and its outlying oases.[11] The literary remains of these ascetics consist primarily of aphorisms or apophthegms, short, memorable sayings, compiled into a number of collections in the monasteries of Palestine.[12] Joseph of Thebes is among the many ascetics included in the collection about whom no biographical information—reliable or otherwise—has been preserved. Though presumably he was Egyptian, either hailing from Thebes or living there, precisely where he lived, in Egypt or Palestine; when he lived, from the fourth to the sixth centuries; and even whether there ever was a "historical" Joseph are all unanswerable. Any cohesive picture of the teachings of this Joseph—whether as a literary construct or a historical person—is further impossible, for tradition attributes only one saying to Joseph. It is, nonetheless, a remarkable one: "Abba Joseph of Thebes said, 'Three deeds (*pragmata*) are honored before the Lord. The first is when someone is sick and temptations are inflicted upon him, and he receives them with gratitude. The second is when someone makes all his deeds pure before the Lord, retaining nothing human. And the third is when someone dwells in submission to a spiritual father and renounces everything of his own will. This one will receive an extraordinary crown. But I, for one, have chosen illness [*tēn astheneian hēirēsamēn*]'."[13] In its form and approach the apophthegm is a classic "word" of the desert, with its memorable list of three elements and its unexpected "punch line," not to mention Joseph's self-deprecatory humility. Joseph's apophthegm shares certain features with contemporary monastic sentiment.[14] The second and third "honored deeds" are commonplace virtues in monastic rhetoric. A disregard for human things, or things of the "world," underlies virtually any type of ascetic "withdrawal," whether that withdrawal be geographical, ethical, social, or some combination of the above.[15] In addition reflexive obedience to an ascetic master is equally central to the Western monastic tradition.

It is the first "honored deed" that is of special interest to Joseph and is indeed enigmatic. Much is left unstated: Why should the ascetic's behavior in sickness rank among the three highest ascetic practices? To what temptations that fall upon the monk specifically or most grievously in time of sickness does Joseph refer? What does Joseph mean in saying he has "chosen illness"? Is he advocating the intentional, voluntary injury of the body so common in monastic hagiography or is he being ironic, or self-deprecating, or something else?

"Choosing illness" in the time of the *Apophthegmata patrum*'s compilation could refer to a variety of ascetic behaviors. It could refer simply to the type of asceticism that Blesilla may have chosen, perhaps not an unusually harsh regimen in itself but one that either puts one at risk of illness or does not relent in the face of it. But another extreme lay in the intentional cultivation of bodily disease or injury as a kind of—perhaps literal—self-mortification, killing the self. Certainly such cultivation of injury and illness is widespread in late ancient ascetic literature. In Palladius's *Lausiac History* Dorotheus was renowned for his self-mortification, building cells every day in the full desert sun. When asked by Palladius, Why are you "'killing your body in such heat?' he answered: 'It kills me, I will kill it.'"[16] Palladius describes Macarius the Alexandrian going to even greater lengths to encourage illness: sitting naked for six months in the malarial marsh of Scetis. Swarmed by ravenous mosquitoes, "he became so swollen that some thought he had elephantiasis," the common ancient term for Hansen's disease, or leprosy.[17] When he returned from the marsh, his voluntary disfigurement had made him unrecognizable apart from his voice.[18] Thinking back to Susan Sontag's characterization of illness as a separate kingdom and citizenship from that of the well and Richard Valantasis's definition of asceticism as the inauguration of a new self, withdrawn from and at odds with the dominant culture, it is not hard to see how useful "choosing illness" could be as an ascetic strategy: Macarius's disease had so radically altered him, he was no longer even recognizable as his former self. In addition as a would-be leper he had achieved an extreme withdrawal nearing social death and a complete loss of citizenship in the kingdom of the well.

While Palladius presents Macarius's choice of illness in a positive light, others were not so sanguine about such choices. We can see this in perhaps the most famous story of "choosing illness," that is, self-induced or factitious illness, that of Simeon the Stylite (c. 386–459), whose *bios* is narrated in two Greek versions and a Syriac version.[19] In the most ancient of the versions, the *Religious History* (*Philotheos historia*), commonly called the *History of the Monks of Syria*, written during Simeon's lifetime by the bishop and theologian Theodoret of Cyrrhus, Simeon is said to have joined a coenobitic monastery early in his career. There he quickly came into conflict with his superiors for outdoing the rest of the monks in fasting. Theodoret claims that the current superior of the community (*tou nun tēs autēs agelēs hēgemoneuontos*) told him that Simeon once secretly fashioned an extremely rough cord of palms and tied them tightly around his bare waist so "as to lacerate in a circle the whole part it went round."[20] After ten days his fellow monks noticed drops of blood trailing the monk, and under duress Simeon removed the rope but refused any medical treatment. After he continued in this manner, inducing other injuries or illnesses in himself, which Theodoret does not specify (*toiauta drōnta horōntes*), "they ordered him to depart from the wresting-school, lest he should be a cause of harm (*blabēs aitios*) to those with a weaker bodily constitution (*tois asthenesteron to sōma diakeimenois*) who might try to emulate (*zēloun*) what was beyond their powers."[21] The leaders of Simeon's monastery worry that other monks might attempt to emulate Simeon; this is precisely, we may note, what the *Life of Antony* calls on its readers to do: "emulate" the lives of the saints. Even in this hagiographical narrative, arguably the most stylistically hagiographical of the various biographical sketches in the *Historia religiosa*, Theodoret shows that elements within society—other monks in particular—could have serious objections to the monk who chooses illness as a form of asceticism.[22]

In the slightly later Greek *Life of Simeon* by Antonius, the episode is magnified in the length of time, in the detail and gruesomeness of Simeon's affliction (he is no longer just bleeding, but the cord had rubbed through his skin causing infection and required fifty days of treatment at the hands of doctors), and in the critical response by the monastery's leaders.[23] Yet for all the controversies, in both *Lives* the factitious illnesses of Simeon are envisioned as proof of his ascetic virtues. In the telling of at least one later poet Simeon's illnesses become the central focus of his triumphant battle against Satan.[24]

In the end, when Joseph of Thebes speaks of "choosing illness," he speaks in the context of this dialectical relationship of illness and asceticism as it relates to both meaning and function. Illness undermines ascetic propriety (as in Simeon's monastery) and may manifest the righteous punishment for the monk's sins (as in Blesilla's case); yet illness may aid in the ascetic project of self-fashioning and transcendence and moreover may reveal their sanctity (in Simeon's and Macarius's cases). All the while health surely signifies the ascetic's spiritual virtue (as in Asella's case).

While Joseph's praise of "choosing illness" might be interpreted as fitting in with either of these attitudes toward ascetic illness, it seems that Joseph promotes an attitude toward illness very much at odds with the types of behaviors characterized by Dorotheus, Macarius, Simeon, and countless others. I wish to postpone any attempt to shed further light on the questions raised by Joseph's apophthegm, except to note that Joseph was in fact not alone in linking the monastic's behavior in sickness with appropriate ascetic practice. The behavior of monastics in the time of sickness, the function that sickness holds in asceticism, and the meaning of ascetic sickness are recurring interests of ascetic thinkers in late antiquity. The meaning and function of sickness in asceticism—as symptoms of excessive *askēsis*, as forms of asceticism, or as signs of ascetic accomplishment—in turn become among the primary loci for the definition of the bounds of ascetic propriety in late ancient Christianity. The prevalence of monastic sickness and the monk's behavior in sickness form common pretexts for defining the limits of proper asceticism and appropriate attitude toward and understanding of the ascetic practices that constitute monasticism in late antiquity.

First I will look at the problem of self-induced illness and ascetic propriety in the ascetic writings of Basil of Caesarea, who sees the self-induced afflictions that would define the practice of monks such as Simeon as threats to monastic discipline and spiritual direction, and—not insignificantly—a threat to church order and orthodoxy. At the same time Basil promotes the experience of illness as a model for the monk's spiritual exercise and progress. Second, I will discuss illness and asceticism in the ascetic writings of Evagrius of Pontus (the *Praktikos* and *On Thoughts*), writing in the generation following Basil and in the tradition of the Cappadocian bishop-theologians. Like Basil, Evagrius is concerned with the behaviors of sick monks, but unlike Basil, he focuses on the causes of such behaviors. Most interestingly in the light of the development of the hagiographical tradition of ascetic health analyzed in the previous chapter, a primary cause of ascetic misbehavior in the face of illness is the misappropriation of role models from hagiography and the Bible. Then I will discuss another important and influential trend in late ancient reflection on illness: the interpretation of illness as a mode of spiritual exercise and asceticism, even as an ascetic practice in and of itself. As representative of this tradition of ascetic illness, I will examine illness in the fifth-century *Life and Regimen of the Blessed and Holy Teacher Syncletica*. Unlike the texts discussed above, the following authors are primarily concerned with critiquing, circumscribing, and redefining what it means to choose illness as a form of practice.

Basil of Caesarea: Immoderate Fasting and Monastic Obedience

In his very public life and career, Basil of Caesarea (330–79) engaged with the realities of illness and suffering on a number of levels. He was a leader, for example, in the establishment of important and influential charitable foundations for the sick.[25] More relevant here are his explorations of illness and its meaning theologically and even personally. These explorations inform his responses to those who "choose illness" in the ascetic communities that looked to him for direction. Before consideration of his disciplinary and ascetic concerns in his *Ascetica*, a look at the theme of illness and its meaning in his *Letters* and the homily *That God Is Not the Cause of Evil* is in order.

It is a well-known aspect of his biography that Basil suffered from ill health for much of his life; one might less charitably describe Basil as obsessed with his own illness, like a latter-day Aelius Aristides, the famous Antonine sufferer.[26] Basil frequently dwells on his ill health in his voluminous correspondence, often detailing his sufferings by way of excusing himself for his inability to travel or his failure to write.[27] He also frequently reads the fevers and fluxes of his own body as a microcosmic reflection of his conflicts in the church body politic over theology and church order. Philip Rousseau describes this tendency well and not sympathetically: "Rather more sinister was the way he wove his illness into his sense of church history."[28] At times Basil explicitly elides his own ailments with those of the church, as he, for example, complains of the "wounds of heretical bites (*dēgmatōn*)" when lamenting his own dental problems, although to be fair, it is not necessarily clear just how seriously Basil intended the comparison to be taken.[29] More often he simply juxtaposes the description of his own fevers and diarrhea (for example) with the controversies consuming the church's body politic.[30] In either case the point is clear: the narrative of his own rebellious and diseased body reflects the larger pathologies of heresy and ecclesiastical discord.

In discussing his own ailments, however, Basil does not deal with asceticism or the larger problem of the moral meaning of illness: Why does the Christian suffer, and how does a just god allow or cause the evils of illness in the world? He takes up these issues in his homily *That God Is Not the Cause of Evil*. For Basil, the questions can lead fools, such as the fool of Psalm 14, to deny the reality of god or to deny his goodness.[31] The meaning of illness, along with other natural evils, thus demands explanation. Basil approaches this question—whence illness if god is good—in a number of ways. Illnesses exist by no evil intent on the part of god but solely because of the choice made by humanity through their free will. Basil proposes the same explanation for the origin of illness seen in the apocryphal *Life of Adam and Eve* in the introduction, an explanation widely shared by late ancient Christian theologians.[32] Humanity was created with bodies in concord with nature and thus healthy, living a "life free from pain in paradise";[33] "but they became ill through a perversion of what is according to nature. For a disruption of health occurs either because of a bad lifestyle (*dia ponēran diaitan*) or because of some other cause of illness. Therefore, God created the body, but not illness; and likewise God created the soul, but not sin. Rather, the soul is made evil through a perversion of what is according to nature."[34] This perversion—an autonomic change in humanity rather than a punishment from god—was set in motion by the devil, driven by envy at the sight of humanity's health in paradise.[35] Basil's characterization of illness as the effect of humanity's fall points to a persistent problem in making sense of illness among the ostensibly holy.

But what of god's omnipotence? As god says, "See now that I, even I, am he; there is no god besides me. I kill and I make alive; I wound and I heal; and no one can deliver from my hand" (Deut. 32:39, NRSV). Basil's deep offense at any suggestion of god's culpability for evil shines through in his reading of god's self-presentation in Deuteronomy. Perhaps drawing on Job 5:17–18 and Hosea 6:1, Basil proposes that the Song of Moses does not mean that god creates illness for some and healing for others—a pattern well attested in the Jewish scriptures.[36] Rather the passage implies that god sends both illness and healing in tandem as a process of salvation to the same person. When he creates evils or illness, he does so only as the precursor to health, as Basil writes: "[H]e transforms them [illnesses] and brings improvement, so that they cease to be evils and participate in the nature of good."[37] Thus god is not the original cause of our ills, even if he may be the proximal cause; the fault lies in humanity's diabolical perversions. Even if god does send illness (as Deuteronomy clearly states), our sufferings are not actually harmful to us; pain and suffering may indeed follow, but they are inflicted on us "to bring us something better."[38] Illness is thus a mode of spiritual direction and spiritual improvement.

Of course Basil is not so glib as to deny that the process of transformation from evil to good or from sick to well is anything other than painful. Drawing on imagery as old as Origen, Basil notes that surgery, cauterizations, and drugs applied by even the most skilled and conscientious physician can be painful or noxious.[39] Yet, he claims, "you do not accuse the physician of any wrong in his cuttings and burnings and complete mutilations of the body; but rather you probably pay him money and you call him a savior, since he has produced disease (*tēn noson*) in a small part of the body to prevent the sickness (*to pathos*) from spreading throughout the whole of it."[40] Basil's readers might well have taken issue with Basil's generalization: ancient patients and their loved ones certainly did criticize doctors for the pain and suffering (and death) they caused in treatment.[41] In any case, as through the pain of medical treatment that cuts off members that are too far gone for treatment, god "sends illness to those for whom it is more profitable to have their limbs constrained than to move unhindered toward sinning."[42] In addition, "bodily sufferings and outward distresses have been invented to halt sin," like the physician's knife or emetic halts the progress of disease.[43] Suffering through the various evils becomes a site for triumph against Satan. While Basil does not make the equation as explicitly as others discussed in this chapter and elsewhere, illness can stand in for or do the work of self-control or asceticism: god afflicts with illness those who cannot control themselves by other means.[44] Basil echoes the common athletic and medical metaphors for asceticism, describing patient suffering as "a training exercise (*gymnasion*) for our souls by the one who plans human affairs with wisdom and foreknowledge, as a physician uses the viper's poison to make medicines for healing (*sōtēriōn pharmakōn*)."[45] In Basil's metaphor illness is both the existential condition of fallen humanity and the treatment or cure for humanity's fallenness, a pedagogue and a replacement for—if not a mode of—ascetic self-control.

Thus in his homily Basil reflects on the meaning of illness in the context of Christian salvation history and touches on the functionality of illness as a mode of ascetic practice. But what of medicine and convalescence? Basil addresses these issues in chapter 55 of his *Longer Rules*: "Whether the use of medical remedies is consistent with the ideal of piety."[46] Basil's response 55 is the longest of the responses in either collection of *Rules* and closes the *Longer Rules*. While the placement here might not necessarily be of special significance, certainly the great length at which Basil devotes his attention to the subject reflects the importance that the problem of ascetic illness played in Basil's thought (and the communities he advised).[47] Basil begins his answer by revisiting the issues that he touches on in his homily *That God Is Not the Cause of Evil*. Humanity was blessed with "immunity from disease" before the fall in "the paradise of delight" and thus had no need of any of the "arts" (*teknai*), for example, medicine, agriculture, and weaving.[48] But following our self-induced fall, god provided humanity with the arts to make up for the "infirmity of nature" (*tēs physeōs asthenes*). "Since our body, so subject to disease, is liable to various kinds of harm," god has provided the art of medicine as a consolation and comfort.[49] The richness of pharmacology, of herbs, metals, and salts, demonstrates the providential role of medicine: clearly god has established the art for the benefit of humanity.

Yet the terminology that Basil chooses in his discussion of the origins and divine sanction of medicine betrays that it is the care of the soul that interests him the most. He refers to humanity's susceptibility to disease with terms that relate to physical disease and to spiritual direction. So if in paradise we "had immunity from injury" (*ei en apatheiai ēmen*), this could just as easily mean that we were in a state of "freedom from the passions" or "emotions," reflective of both Stoic terminology and widespread late ancient Christian characterizations of the goal of the ascetic life.[50] Basil's characterization of our present precarious position also points to physical disease and to passionate entanglements, *to empathes hēmōn sōma*, which Clarke renders as "our body, so subject to disease" and Silvas renders as "Since our body is susceptible to conditions." Basil's choice of *empathes* could also be rendered "We are in a state of emotion" or "subject to passion."[51] The semantic ambiguity between bodily illness and the passions is important for Basil's goal in comparing medicine with the cure of souls.

Distinct from much early Christian elaboration of the "cure of souls" is Basil's insistence on the ascetic utility of illness as a mode of spiritual direction. So the sick should avoid using medicine improperly (that is, merely to heal the body). Rather they should recognize that the process of treatment and recovery is a type (*typon*) for something far more important. He writes, "[A]ccept the use of its [medicine's] remedies as designed for the glory of God and a type of the care of souls (*typon tēs tōn psykhōn epimeleias*)."[52] In this sense Basil's interest in *Longer Rules* 55 expands on his description of medicine elsewhere in his ascetic corpus, where medicine is primarily understood as a metaphor for spiritual care. In *Longer Rules* 55 the phases of illness, treatment, and convalescence typify aspects of spiritual direction. Just as the patient must sometimes undergo painful treatments, the monk must "accept the cutting effects of the word that exposes (*ta tmētika tou elenktikou logou*) and the bitter drugs of penalties for the cure of the soul."[53] Chronic diseases show "that we ought to amend the sins of the soul by sustained prayer and prolonged repentance and a more laborious struggle than reason would suggest to us is sufficient for our healing."[54] Such medical analogies are by now familiar. What is more important in the *Longer Rules* is that Basil moves beyond the mere typological comparison of medical healing to the cure of souls. Here the process of illness, treatment (or its failure), and convalescence is itself a form of "instruction" in the care of the self: "Often, when we have contracted illnesses (*tais nosois*) for our instruction (*pros paideian*), we are sentenced to undergo a cure (*therapeian*) by painful means as part of the instruction. And so right reason teaches us not to shrink from cuttings or cauterizations or the pains caused by bitter and burdensome drugs or privation of food or a strict regimen or abstinence from harmful things, since—I say it again—the object of benefiting the soul is being assured, for it is being taught by way of example how to take care of itself."[55] Thus illness might not be considered an "evil" at all but rather an opportunity (through its endurance and treatment) for training the self to cure the soul along with the body.

For all the benefits of medicine, however, it is important that the sufferer reflect on the cause of the diseases and their moral meaning, for not all diseases are of natural causes (*physeōs*) or from diet (*diaitēs*) or any other bodily cause (*tinōn allōn sōmatikōn arkhōn*). There are several other possible causes of diseases, and in such cases medicine will not likely benefit the sufferer. First, "often illnesses are scourges for sins, sent for our conversion." In this case the proper approach to illness is to acknowledge and confess the sin, followed by patient endurance of the illness without any recourse to medicine. Still other times illness is brought about upon the innocent through Satan, just as he tempted Job. Other times the righteous are condemned "to bear their sufferings even unto death" (citing Phil. 2:8), such as Lazarus, who is never recorded as either requesting or receiving any medical assistance, just suffering and dying. As John Cassian argues in his chapter "On the Deaths of Some Holy People," according to Basil such sufferings unto death benefit both sufferer and observers. Lazarus found rest in the bosom of Abraham (compare Luke 16:20–25) and also serves as an example to others. Last, again like Cassian and like John Chrysostom's homilies, sometimes the saints suffer illness to demonstrate their human nature to skeptics.[56] In all such cases medicine holds no benefit. It would be a greater danger (*mallon kindunos*) "for them to be led astray from right reason into a craze for bodily health."[57]

Illness also aids in ascetic self-control (*enkrateia*), argues Basil. The dietary regimen advocated by a doctor works hand in hand with Christian asceticism: "it cuts out luxury and condemns satiety and banishes as unsuitable a rich diet and superfluous preparations of condiments. For the most part it calls want the mother of health (*tēn endeian mētera tēs hygeias*), so that in this respect, too, its counsels are not without use to us."[58] Here Basil highlights the art of medicine's preventative regimens as complementary to the ascetic life.[59]

But what of those "who have brought illness on themselves from a disordered lifestyle" or, more controversially, those who intentionally endanger their health through excessive asceticism, in a sense choosing illness?[60] Basil addresses these concerns in more detail in his *Shorter Rules*.

That this was a very real threat in Basil's Cappadocia is understandable. On a basic level, Asia Minor had been a site for controversial ascetic practice in the formative decades of Basil's career, especially among the enthusiastic followers of Eustathius of Sebaste (c. 300–c. 377). Eustathius and his followers went beyond promoting virginity, strict diet, austere dress, and the avoidance of meat, going so far as to condemn marriage altogether. They furthermore (at least according to their opponents) fostered a prominent role for women, encouraged slaves to abandon their masters, and promoted the independence of virgins and ascetics from the constraints of the church hierarchy and liturgical cycle.[61] Sometime in the mid-fourth century, perhaps A.D. 340, a council was convened in the city of Gangra in Paphlagonia and charged with regulating these perceived ascetic excesses and bringing them into line with more moderate, profamily values.[62] The twenty canons from the Council of Gangra anathematize, among others, those who forbid meat eating, criticize the institution of marriage, encourage slaves to flee, and refuse to worship with married clergy, as well as women who wear men's clothing or cut their hair. Most relevant for Basil's concerns with choosing illness are the canons against dietary impropriety, which, in addition to anathematizing those who condemn meat eating, also anathematize those who fast on the Lord's day and those who do not fast on fast days, at least without being sick.[63]

While the criticism of Eustathian "enthusiasm" no doubt lies beneath Basil's own approach to ascetic propriety, Basil's specific concern about illness within ascetic practice, in particular the tendency of monks to induce illness through extreme fasting, is not among the ascetic behaviors condemned by the Council of Gangra.[64] Rather it is the adherence to the common liturgical life of fasting and feasting that attracts the attention of the thirteen bishops at Gangra. Something else is at work here. Basil's concerns share more in common with the disputes around Simeon's *askēsis* that Theodoret would describe in the next century.

In the midst of Basil's praise of illness as both a model for spiritual improvement and a stand-in for asceticism, as well as the general atmosphere of ascetic enthusiasm in Anatolia, it is not hard to anticipate that the principles of moderation and uniformity in asceticism would be difficult to enforce in the coenobia of late fourth-century Cappadocia. Several questions, in fact, regard the treatment of those who desire to "practice abstinence beyond [their] strength" (*enkrateuesthai huper dunamin*).[65] The first such query regards monastics who are unable to obey the rules of the monastery because they have been weakened (or perhaps fallen ill) from their self-abnegation. Must his superiors and brethren allow the monk to fail to fulfill "the commandment set before him"? This situation poses a dilemma for the superior, who has two basic options: either to allow a dispensation for the monk (thus breaking the common rule and sowing the seeds of discord) or not to allow a dispensation (which might either be ineffectual or injure the monk further). In recognition of the undesirability of both of these options Basil offers no direct answer. Rather he answers by questioning and redefining the very premises of the question. Such extreme ascetic "self-control" (*enkrateia*)—in Basil's view—cannot accurately be described as abstinence, since "abstinence (*enkrateia*) consists not in refraining from material foods [as one might assume], but in complete giving up of one's own will."[66] Thus one cannot practice true abstinence beyond one's strength, for excess negates the fundamental principle of asceticism itself (or *enkrateia* in Basil's terminology): reflexive obedience to a spiritual master. Beyond this clarification of terminology, however, Basil declines to advise on precisely what a superior should do in the situation addressed.

Basil continues this line of reasoning elsewhere in the *Shorter Rules*. What about those who injure themselves through "immoderate fasting" (*dia to ametrōs nēsteuein*) and therefore require special food? Should these ambitious ascetics be allowed such special considerations?[67] Basil again answers by examining the premises of the question: "Times of fasting are not dictated by the wishes (*to thelēma*) of the individual but by the needs (*hē khreia*) of those who have embraced the religious life."[68] Thus no one should have the option to pursue immoderate fasting in the first place. However, as long as anyone "fasts in such fashion [that is, according to the needs of the community] he is counted worthy of receiving power to fast."[69] Basil's responses to questions of excessive fasting and its injury to the body all highlight obedience as a basic principle of monasticism. So he responds to the problem of monks who decide to abstain from certain foods normally allowed in the community, a question that refers more likely to the refusal of food and water out of ascetic interest rather than mere preference: "Is it right for a man to decide to abstain, for example, for a given time from something to eat or drink?"[70] He follows up on this with two more related answers: whether anyone "should be allowed to fast or watch more than the rest, according to his own will"; and what monks who have been weakened by fasting should do about their manual labors.[71] The questions—again—are framed incorrectly: no one should choose to abstain from anything, for "every judgment of a private will is dangerous."[72] Asceticism by Basil's definition is communal and subject to common orders. Furthermore any decision to fast more than one's fellow monks undermines the ascetic spirit, rooted rather in the destructive "passion (*pathos*) of contentiousness arising from vainglory."[73]

Excessive asceticism, and the weakness and injury that follow it, undermines other fundamentals of monasticism, such as manual labor and service unto others. So another asks, if fasting hinders work, which is the more highly valued asceticism: work or fasting?[74] Basil again declines to answer the question posed, instead advising that in true asceticism nothing should be in excess: "We should make use of both fasting and eating in a fashion appropriate to piety; in order that we may fast when God's commandment must be accomplished in fasting, and when again the commandment of God demands food to strengthen the body, that we may eat, not as gluttons, but as God's workmen."[75] The very idea of excessive asceticism—or asceticism that leads to illness or injury—is fundamentally incompatible with the monastic life and indeed cannot be classified as asceticism at all. Asceticism entails not a level of fasting, number of psalms, or length of vigil; rather asceticism is total subjugation of the will to the superior of the monastery and unthinking obedience to the common rule of the coenobium. The idea of a monk punishing his body into illness should be utterly unthinkable in such an environment.

In the *Longer Rules*, Basil touches on similar themes. One question posed to the bishop revolves around the definition of "self-control" (*enkrateia*). It appears that the meaning of asceticism was sufficiently unclear and the predilection toward illness-inducing asceticism sufficiently common that Basil goes so far as to clarify, "[B]y self-control we do not at all mean complete abstinence from food—this would indeed be the violent dissolution of life."[76] The true ascetic, rather, practices "abstinence from pleasures" (*apokhēn tōn hēdeōn*).[77] Basil returns to this theme in a number of his responses in the *Longer Rules*, complementing his approach in the *Shorter Rules*.[78] Uniting his various responses is an approach to ascetic illness that appears at odds, at least superficially, with that of Joseph of Thebes. Basil is adamant that ascetics (true ascetics at least) should not be "choosing" anything, let alone illness.

To review, Basil addresses the problem of monks who choose illness or injure themselves through excessive fasting by framing his response within the context of the core meaning of asceticism, illness, and medicine as part of god's providence. Basil emphasizes the centrality of obedience to one's superior and to a community rule in practicing self-control (*enkrateia*). He thus casts excessive self-mortification, especially any form of fasting that produces illness or injury, as not authentically ascetic at all but rather self-willed vainglory. In addition, although he acknowledges that there are cases of affliction in which medicine serves no purpose, he generally praises the value of medicine. The process of illness, treatment, and convalescence not only functions as a model for the proper training of the self and the soul but also holds other benefits for the ascetic. The transformation of diseased flesh to health provides valuable lessons as a type for spiritual healing and conversion. The practice of medicine furthermore complements the ascetic practices of the ascetic, fostering a disciplined control of the body.

Evagrius of Pontus: The Misappropriation of Role Models

Compared to the scant information preserved about many of the desert fathers, we are fortunate to have two, a longer and a shorter—perhaps abridged or expurgated—versions of a *bios* of Evagrius, both of which are part of Palladius's *Lausiac History*. The existence of dual expurgated and unexpurgated versions of Evagriana is seen elsewhere, such as in Evagrius's controversial *Kephalaia gnostica*, which is preserved in two Syriac versions.[79] Of his *bios* the shorter is preserved as part of the Greek version of the *Lausiac History*, while the longer is preserved in a fragmentary Coptic version. Whether the Coptic text is part of a separately transmitted life or of a different recension of the *Lausiac History* is an open question.[80]

In contrast to such popular Lives as Antony's, written by those with little in the way of personal contact with the saint, Palladius had spent nearly a decade in the company of Evagrius and his contemporaries and remained devoted to his teacher throughout the controversies that coalesced around the teachings of Evagrius and other Origenists. Palladius describes his devotion and debt to Evagrius in the Coptic fragment: "Indeed, it was also he who taught me the way of life in Christ and he who helped me understand Holy Scripture . . . for the whole time I was in that monastic settlement I was with him, each of us living enclosed and apart. I was by his side Saturday night and during the day on Sunday."[81] If the *bios* presents a personal portrait of Evagrius, it is also at times a disarmingly unflattering one. Palladius details Evagrius's significant failings, particularly his weakness for urbane dissolution and lustful thoughts, even an affair—consummated or not—with a married woman in Constantinople.

The two versions of Palladius's description of Evagrius's way of life describe an ascetic well within the mainstream of hagiographic conventions. Evagrius endures a harsh renunciation and painful—even torturous—mortifications of the body, although perhaps not going as far as the Lives of Antony and Simeon describe the privations of their heroes. Yet the two versions are not uniform. According to the Greek version of the *Lausiac History*—the version more familiar to students of late ancient monasticism today—Evagrius was so tormented by the demon or thought of lust that he spent a winter standing naked in a well in order to bring his passions under control, and "his flesh froze." Even then the demon returned, and Evagrius spent another forty days exposed to the elements, so that "his body grew welts in the same way brute animals do."[82] He never bathed and never ate greens, fruit, or, Palladius claims, any cooked food.[83] Both versions depict Evagrius heroically neglecting his body's health. When after sixteen years in the desert, according to the Greek version, his "body required food prepared over a fire, because of his weak stomach," he still refused bread and accepted only gruel or herbs as a comfort.[84]

The Coptic version is considerably more detailed. Given Palladius's tendency toward graphic descriptions of monastic illness in the stories of

Benjamin and Stephen (discussed in Chapter 1), this has the air of an authentically Palladian description. In the Coptic version he hurts his "bowels" (*epefsahoun*), "suffering pain in his anus" (*eafci mkah henmanphen mōou ebol nhemsi*).[85] In another telling detail, the Coptic version makes it clear that it was not his body that compelled him to change his diet but his elders: they "made him change his ascetic practice" (*anihelloi threfšibti ntefaskusis* [for *askēsis*]).[86] In such details Evagrius is reminiscent of monastic stars of hagiographic fame who cared nothing for the fates of their bodies, perhaps echoing the type of tension that Theodoret would describe at the self-harming asceticism of Simeon in the fifth century. In this hagiographic rendering, Evagrius lived out Antony's words, which themselves echo generations of philosophical and spiritual direction: "As we rise daily, let us suppose that we shall not survive till evening."[87]

How reliably Palladius preserved the life of his teacher is difficult to determine. But Evagrius's own teachings at least present a different picture: a monastic elder who looked with suspicion upon the hagiographic norms of excessive asceticism. In his practical and ascetic writings, written as guidance for aspiring monks, he instead underscores the centrality of a disciplined care of the body's health for ascetic progress, a concern that he contrasts with the models provided in popular monastic hagiographies. It is thus no accident that in his introductory treatise on the practice of monasticism, the *Praktikos*, or *The Monk*, Evagrius twists the famous maxim of Antony that the monk should live each day as his last.[88] Instead of attributing the saying to Antony, Evagrius quotes his "saintly teacher," probably Macarius the Great (also known as Macarius the Egyptian), Antony's contemporary and perhaps rival: "Our saintly teacher with his great experience in the practical life (*praktikōtatos*) used to say: The monk must ever hold himself ready as though he were to die tomorrow, *and in turn must treat the body as though he would have to live with it for many years.* The first practice, he would say, cuts off the thoughts of acedia and makes the monk more zealous; the latter keeps the body healthy (*to de sōon diaphulattei to sōma*) and always maintains its abstinence (*enkrateian*) in balance (*isēn*)."[89] The allusion to Antony's maxim is immediately clear to anyone familiar with the *Life of Antony* but is here subverted so that the meaning is quite different from Antony's version.[90] Evagrius subtly but unmistakably criticizes the model of asceticism promoted by the *Life of Antony* as not "practical," as opposed to the advice of the "eminently practical" (*praktikōtatos*) Macarius. Echoing elements of the Basilian ascetic writings, such as the spurious but contemporary *Sermo asceticus*, Evagrius emphasizes the need for moderation or balance in abstinence to enable true, enduring asceticism.[91] So elsewhere in his practical treatise he argues for moderation in all ascetic practices: "But these practices [that is, reading, vigils, prayer, fasting, work, withdrawal, psalmody, patience, and mercy] are to be engaged in at the appropriate times and in due measure, for what is done without due measure or not at the opportune moment lasts but a little while; and what is short-lived is more harmful than profitable."[92] Such concern with the maintenance of bodily health (*to de sōon diaphulattei to sōma*) is a central component of Evagrius's ascetic program, setting his program against the more extreme privations of the hagiographer's Antony and his imitators.[93]

Writing in the tradition of Origenist-influenced asceticism seen in the *Letters* of Antony, Evagrius recognizes the impulse toward immoderate or extreme asceticism as symptomatic of the influence of demons, who harass the monk with evil thoughts (*logismoi*).[94] Evagrius makes it clear, however, that in contrast with the privations of the saints who never alter their asceticism in the face of illness, for monks in the world of practical asceticism, "It is not possible on every occasion to fulfil the habitual rule."[95] Yet it is a constant temptation from the demons, "hindering what can be done and forcing us to do what cannot be done."[96] This temptation is especially prevalent—and especially dangerous—among the sick: "And so they prevent the sick (*tous asthenountas*) from giving thanks for their sufferings (or pain, *epi tais algēdosi*) and acting patiently towards those who are looking after them; in turn, they encourage them to practice abstinence even while they are weak (*atonountas de palin enkrateuesthai*) and to say the psalms standing even when they feel weighed down."[97] Evagrius identifies this demon that pushes the monk to extreme self-denial as the demon of gluttony (*ho tēs gastrimargias . . . daimōn*), who, having failed to tempt the monk to overeat, drives the monk with the desire for "extreme asceticism" (*askēseōs akrotatēs*).[98]

Tracing the compulsion toward health-damaging asceticism to demonic temptation is not new to Evagrius. In the *Life of Antony*, no less, Antony describes the trickery of demons who take the form of monks to compel them through competition not to sleep or to go entirely without food.[99] What is new and significant in Evagrius's interpretation of such demonic activity is that he identifies the means of demonic temptation as—insidiously—the very foundations of the monastic life: the Bible and the Lives of the saints. In his treatise *On Thoughts*, evocative of Athanasius's statements that he anticipates his readers wanting "to emulate [Antony's] purpose (*zēlōsai tēn ekeinou prothesin*)" and that "Antony's life (or *Life*) is a sufficient model of asceticism for the monk (*esti gar monakhois hikanos kharaktēr pros askēsin ho Antōniou bios*),"[100] Evagrius claims that the demons of gluttony and acedia, which in this case imitates gluttony, compel the monk to "become their imitator" (*toutōn mimētēn genesthai katanankazei*) and call them to compete (*eis zēlon proskaloumenos*) with biblical and hagiographical heroes.[101] They bring to mind, for example, the divinely aided asceticism of Daniel and his companions, who fasted from impure food in the court of Nebuchadnezzar; the boys lived on vegetables and water, yet remained visibly healthier than those of the king's court who feasted on rich food and wine (Dan. 1:3–21). They also call up images of John the Baptist, who ate only locusts and honey and eschewed even the relatively modest garb of the monk (Mark 1:6 par.).[102]

Also dangerous for the monk are the stories about the great ascetic masters: "[The Demon] evokes the memory of certain other anchorites who have always lived in this way or who began to [and by implication had to abandon it], and he compels him to become their imitator so that in pursuing an immoderate abstinence (*tēn ametron . . . enkrateian*) he may fail to attain even a moderate one, the body not being strong enough because of its weaknesses (or infirmity, *dia tēn oikeian astheneian*)."[103] We should not be surprised that Evagrius singles out the figure of "Antony, the very first of the anchorites," as an especially dangerous exemplar, driving the monastic to undertake "the prolonged and inhumane withdrawal" (*tēn khronian kai apanthrōpon anakhōrēsin*).[104] Such strict asceticism is demonic, and disastrous for the monastic. One way or another the monk leaves the monastery: either through premature death by pushing the body beyond its natural limits or through the loss of will and the sense of shame at competing with—and inevitably losing to—the figures of hagiography and the Bible. Thus in contrast with the intentional, voluntary courting of illness that Evagrius is described as undertaking in his *bioi*, Evagrius in his own teaching warns against choosing illness and disregarding the care of the body. Evagrius's preserved teachings highlight the risks posed by excessive asceticism and factitious illness rather than the spiritual benefits of suffering disease.

Amma Syncletica: Illness as the Great Asceticism

Written in the century after Evagrius and in the Evagrian tradition, the *Life and Regimen of the Blessed and Holy Teacher Syncletica* presents a complex reflection on how to make sense of the illness of the ascetic and the risks and potentials for embracing illness as an ascetic practice. Much as the *Life of Antony* is constructed by framing extended paraenetic discourses with biographical prologue and epilogue, the author of the *Life of Syncletica* has bracketed a large corpus of ascetic teachings attributed to Syncletica (chapters 22–102) within a largely conventional biographical introduction (1–21) and a narration of Syncletica's death (103–13). The *Life of Antony* exerts a clear influence on the hagiographer's description of Syncletica's early life.[105] Like Antony, Syncletica was something of an aristocrat and a beautiful one at that, sought by many suitors.[106] She, like Antony, never took to the life of the world but always inclined toward asceticism.[107] Also like Antony, she lost her parents as a young adult, and she was left in charge of a sister, at which point she liquidated her estate for the benefit of the poor and took up the monastic life.[108]

In addition Syncletica's hagiographer based his description of her ascetic practice on Antony's model. Much as Athanasius emphasizes the physiological change apparent in the ascetic, Syncletica's hagiographer notes that even from her youth Syncletica had a bodily constitution fundamentally different from that of her peers: her health was maintained by strict fasting, which the author calls a *sōtērios pharmakos*, a health-preserving remedy. If ever she diverged from her ascetic regimen, she became ill: "Her face was pale, and the weight of her body fell."[109] Thus health reflects her excellence in asceticism; illness points to ascetic or moral shortcomings. In contrast to the ascetic ideals promoted by Basil and Evagrius, the hagiographer portrays Syncletica as an ascetic superstar, "injuring her body through manifold sufferings [*ponōn*]."[110]

Her ascetic career, according to the *Life*, was crowned by a gruesome final illness cast upon her by the devil, who "defeated by health" then "makes the body sick."[111] The hagiographer took considerable care describing the particulars of her suffering. The devil began by torturing her with high fevers and infected her lungs, which—consumed by disease—were then coughed up in her sputum (*ptusmatōn*).[112] Her body wasted away. But the worst was yet to come. Next, "having caused pain in one tooth, [the devil] made her gums putrid in like manner. And the bone fell out; the spreading passed into the whole jaw, and became decay of the body pressing on the neighboring parts; and in forty days the bone was worm-eaten. The surrounding spaces were all becoming black. And the bone itself was corrupted, and little by little wasted away; putrefaction and the heaviest stench governed her whole body so that the ones who served her suffered more than she did."[113] Syncletica has not, as David Brakke notes, "chosen to be ill," but she has chosen a particular way to be ill, at first resisting any sort of medical treatment.[114] Syncletica's illness serves as a mode of self-transformation, adapting the Pauline dialectic of weakness and strength (2 Cor. 12:10). Syncletica's illness (*astheneia*, or weakness) is but a ruse in her battle with the devil, serving to reveal her "manliness" (*andreia*) and the strength of her body (*Dynamei de theiai to holon parakrateito sōma*).[115] Her illness also underscores the gulf between the saint and her followers. Her refusal to accept treatment—realizing that the source was diabolical, perhaps echoing the types of concerns of Basil in his *Longer Rules* 55—reveals her manliness (*andreia*), at the same time laying bare the weakness (*astheneia*) of her followers, who plead with her to cover the stench for their own benefit.[116]

Ultimately she accepts medical treatment, although the hagiographer betrays his ambivalence about such a holy ascetic resorting to medical care. He even has the physician describe his application not as curing or treating but as anointing the dead part of her body for burial.[117]

In presenting illness as a mode of manliness and strength, Syncletica's hagiographer draws on a theme seen in Basil's writings. That is, illness has value in a number of ways, not least of which is that illness does much of the work of asceticism. Syncletica does not—contrary to Evagrius's recommendation—lessen her asceticism and comfort her body, but neither does she increase her austerities. Rather her illness takes the place of asceticism and increases her austerities. Because of her illness, fasting was increased: "she was without nourishment; for how was she able to take meals, when she was ruled by such putrefaction and stench?" She also went without sleep.[118] Sickness thus entailed no lessening of her asceticism but aided her abnegation of bodily needs.

It is this latter portion of her *Life* that has received the most attention and has inspired a number of thoughtful readings in the past few years.[119] Here I will focus in more detail on her teachings, encapsulated as a collection of apophthegmata in the hagiographic depiction of Syncletica's brutal ascetic suffering. The aphorisms attributed to Syncletica in her *Life* and in the related (but more limited) corpus of sayings transmitted in the alphabetic series of the *Apophthegmata patrum* do not form an entirely coherent and consistent picture of the ascetic life.[120] This is the case with the sayings traditions of late ancient monasticism in general. It is not possible to be certain of the authenticity of all sayings attributed to any personage, and just as important, the context of most sayings has been stripped away. Nonetheless in the teachings transmitted under her name, a picture emerges of Syncletica as a monastic leader deeply concerned with the proclivity of her charges to injure themselves through excessive asceticism, and furthermore concerned to establish a positive and productive meaning and utility for illness as a type of ascetic practice in and of itself. Syncletica's teachings expand on elements found in Basil and Evagrius, focusing on moderation and self-control as the defining characteristics of asceticism and distinguishing true asceticism from that under the influence of demons.

Syncletica approaches the issue of ascetic self-harm, those who choose illness, much as Basil does, by defining core terms. Asceticism (*askēsis*) in Syncletica's teachings does not entail an ever-increasing level of privation or even a level of privation that the ascetic should maintain until death, as is encouraged in the foundational ascetic hagiography of Antony, in such later derivatives as Jerome's *Life of Paul of Thebes*, and indeed in some parts of the biographical frame to her own *Life and Regimen*. In fact proper asceticism may not be defined by any of the typical ascetic works: prayer, fasting, vigils, or manual labor. Rather true asceticism is defined by self-control (*sōphrosyne*).

Self-control for Syncletica entails a renunciation of excessive asceticism just as it does excessive pleasures. She distinguishes two categories of ascetic behavior. On the one hand is "royal and divine asceticism" (*tēn theian kai basilikēn askēsis*). On the other is "tyrannical and demonical" (*tēs tyrannikēs kai daimoniōdous*) asceticism, "a discipline (*askēsis*) that is encouraged by the Enemy."[121] Syncletica ominously notes that those who "practice this discipline" are "[the enemy's] disciples" (*mathētai*).[122] The difference between the two asceticisms, of god and the devil, may be difficult to discern, as one might expect from Evagrius's criticisms of extreme asceticism: any "enemy" who works through asceticism, as he works through the Bible and the Lives of the saints, is subtle indeed. The demonic ascetic, Syncletica says, is like counterfeit (though not adulterated) gold money, masquerading with a false stamp as gold stamped with the emperor's true sigil. It is thus imperative for monks to be "good money changers," adapting Jesus's words in Matthew 25:27. What is so deceptive about this false asceticism is that it consists of the same practices as the royal and divine discipline, "fasting, self-control, and almsgiving," just as the counterfeit gold in Syncletica's analogy "is the same, but there is a difference in the impression."[123]

The devil may attack the monk's soul with fake asceticism either when it is "sluggish and slothful" (*bradeian kai nōthran*) or when it "considers itself zealous and diligent in asceticism" (*dokousan autēn spoudaian einai kai epiponon pros askēsin*). The death-dealing asceticism of the devil is a prime threat to the monk, which she describes in extreme terms: "This weapon [that is, asceticism] is the ultimate and chief of all evils" (*eskhaton kai koruphaiotaton pantōn esti tōn kakōn).* The difference between the two ascetic types lies not in methods of bodily control or amount of food, water, or sleep but in the presence of moderation or balance (*summetrias*). Lacking moderation, the asceticism of the enemy is "tyrannical": the diabolical asceticism, not the ascetic, is in control. Such ascetic temptation is "[g]rievous and deadly," grounded in the mistaken conviction, planted by the devil, that the ascetic's soul "has grasped matters that are incomprehensible to the majority and that it is superior in fasting."[124] Like Evagrius before her, Syncletica highlights the dangers that sainthood poses to the health of the novice. Syncletica states that the devil "suggests to the soul a host of heroic [or manly] deeds" (*andragathēmatōn*), following the example of Syncletica herself, renowned for her own "manly deeds."[125] In tempting the monk to fast beyond her abilities and to emulate the fantastic deeds of others, the soul "perishes and is destroyed, smitten with a wound hard to heal" (*dusiatōi helkei plēgeisa*).[126] It is not said but perhaps goes without saying that the body too perishes from the wounds of excessive asceticism.

In contrast to the devil's asceticism, Syncletica generally advocates for a balance or uniformity in fasting. So she advises, "For you, through your whole life, there should be a single rule for fasting. Do not fast for four or five days and on the next day dissipate your strength with a surplus of foods."[127] In addition asceticism should be indexed to the age and health of the monk: "When you are young and healthy, fast; for old age will come with illness" (*meta astheneias*).[128] For the ascetic whose arrogant intensity leads her down the path not only to death but also to damnation, a swift intervention is needed. If she is an anchorite, she is to be forced into a coenobium (*en koinobiōi eiserkhesthō*) with its stricter rules and close supervision by experienced and tested monks. Echoing Basil, she argues that "in a coenobium, we prefer obedience (*hupokoē*) to asceticism (*askēsis*). The latter teaches pride, the former humility."[129] There the excessive asceticism will be countered by forcing the monastic to eat twice a day, twice the amount normally allowed for coenobitic monks.[130] The underlying psychic cause of excessive asceticism, arrogance, is also to be countered. She is to "be censured by her associates and rebuked; yes, she should be censured as vigorously as someone who is doing nothing important."[131] In a statement that may reflect Evagrius's concern with those who harm themselves trying to emulate Antony and John the Baptist, "the most renowned lives of the saints should be presented for interpretation (*prosagesthōsan . . . eis exēgēsin*)."[132] That is, the Lives of the saints require the authoritative reading of a superior—they do not speak on their own. In this sense Syncletica's own teachings undermine her image as an unwavering advocate of bodily mortifi-cations and austere asceticism, so fostered by her hagiographer's focus on her asceticism and sufferings.

More important, Syncletica reads the illness of the ascetic as a possible sign of demonically inspired asceticism. In fact this type of ascetic self-hurt is a "disease" (*nosos*), the "ultimate and chief of all evils," brought on "through an excess of asceticism" (*di'hyperbolēn askēseōs*).[133] We need not draw a fine distinction between disease of the body and that of the soul in this case, as the two are intimately intertwined in Syncletica's thought, a point observed by others.[134] Discerning this evil disease of asceticism is thus an urgent concern of the superior, to be cured by the administration of a nonascetic diet and the guided reading of hagiography.

If demonic asceticism is a death-dealing "disease," what does the monk—and her superior—do in the case of other types of disease (*hē nosos*), illness (*tēn astheneian*), and bodily injury (*tēn plēgēn tou sōmatos*)?[135] Syncletica does not detail the process of discernment between nondemonic illness and the disease of tyrannical and demonic asceticism; one can imagine that it could be difficult to distinguish in some cases. Regardless, establishing the meaning of nondemonic illness is just as central to Syncletica's ascetic program. As Basil had argued, nondemonic illness may have special spiritual and ascetic ben-efits, but not because it increases the monk's suffering. "Let us," she counsels, "not be saddened if we are unable to stand for prayer or to sing Psalms aloud because of the illness and injury of our body (*tēn astheneian kai tēn plēgēn tou sōmatos*)."[136] Since the royal road of asceticism entails bodily suffering of a moderate and stable level, involuntary sufferings—such as those caused by bodily illness—effectively preempt the need for voluntary sufferings. Since the goal of asceticism is the "purification (*kathairesin*) of desires" and the control of "shameful pleasures," and since illness necessarily accomplishes these same goals, albeit involuntarily, there is no longer a need for asceticism in times of illness.[137] So Syncletica says in the *Apophthegmata patrum*, "Truly fasting and sleeping on the ground are set before us because of our sensuality. If illness then weakens this sensuality the reason for these practices is superfluous [or excessive (*perittos*)]."[138]

A longer version is recorded in her *Life*: "But why do I say superfluous? Because potentially fatal lapses have been checked by illness (*tēi nosōi*) as if by some strong and powerful medication (*meizoni tini iskhuroterōi pharmakōi*). This is the great asceticism (*hē megalē askēsis*): to remain strong in illness (*to en tais nosois enkarterein*), and to offer up hymns of thanksgiving to the

Almighty."[139] She continues, echoing Basil's counsel in his *Longer Rules* 55: "Are we deprived of our eyes? Let us not take it amiss; we have lost the instruments of insatiable desire, and yet with our inner eyes we contemplate as in a mirror the glory of the Lord. Have we been struck deaf? Let us give thanks that we have completely lost useless noise. Have we suffered damage to our hands? Nonetheless we still have our inner hands well prepared for war against the Enemy. Is illness in control throughout our whole body? Still the health of the inner person will increase all the more."[140] In Syncletica's counsel, disease becomes a remedy for the ills of humanity's fallen existence: illness tamps down physical desires, overwhelms the temptations to gluttony, and drives away lust.[141] Furthermore, "illness controls the whole body" (*arrhōstia kath'holon to sōma kratei*), displacing the ascetic control of the body normally incumbent on the monk herself. Since illness does the ascetic work formerly up to the ascetic, all other voluntary sufferings are rendered excessive (*perittos*).[142] The only expectation of the sick ascetic is to "persevere" and give thanks—though in times of suffering this may be difficult indeed. As a counterpoint to the illness of demonic asceticism, the "ultimate and chief of all evils," to persevere involuntary illness with thanksgiving is a great form of asceticism indeed, *hē megalē askēsis*.

Conclusion

For Basil, the temptation to excessive asceticism—to choose sickness—undermines what he sees as the core fundamental characteristics of asceticism: a focus on the divine and utter obedience to one's monastic superior and the monastic rule. The sick monk renders himself unable to comply with the monastic rule, undermining the very basis of asceticism. Yet Basil sees in sickness and convalescence (or its failure) a typological model for spiritual progress.

Evagrius of Pontus condemns such asceticism in harsher terms, connecting the drive to extreme mortification as a demonic temptation, as dangerous as temptations to overeating or fornication. Demons trick monks into taking Antony and others too literally as role models, thus damaging their health and shaming them by their inevitable failure to equal the ascetic greats of hagiography. Demons furthermore tempt the sick to continue their ascetic practices even in the midst of pains and fevers.

Syncletica similarly sees the urge to excessive asceticism—and the refusal to cease ascetic practice in time of sickness—as a symptom of demonic agency.

Like Basil, Syncletica insists that true asceticism consists not of any particular practice but of self-control. Syncletica further insists that asceticism consists not of a fixed level of privation but of the control of passions. Thus in the case of sick monks voluntary asceticism is unnecessary and is indeed to be condemned, since the involuntary suffering of disease controls desires more effectively than does any voluntary privation. The thankful endurance of illness is the great asceticism.

This context prompts a return to the controversies that swirled around the sick ascetic Blesilla and to Joseph of Thebes, who claims to have "chosen" illness as a practice approved by god. It is interesting to note how far Jerome's explication of Blesilla's suffering and death is from the well-developed strategies for making meaning of illness discussed here. Jerome's understanding of Blesilla's illness as a pedagogical punishment for prior sinfulness (in her case vanity) differs from the related traditions of the Cappadocian and Origenist teachers of the east.

Joseph's aphorism on ascetic illness lies much closer to the traditions discussed in this chapter. Judging by the controversy engendered by sickness and asceticism, it is not surprising that Joseph would consider a certain manner of behavior in sickness to be one of the three ascetic deeds most honored by God. In fact, as he considers obedience the most honored ascetic practice, Joseph is rather modest in his valuation when compared to Syncletica, who labels perseverance and thanksgiving in sickness as the great asceticism. Joseph is certainly not alone in speaking of the temptations that are inflicted upon the sick: judging by the treatments of Basil, Evagrius, and Syncletica, the temptations that come upon the sick were considerable. While one might expect such temptations to include primarily indulging in luxuries and comforting the body, this is not borne out by Basil, Evagrius, and Syncletica. In point of fact, the temptations that befall the sick are not temptations to lessen their asceticism. Quite to the contrary, the most prevalent temptations are to continue their *askēsis* in spite of their illness. Such temptations include the demonic enticements to imitate the role models of the Bible and hagiography and to impose extra voluntary ascetic burdens upon the sick body. These, I submit, are the "temptations" to which Joseph refers. Thus when Joseph says "I have chosen sickness," he has not chosen to injure his body voluntarily as did Simeon or Dorotheus. Rather by "choosing illness," Joseph has opted to undertake a difficult asceticism indeed: with patience and thanksgiving to accept—and resist—the temptations that befall the monastic in sickness, the temptations to continue his voluntary privations in the face of involuntary sufferings.

By framing this endurance of illness (à la Syncletica) as a "choice," Joseph helps—within the context of controversy and competition over ascetic propriety and authority—to frame illness (an involuntary state not normally considered ascetic) as a type of ascetic spiritual exercise. We may recall Hadot's definition, based on Greco-Roman traditions, of spiritual exercises as "voluntary."[143] Slipping on a banana peel or getting cancer are not voluntary and thus would not normally (in the ancient context of which Hadot writes) be considered ascetic, although they might well result in bodily mortification. By framing illness (or a proper mode of being ill) as a choice (*haireō*), Joseph, in line with other authors examined here, transforms illness into asceticism, a spiritual exercise.

The next two chapters explore how the spiritual exercise of illness would be elaborated in the realm of hagiography and in the more practical world of monastic spiritual direction.

Chapter 5

Pestilence and Sainthood: The Great Coptic *Life of Our Father Pachomius*

The Great Coptic *Life of Our Father Pachomius* presents a sustained meditation on the meaning of chronic illness within the life of a saint. The approach that the Great Coptic *Life* takes differs—quite intentionally—from the model promoted in Antony's *Life* and reflects in various ways the controversies concerning the uses and risks of illness as an ascetic practice discussed in the previous chapters. The Great Coptic *Life* throughout presents a narrative interpretation of the meaning and utility of illness within ascetic practice. In short, the *Life* radically critiques the hagiographical model of the healthy saint promoted by the *Life of Antony* and others, not only defending the sanctity and authority of Pachomius as a chronically ill monk but also elaborating a vision of enduring illness as a marker of sanctity, imitating the specific ascetic performances of his master Palamon and the sufferings of the martyrs.

The Great Coptic *Life of Our Father Pachomius* does not bear the same prestige and cultural influence as the *Life* of his influential contemporary Antony. While Antony's *Life* would become the archetype for Christian hagiography, the Coptic *Life* of the founder of the coenobitic monastic tradition is more rarely read. There are understandable reasons for the neglect. While the *Life of Antony* is more or less cohesive and easily read in a sitting, the Great Coptic *Life of Our Father Pachomius* (or simply here the Great Coptic *Life* or the *Life*) is a sprawling collection of traditions several times the length of Antony's *bios*, continuing its chronicle even long after the death of Pachomius to include the careers of later successors. Its use as a source for the "historical Pachomius" is just as or even more compromised than the *Life of Antony* is for its hero, as it was composed at an unknown time by an unknown author. It is furthermore only one of a number of *Lives* of Pachomius in Coptic, Greek, and Arabic, whose stemmatic relationships are still contested. The Great Coptic *Life* may also suffer a marginality due to its Coptic-ness, as have so many facets of the literary and material culture of late ancient Egypt.[1] Yet for all of its bulk, the Great Coptic *Life* is coherent thematically and theologically. In the context of late ancient hagiography the Great Coptic *Life* is a literary work along the lines of the *Life of Antony*, a complex meditation on the life of the founder of coenobitic asceticism.

The Great Coptic *Life*'s vision of Pachomius as a model for the sick saint has been largely overlooked. Studies of the biographical elements of the Pachomian narrative have hardly even noticed Pachomius's chronically poor health. Philip Rousseau, in his still indispensable monograph on Pachomius, mentions his illness only briefly, and then only in the context of Theodore's demotion.[2] Henry Chadwick in his oft-cited essay "Pachomios and the Idea of Sanctity" does not touch on the issue at all, though Pachomius's illness is integral to the idea of sanctity in the *Life*.[3] Nor does Heinrich Bacht note the prevalence of Pachomius's illnesses (although he makes a point of his drawn-out death in the plague).[4] Mark Burrows, while presenting Pachomius in terms evocative of Antony in Athanasius's *Life*, never notes that the "visibility of god" in our father Pachomius, whom Burrows describes as the "singular bearer of *ho logos tou theou*" and a "*teleios anthrōpos*," is a chronically ill "perfect man" and bearer of the word.[5] This is a far cry from Antony, whose bearing of the word manifests in longevity and freedom from disease. A similar lacuna is visible in Peter Brown's description of Pachomius of the Greek *Life* as a *representatio Christi*; asceticism, as Brown puts it, "was a way of passing on . . . the mighty image of the presence of Christ among men."[6] While this may hold without too great difficulty for the Greek *Life*, the Great Coptic *Life* poses an important problem of just what kind of *representatio* a chronically sick saint presents.

This chapter shows that it is through illness, especially his own but also those of others, that the peculiar sanctity of Pachomius is established; as such, illness is a central structuring element in the Great Coptic *Life* of Pachomius. Drawing on the themes explored in the previous chapters and the Introduction, I show that the author of the Great Coptic *Life* is quite aware that a chronically ill saint flies in the face of hagiographical conventions; at the same time the *Life* reflects late ancient Christian perspectives on the potential utility of illness as a mode of spiritual advancement and spiritual direction (though not clearly dependent on the sources and traditions discussed in Chapters 1 and 4). The Great Coptic *Life*'s approach to the chronically ill saint negotiates the dialectic between these understandings of health and illness as a component of asceticism.

Pachomius's Early Life: Asceticism and Pestilence in the Village of Šeneset

The Great Coptic *Life* begins by placing the *Life of Our Father Pachomius* within the context of the broad sweep of Christian salvation history, a familiar aspect of monastic writing witnessed as early as Antony's *Letters*. It will be clear, however, that the *Life of Pachomius* elaborates ascetic health entirely differently than does Antony, or his biographer for that matter. In its survey of biblical and ecclesiastical history the *Life* intertwines two themes that will echo throughout the narrative: fatherhood and martyrdom. "The Word of God," begins the *Life*, "who made all things, came to our father Abraham and ordered him to sacrifice his only son. . . . After our father Abraham, he spoke to Moses, his prophet and servant, and to all the prophets; then he appeared and spoke as man and as the seed of Abraham."[7] Note that the two primary biblical models, apart from Christ incarnate, were blessed with long, healthy lives: 175 years for Abraham and 120 years for Moses. Not atypical of monastic narrative, postresurrection salvation history pivots at the persecution and suffering of the martyrs, followed by the rise of asceticism: "Many martyrs offered themselves to various tortures unto death and received the crown. . . . Then faith increased greatly in the holy Churches in every land, and monasteries and places for ascetics began to appear, for those who were the first monks had seen the endurance of the martyrs. . . . Then they offered their souls and bodies to God in strict askesis and with a befitting reverence, not only because they looked day and night to the holy Cross, but also because they saw the martyrs take up their cross. They saw them and imitated them."[8] The Great Coptic *Life* thus quickly segues from the lives of the patriarchs, blessed by god with longevity and health, to their descendants the martyrs, tortured and suffering and dying (prematurely) for the cross and yet compensated for their suffering with an assurance of a prompt translation to paradise after their passing. It is to the latter—the suffering martyrs—that monks look as a model.

Pachomius's own call to asceticism follows his conversion to the Christian life while imprisoned as a conscript for Constantine's war with the Persians.[9] Released from the army without seeing battle, Pachomius made good on his prison-house promise. Settling in a sparsely inhabited village called Šeneset, he began the life of a village solitary. The description of his lifestyle resembles those ur-ascetics of the *Life of Antony* who lived on the outskirts of the village.[10] Yet it is worth noting that while Pachomius refers to himself as *monakhos*, his asceticism is not described in any detail, apart from his "tending to some greens and date-palms for his bodily needs," a rather modest asceticism in any case.[11] It was as a servant rather than an ascetic athlete that he made his fame and his ascetic program, as the *Life* makes clear. It was by his "charity" (*tefmetmairōmi*) that he "made progress" (*naferprokoptin*, Gr. *prokoptein*, a standard characterization of asceticism in late antiquity).[12] While at first Šeneset had few residents, he attracted a large following who left their homes to settle in Šeneset due to his willingness to converse with, console, and sometimes feed others in need.[13] The *Life* insists that his followers' attraction was not merely to his charity; "in fact it was because of his way of life (*anastrophē*) that many people came to be in that place."[14]

Pachomius's experiment in village asceticism in Šeneset would not last long. A great pestilence (*ouništi nšōni nloimos*) soon fell upon the community, killing many, although the *Life* does not provide the body count, as it will for a later plague that ravages the monasteries. Pachomius distinguishes himself by serving the sick, particularly in gathering firewood from the large grove of thorn trees (*acacia nilotica*) nearby. The *Life* is silent on how the villagers treated themselves or otherwise coped with the illness; the focus is on Pachomius. Regardless, Pachomius is presented not as curer or healer but merely as servant: "He simply served them (*aplōs* [Gr. *haplōs*] *naferdiakonin erōou*) until god should bless them with healing."[15] The episode is an important component of the Great Coptic *Life*. Pachomius's ascetic mission lies not in reclaiming humanity's long-lost health but in humble servitude, patiently enduring the world's endemic disease, and aiding however imperfectly other sufferers. The plague of Šeneset, furthermore, is the catalyst for the turning point in Pachomius's ascetic career: his call into the desert to apprentice with the anchorite Palamon.

As a point of contrast, take the parallel in the Greek *Vita Prima*, probably the more familiar version of Pachomius's call to the desert. Pachomius dreams of "dew of heaven" descending upon him, turning to honey in his hand, and dropping on the ground, a not unconventional symbol of Pachomius bringing sanctity to the earth. In the Greek version the would-be monk immediately heads off in search of the local anchorite Palamon.[16]

While the vision is similar in the Coptic *Life,* it is separated by a period of up to three years from his journey to Palamon.[17] In the Great Coptic *Life* it is the great plague of Šeneset, rather than any vision, that drives Pachomius to realize that his career must take him outside the village. With a faintly bitter tone in the saint's mouth, the *Life* notes,

> When they had been healed of their illness, he reflected, saying, "This labor, taking care of the sick in the villages, is not for monks, but only for clergy and some faithful elders. From today on I shall not undertake to do this work, so that another might not put his hand to this labor, and a scandal meet him for this reason, and so that the saying might not pertain to me, 'A soul for a soul'" (Ex. 21:23, Lev. 24:18). For it is written, "Pure and undefiled worship before God and the Father is this: to visit the orphans and the widows, and to keep unblemished by the world" (Jam. 1:27). And after three years in that place, he saw that great throngs had surrounded him, so that he was greatly distressed, for they did not allow him any solitude. Then he sought to become a monk and to go into seclusion (*eše naf etianakhōrēsis*).[18]

The contrast with the Greek version is stark. In the Great Coptic *Life* it is the pestilence in the community and the related distress (*hojhej*) it entailed that drive Pachomius to realize that he could not remain as a village monk. He had to find a new way, which would culminate in the Koinonia, by way of Palamon's desert cell. In this community of celibates (the "orphans and widows" of the Epistle of James quoted by the *Life*) Pachomius would keep himself "uncontaminated" or "unblemished" (*atacni*) from the world.[19] Yet in an irony perhaps not unintended by the Great Coptic *Life*, while he might successfully escape the contamination of the world, the contamination and blemishes of pestilence would follow Pachomius throughout his life in the cloister.

The plague of Šeneset is unique to the Great Coptic *Life*. Admittedly the other Coptic versions are preserved only fragmentarily. It is conceivable, for example, that such a plague narrative could have been in the First Sahidic *Life of Pachomius*, which is generally regarded as preserving a very early and "unrefined" stratum in Pachomian tradition due to its controversial narrative of the saint's early and humiliating failure to organize a community (not preserved in other traditions).[20] It is also not out of the question that a similar narrative could have been included in one or more of the other extremely fragmentary Sahidic *Lives*. As it stands, however, the contrast is quite clear between the two relatively complete ancient versions, the Great Coptic and the Greek. In contrast to the Greek *Vita Prima*, the plague of Šeneset looms large in the biography of Pachomius in the Great Coptic *Life*. The Great Coptic *Life* of Pachomius—to a degree unmatched by the Greek—will be punctuated throughout by outbreaks of illness, either epidemic among the communities or limited to Pachomius himself. His *Life*, in fact, preserves no fewer than six major episodes of illness suffered by the saint from early in his career until his death and many more episodes of illness suffered by others, including plagues that ravage his community after his death, taking with them two of the three successors to Pachomius. Illness and pestilence, particularly afflicting the holy, are dominant structuring elements in the *Life*, a fact foregrounded by this early plague: the very impetus for Pachomius's ascetic journey to the desert, a journey that will eventually lead him back to another type of village—the coenobium.

Health and Manliness: Pachomius Joins the Army

Pachomius's considerable weakness and illness are issues that the Great Coptic *Life* returns to repeatedly and pointedly. This is especially clear in comparison with the shorter, independent Greek *Vita Prima*. An example of this may be seen in the early conscription of Pachomius into Constantine's army, an episode shared by the Great Coptic *Life* and the Greek *Vita Prima*. The Coptic *Life* reports that "the youth Pachomius was himself conscripted when he was twenty years old, although he was not very strong (*kegar nafoi njōri an pe*). But because of the great mass that they had conscripted, he too was conscripted with them."[21] The Greek *Vita Prima* notes that Pachomius was conscripted at age twenty; yet it says nothing about his strength or constitution. Otherwise the accounts are quite the same.[22]

Why would the Coptic *Life* deem it significant to present Pachomius as an unlikely candidate for military service though in the prime of his life and prior to undertaking a potentially weakening ascetic practice? The Coptic word used here, Bohairic *jōri*=Sahidic *jōōre*, marks the strong, powerful, and youthful; it translates Greek words such as *iskhuros, dunatos, krataios, andreios, eumegethēs*: strong, powerful, manly.[23] This saint is quite the opposite: weak, unmanly.

The introduction of Pachomius's bodily infirmity into this passage is emblematic of the Coptic author's distinct approach toward the meaning of the saint's illness. The source shared with the Greek *Vita Prima* probably had no such claim, unless it was removed by the Greek hagiographer (possible but unlikely). Rather it seems a later addition, since Pachomius's bodily infirmity does not otherwise play a significant role in the conscription narrative. Instead of adding texture or explanation to this early episode, the mention of Pachomius's weakness looks ahead to his career as a chronically ill saint.

As will already be clear from previous chapters, to describe a saint as "not strong" is quite unusual in the context of late ancient hagiographical conventions. While there are certainly sick saints, it is highly unusual to highlight the constitutional infirmity of the saintly protagonist at the beginning of a Life, especially in the full bloom of manhood at age twenty. Compare the *Life of Syncletica*, discussed in Chapter 4, whose hagiographer contrasts her ostensible feminine weakness and illness (*astheneia*) with her authentically manly mind, manly good deeds (*andragathēmata*), and strong body.[24] Her weakness baits the trap for the devil, to be defeated by her manliness. As witnessed widely in late ancient hagiography, any weakness presages a countervailing strength. While Antony, Simeon, or Syncletica might be broken or beaten by ascetic practice and demonic assault, they are nonetheless, as Hemingway might say, strong at the broken places.

It is furthermore unusual to present the protagonist as weak or not manly (Greek *andreios*=Coptic *jōri*) in the context of presenting the monk as the new martyr. The Coptic author draws this comparison in the *Life*'s prologue and will—discussed below—frame Pachomius's final illness and death as nothing less than a martyrdom. As readers of early martyrology will note, martyrs are strong, and female martyrs and confessors as early as Thecla and Perpetua are known for taking on masculine characteristics. A rhetoric of manliness runs throughout early Christian martyrdom narratives and even Jewish martyrology, such as the influential narratives in 2 and 4 Maccabees. The rhetoric of masculinity pertains not only to women but also to others who diverge from ancient ideals of masculinity, such as youths and the aged. A rhetoric of masculinity, Stephanie Cobb argues, is central to the Christian critique of Roman imperial culture, as martyrological narrative transforms subjects gendered as feminine by the dominant culture into exemplars of masculinity, at the same time feminizing the forces of power and juridical violence in the terms of the dominant culture (they are cast as lacking reason and at the control of the passions, frequently described as characterizing women).[25]

In light of this deep-seated Christian faith in the masculinity of the martyrs, it is all the more remarkable that the Great Coptic *Life* insists that Pachomius, who should be near the peak of his manliness at the time of his conscription, is anything but strong and manly. Pachomius's weakness, even in times of relative health, will continue to appear in the narrative. On one occasion Theodore visits Pachomius "while his body was not strong" (*erepefsōma oi n[at]jom erof*). Later in the *Life* his weakness will even be a source of criticism from another monk, who ridicules Pachomius as a "weak senior monk" (*paihello natjom*).[26] When the Coptic *Life* characterizes Pachomius as infirm and a poor candidate for military service and further repeatedly characterizes the father as "not strong" or "infirm" (*atjom*), it calls the readers' attention to a sharp disjunction between the Great Coptic *Life* and other famous Lives of ascetics and martyrs. As will become clear, the *Life*'s characterization of Pachomius as the weak soldier and the sick saint will continue to be relevant, even as the Great Coptic *Life* (again in contrast to other versions) characterizes Pachomius as a martyr in his death.

It seems a fair characterization of martyrological narrative that the weak become strong and the feminized become masculinized. Mathew Kuefler notes, however, that such a directional transformation was not universal, that is, entailing the rejection of the label of "unmanly" or "weak": "[S]ome Christian men were willing to accept this label of weakness and unmanliness as part of the humility required by patience and to leave the retribution for such attacks to God."[27] While this line of martyr narrative is not the most visible in recent scholarship on gender and martyrdom, it goes a long way toward explaining Pachomius's unsuitability for military service, his near constant illness, and his death as a "martyr" to the plague. Like the Christians described in Kuefler's quote above, Pachomius's hagiographers were concerned to show his absolute humility, a typically praised virtue among monks but exceptionally difficult to achieve as a leader of a federation of coenobitic monasteries. Philip Rousseau has noted the importance of humility in the memory of Pachomius's followers, humility (and patience) before his junior monks even in the face of contempt and abuse.[28] While I will return to this later, in brief, the Great Coptic *Life*'s embrace of the label of weakness for the young soldier Pachomius points to his constant, humble, patient, and even passive endurance (all martyrological values) of illness as a consummation of the martyr's quest.[29]

Pachomius and Palamon

Pachomius's own experiences with chronic illness are prefaced by his encounters with his master Palamon, whose ascetically induced illness establishes a complicating precedent, reflecting the kinds of controversies about the meaning and function of illness as an ascetic practice discussed in the previous chapter. After Pachomius joined Palamon as his disciple, the two "lived together as one man, practicing a hard and exhausting asceticism."[30] Palamon was at first unsure of Pachomius's ability to bear Palamon's ascetic program and so began a process of testing him in the various practices, vigils, prayers, and manual labors to see "if he could endure without growing weary" (*jean fnaerhupomenin ešt[em]ernkakin*).[31] Veilleux translates the passage a bit more pointedly, "to see if he would hold out without getting sick," which is certainly possible given Pachomius's and Palamon's impending illnesses.[32] This passage, like so many others relating to Pachomius's (and Palamon's) bodily constitution, is unique to the Coptic *Life* and not included in the parallel Greek *Vita Prima*. While the phenomenon of an anchorite testing the ascetic aspirant is a common one, here Palamon's testing of Pachomius echoes the *Life*'s earlier mention of Pachomius's bodily infirmity.

Nonetheless, Pachomius endures all the ascetic practices taught by Palamon despite his lack of strength, and the two become "as one man" until Palamon's own *askēsis* catches up with him. Unlike the hagiographies of Antony, Paul, and Onnophrius discussed in Chapter 3, asceticism in the Great Coptic *Life* does not induce or maintain health, and the meaning of illness for the saint, here and elsewhere in the Greek Coptic *Life*, is at the very least ambiguous; it will later prove contentious. Thus the *Life* describes Palamon's illness:

The Old Man Abba Palamon fell ill in his spleen due to the magnitude of his ascetic practices (*pašai nniaskēsis*), especially because of his old age, inasmuch as he gave himself no relief in his exercises (*henipolētia*, read *hennipoliteia*). His neighbors and some other elders visiting from afar saw him suffering in illness (*henphisi mpišōni*), and they brought a great master doctor (*sah nsēini*) to him, so that perhaps he might be able to heal him. When he went in to him, the doctor said to them, "It is no matter for a doctor, only the suffering of ascetic practices. So now if he will listen and eat a bit of appropriate food, he will recover."[33]

Palamon's illness evokes Athanasius's description of Antony in old age, never relenting in his *askēsis* and yet enjoying perfect health until death at 105. The Great Coptic *Life*, in contrast, traces Palamon's affliction of the spleen to his ascetic rigor. His illness furthermore does not signify Satan's torments (as did Syncletica's cancer), nor does it result from self-torturing or transgressions of ascetic norms (as we saw variously in Chapter 4). It is a simple function of his asceticism. According to the esteemed doctor, the cure is simple: Palamon must lessen his asceticism, if even only slightly.

In both the Coptic and Greek versions, Palamon takes this advice and eats a diet appropriate for the sick, but failing to see any improvement after a few days (*hanehoou*), he concludes that the treatment will not work. In the context of ancient medical practice (or modern for that matter) a few days is an extraordinarily short time to expect relief from dietary therapy. The *Life* rather plainly implies that Palamon simply had no interest in seeing his treatment through. Instead he interpreted his illness as an opportunity to emulate the martyrs of old. "Do not think," Palamon says, "that recovery (*mton*) is from perishable foods, but recovery and strength (*jom*) is from our Lord Jesus Christ. For if the martyrs of Christ endured their limbs to be cut off and were beheaded and burned in the fire, and they endured unto death in the faith in god that is theirs, then I am worthy to be sick (*erjōb*) because of an insignificant (*elakhiston*) illness. Although I obeyed you, and was persuaded by you, and ate the foods considered to strengthen the body, look, no relief has come to me."[34] Palamon's words reflect Paul's ubiquitous words to the Corinthians, as well as the gendered rhetoric of martyrological narratives; through endurance of sickness or weakness (*erjōb*) he will gain strength (*jom*) from Christ.

Yet here again the *Life's* interpretation of the meaning of the saint's illness is conflicted and ambivalent. While the Greek and Coptic traditions diverge at this point, both grapple with a complicating factor: Palamon did not receive the kind of enduring health from Christ that one might expect from such hagiographies as the *Lives* of Antony and Onnophrius. In the Greek *Vita Prima*, Palamon boldly predicts, "So if I return to the rigorous *askēsis* in which is all comfort I will be healed."[35] Palamon's confidence in asceticism was misplaced, since he was dead a month later.[36] The Greek *Life's* stark presentation of Palamon's death leaves the question of meaning unanswered. The Coptic version complicates the matter. Although Palamon declines to continue treatment, gone is Palamon's bold confidence that he would be cured by his *askēsis*. Yet in the Coptic he is cured, however briefly: "And thus he returned again to his ascetic practices (*nefaskēsis*) in great suffering, until the Lord saw the constancy of his strength (*ntefmetjōri*) and gave him comfort (*nteftimton*) and healed him (*nteftalcof*) from his illness."[37] Thus in the Great Coptic *Life*, Palamon's endurance approximates the sort of ascetic healing typical of late ancient hagiography. Yet even here the meaning of the saint's illness and recovery is less than straightforward. While the contrast between the enduring strength of the senior monk Palamon and the "not strong" (*oujōri an pe*) young Pachomius stands out, Palamon nonetheless dies shortly after this "cure" (*talco*). This fact is perhaps intentionally obscured by the Coptic *Life*, by inserting the story of Pachomius's vocation to coenobitic monasticism in between Palamon's "cure" (*talco*) and his death shortly thereafter.[38]

In the Great Coptic *Life*, Palamon's illness, cure, and death frame Pachomius's vocation to coenobitic monasticism and foreground Palamon's illness behavior as the model for Pachomius's later mimetic ascetic practices (more below). While in the Greek *Vita Prima* Pachomius receives his vision to found a new community before Palamon falls ill, in the Great Coptic *Life* only after Palamon has fallen ill and has been at least temporarily healed does Pachomius receive his transformative vision to establish the Koinonia. The *Life* emphasizes that in response to Palamon's splenetic sufferings and his refusal to relent in his asceticism, "The young Pachomius strove to emulate (*khoh*) him in everything that he undertook."[39] Unlike his vision, Pachomius's explicit imitation of Palamon's suffering is not included in the Greek parallel. Following is the famous call of Pachomius from a heavenly voice to establish a community of monks at the abandoned village of Tabenesse. Despite the radical change that Pachomius would make in his ascetic practice by following the vision shown him in the abandoned village of Tabenesse, in the Great Coptic *Life* Pachomius would indeed imitate the works of his master, not least through chronic illness.

Pachomius in the Koinonia: The Chronically Ill Saint

From the start the Great Coptic *Life* presents Pachomius's life in the Koinonia as a world apart from the paradisiacal *politeia* of Antony, Paul, or the monks of Isidore's monastery in the *History of the Monks in Egypt*. The Koinonia is not a realm of prelapsarian health and happiness or the "peaceable kingdom" of humanity and animals.[40] Pachomius and his first inmate, his brother John, undertake the harsh asceticism typical of late ancient hagiography, with the result that "their feet were swollen from the pain, as they had stood on them all night, and with the result that their hands were [as if] dipped in blood, since they were not able to withdraw them at all due to the multitude of gnats feeding on them."[41] Other creatures are no more charitable to the monks than the gnats. Pachomius's control over the beasts is not through peaceful concord but rather through conflict, such as hurling water in a hostile crocodile's face and cursing it, a far cry from the *History of the Monks in Egypt*'s paradisiacal desert, where Apa Helle rides across the Nile on a crocodile's back.[42] In addition, far from the health of Isidore's monks in the *History of the Monks in Egypt*, the Coptic *Life* characterizes Pachomius's monks as frequently sick.

While there is no doubt that the Pachomian literature in general and the Coptic *Life* in particular place a high value on the compassionate care of sick monks, the Great Coptic *Life* also promotes illness as a mode of asceticism, though within certain limits.[43] In one such case Pachomius's heir apparent Theodore comes to him with a question about a headache (*paipathos nšōni [et] ḥentaapha*). Contrary to the usual advice given in the Pachomian literature, the father counsels Theodore no treatment, just patience: "It is right for the faithful person that the illness remain ten years in his body without him telling anyone, except for an obvious disease that he cannot conceal."[44] The patient endurance of involuntary illness features regularly in the Great Coptic *Life*.

That is not to say that no one is healed in the Coptic *Life*. Pachomius is regularly presented as a charismatic healer, especially of nonmonastic supplicants. Pachomius heals a demon-possessed woman by sending blessed oil, which is vicariously applied to her.[45] He inadvertently heals a woman suffering from a flow of blood in a repurposing of Mark 9:18–22, though instead of becoming angry as did Jesus, "The man of god Apa Pachomius grieved to the point of death on account of this deed, because he had always fled from human glory."[46] In addition with blessed bread and oil he heals a demoniac boy.[47] But alongside the narratives of healing, the Coptic *Life* emphasizes the unreliability of charismatic healing and its secondary importance. Pachomius was known to fail at healing, and the *Life* presents him as downplaying the significance of healing. "Do not think," says Pachomius, "that bodily healings are [true] healings."[48] Rather, spiritual healings are the true healings. While such sentiments and justifications of the failure of charismatic healers are by no means unique to the Pachomian *Life* (compare the *Life of Antony* 56), the prominent placement of these caveats at this particular point indicates their special importance. It is in illness, not healing, that the *Life* finds the height of sainthood.

Directly following the narrative of Pachomius's failures to heal and his praise of spiritual healings as far more important than those of bodily illnesses, Pachomius falls (bodily) ill, his first of six major episodes of illness: "It happened once that our father Pachomius was somewhere with the brothers reaping . . . and our father Pachomius returned one evening and laid down on a mat with his body heavy."[49] Pachomius's behavior imitates Palamon's illness behavior. Much as Palamon rejected even the modest dietary changes prescribed by the physician, Pachomius refuses any special accommodations in his illness, a comfortable blanket and the offer of some dates. Rather "he remained lying down sick for two days without food," all the while rising every so often (*katakouji*) to pray. Without medical care and without significantly altering his diet, "on the third day he was relieved (*afasiai*) of the illness. He rose, went back, and even ate with all the brothers."[50]

The parallel in the Greek *Vita Prima* takes this episode in a different direction, making it clear that Pachomius was not sick in body but afflicted by demonic thoughts.[51] In the Greek *Vita Prima* but not in the Coptic *Life*, the problem of demonic illness is depicted as a special interest of Pachomius. So, "[t]hrough the discernment of the spirit, he also tested the nature of the different states of health, because the demons try to impede the faithful in every way." In the case of this specific illness, Pachomius is not "cured"; he realizes that he was never sick: "[H]e girded up his loins and went to eat at the table of the healthy brothers, realizing that the disease was not natural (*mē physikē*). And he gave thanks to God who had strengthened him. And so, when he saw another [in the same situation] he straightened him out so that he would not be mocked by the enemy."[52] While later in the Great Coptic *Life* Pachomius asserts that some diseases could in fact merely be demonic *phantasia* (*SBo* 107) and even disbelieves in the substantiality of his own illness (*SBo* 117), in this case the contrast with the Greek parallel is clear: Pachomius's illness is bodily and natural, just as Palamon's was before him.

The nondemonic etiology of his illness in the Coptic *Life* further sets Pachomius's illness against other models of ascetic suffering, such as Antony and Syncletica (as different as their respective outcomes were). While there is no question of Pachomius's exceptionality, his illness is presented as mundane, lacking the theatricality of an Antony or the grotesque melodrama of a Syncletica. On the other hand, Pachomius's refusal to alter his *askēsis* in illness also differs from what is advocated by Evagrius (or, in the next chapter, Barsanuphius) and is even different from his rules for other Pachomian monks. Pachomius is an exception, and through his illness his exceptionality is revealed and maintained.

Pachomius's next illness follows directly. Again the Great Coptic *Life* portrays Pachomius as imitating Palamon's behavior, here even identifying the very same cause for illness: excessive asceticism, *pašai nniaskēsis* and *phisi nniaskēsis* in the case of Palamon, *phouo nniaskēsis* in the case of Pachomius: "Another time he fell so ill that he was pained to the point of death due to his excessive ascetic practices. They carried him to where the sick brothers were lying (perhaps the infirmary, *epima erenisnēou etšōni nkot nhētf*) so that they might get him to eat a few vegetables there."[53] Two details are worth noting here: first, Pachomius is described as being taken ("lifted" or "gathered") to the monastic infirmary by others, not at his own request, which is not unexpected considering that he is described as "at the point of death" (*šaehrēi ephmou*); second, while the narrative seems to present his expected diet of "a few vegetables" (*kouji nouoti*) as typical of sick food, these would hardly be out of place in a typical diet for the healthy as well.[54] In fact the episode underscores that while Pachomius adamantly urged all manner of ascetic rules to be suspended when caring for monks in need, he would never lessen his own asceticism.

That Pachomius's diet in sickness is that of a normal "healthy" monk and not that accorded to the sick (at least some sick) is noted by the *Life*. So the *Life* directly continues with the story of another sick brother who, wasting away from a lengthy illness, begs the brothers in charge to give him some meat, a request roundly refused by the brothers as "not our custom" (*tensunēthia an te*). The sick monk appeals to Pachomius, and when the saint sees the boy's condition and hears of the infirmarians' hard-heartedness, he groans, weeps, and condemns them for their neglect and for failing to recognize the different ascetic demands between the healthy and the sick. The chastened monks buy a young goat and prepare it for the sick monk. But for Pachomius, also lying sick, "they brought the few cooked vegetables for our father Pachomius, and he ate them with thanksgiving, just as any of the brothers in his monastery (*mphrēti nouai nnisnēou*)."[55] The point is clear. For all of Pachomius's charity and forbearance toward the monks in the monastery, even going so far as to allow meat to be prepared in the infirmary, he would not lessen his own asceticism although at the point of death himself. While Pachomius's recovery is not narrated, the *Life* implies that Pachomius again recovered his health without lessening his asceticism in any significant way or accepting medical care.

Following his recovery the *Life* narrates the growth of the Pachomian federation, as Pachomius founds new monasteries and already established communities petition to place themselves under the community rule. Pachomius's protégé Theodore also joins the community. This is followed by Pachomius's third illness. Here again Pachomius imitates Palamon's earlier behavior: "it happened again one day that our father Pachomius was lying down sick (*ef-nkot efšōni*), and they brought him a bit of good fish sauce for him to eat, since he was ill (*jefšōni*)."[56] The fish sauce in question here is *garelaion* (Coptic *karella*), a paste of the ubiquitous Greco-Roman garum with wine and/or oil.[57] In this case it is stated later in the narrative that the fish sauce was a condiment added to a bit of greens (*pikouji nouoti*). While the use of salted fish products such as garum and its derivatives would have been quite at home in caring for the sick in coenobitic communities of the fourth and fifth centuries, Pachomius again rejects this help outright:[58]

> And when he saw [the fish sauce] he said to Theodore, "Bring a jug of water." And when he had brought it, he poured [water] into it and stirred with his hand until the oil that was in it spilled out. Then he said to Theodore, "Pour water over my hands so I may wash them." He washed his hands and poured water over Theodore's feet. Then [Theodore] asked him, "What is this that you've done, Father?" Our father Pachomius said to him, "I poured water into the bit of vegetables and destroyed the sweetness of its pleasure (*hudonē*, for *hēdonē*) so that it would not be for me a fleshly desire (*epithumia*). As for the water that you poured over my hands, as if washing them, because you washed my hands, I in turn washed your feet. This is what I've done, so that I might not be judged because you were a servant to me. Rather it is right for me to serve everyone."[59]

Pachomius's reaction to being offered a common foodstuff for the sick comes off as impetuous; it borders on violent as he not only refuses the condiment but also ruins it. He pours water over the seasoned vegetables as if cleansing them of pollution. The impression of cleansing is reinforced by pouring water over the feet of Theodore. While Pachomius is presented as rhetorically framing this cleansing as an *imitatio Christi*, the fact that he pours water over Theodore's feet just as he pours water over the vegetables, described with the same verb *jōš* (Sahidic *cōš*), suggests the removal of pollution or the stain of sin.

In cleansing his food and protégé, Pachomius imitates not only Christ but—even more important—also Palamon. During Pachomius's apprenticeship with Palamon, as the Great Coptic *Life* narrates, Pachomius once brought him vegetables with oil and salt. When Palamon saw this, he struck Pachomius and ordered vegetables without oil or vinegar, served only with salt mixed with ashes. Pachomius then dutifully poured out the oil and salt and replaced the condiment with salt mixed with ashes.[60] While Palamon ruins the condiment with ash and Pachomius with water, the parallel is unmistakable. Furthermore in Palamon's first instruction to Pachomius upon accepting him as a disciple, Palamon explains that the use of oil and wine (both of which would have been in the fish sauce) was forbidden, as was meat, as reflected in

Pachomius's previous illness.[61] Thus while oil and salted fish would have been familiar components of sick food in late ancient monasteries of Upper Egypt, Pachomius in the Great Coptic *Life* invokes the far more stringent rule of Palamon to emulate.

The first three illnesses of Pachomius present the saint as emulating the model and the teachings about ascetic behavior in illness laid down by his master Palamon. In the first Pachomius adamantly refuses any special allowances for the care of his body in illness, turning down food and comfort. Like Palamon, at least in the Coptic *Life*'s version, he recovers without resorting to medicine or even basic hygiene but simply through fasting and prayer. In his second illness he is at the point of death, and the cause of illness is the same as Palamon's: excessive asceticism. Yet again Pachomius refuses to alter his regimen and rejects special treatment. Nevertheless he insists that all manner of accommodations should be made for regular sick monks, even as far as violating Palamon's ban on meat. Then Pachomius falls ill again, this time imitating the early command of Palamon to adulterate or ruin condiments in order to destroy any pleasure one might take from them, as well as Palamon's unusual ban on oil and vinegar. These three episodes establish Pachomius's illness as a central motif in the narrative. The *Life* presents Pachomius as an exceptional figure, not promoting (at least explicitly) his own behaviors as a norm for the rank and file. Pachomius's illness behavior aligns him in imitation of his ascetic master Palamon, embracing an unrelenting ascetic regimen in the face of illness, illness either caused by the ascetic practices themselves or as the expected side effect of fallen human existence. Illness is not the terrain of battle against the demons; nor is it a failure of ascetic practice or resolve. It is a faithful imitation of the ascetic regimen established for him by his master Palamon. And if Palamon's end is any indication, Pachomius's endurance of chronic illness promises not an ascetic transformation into luminous health but only ascetic endurance of sickness unto death. This is precisely what is in store for the saint.

Pachomius's next illness in the Coptic *Life* and the two that follow form a loosely constructed unit, foreshadowing the departure of Pachomius to paradise and the subsequent conflicts over leadership that would threaten the unity of the Koinonia. The next illness dwells less on the behavior of Pachomius than on the reaction of his fellow monks to his illness. With its characteristic looseness of chronology, the *Life* states, "And it happened that on another occasion our father Pachomius fell ill (*afšōni*), such that he was pained (*ethrefmkah*) to the point of death."[62] This is now the third time that Pachomius is described as near death; in addition to the infirmary episode, Pachomius nearly died in an earlier visionary experience, although the *Life* does not characterize this as an illness or injury.[63]

In contrast to the reaction described in the past two near-death experiences, Pachomius's followers sense that the end is near, and they fear for the future of the monastic federation without their father Pachomius's leadership. The leaders of the monasteries and the monks of Pachomius's monastery at Pbow beg Theodore to agree to lead them in the eventuality of Pachomius's death. In what sounds like pious apologetics, the *Life* emphasizes that Theodore did answer their call immediately, "because he did not desire to be in the position of leadership and the vain glory of this work because of his great humility."[64] But in the face of their repeated entreaties, he was persuaded and was thus drafted as the father-in-waiting.

The *Life* makes it clear that had Pachomius died as the elders of the communities feared, Theodore would have been duly acclaimed as the next father of the Koinonia and would have accepted the call. Their plans, however, came to Pachomius's attention, and when Pachomius had recovered a bit (*etafmton noukouji ebol hapišōni*), he called for a public confession of sins among all the brothers, at which Theodore confessed that he had agreed to succeed Pachomius, a sin of vainglory (*ōou efšouit*).[65] While the *Life* is nothing short of apologetic in its defense of Theodore's sanctity and dutifulness, the underlying repercussions are straightforward: Pachomius sends him to a "place apart" (*ouma eforf*)—perhaps a hermit's cell—to repent until god should forgive him. While doing penance Theodore is repeatedly confronted by monks who either commiserate with him by criticizing Pachomius or accuse Theodore of even more grievous sins. It is perhaps in response to the significant disruption that Theodore's grieving and weeping presence was causing in the monastery that Pachomius sends him abroad. While the *Life* frames Pachomius's order as sending Theodore to visit and console the other monasteries in the federation, Theodore's departure from the monastery functions as exile, an event which plants the seeds for the conflicts in the Koinonia after Pachomius's death: a division between the partisans of Theodore and those of the monks whom Pachomius would actually name his successor, the short-lived Petronius followed by the pious but ineffective Horsiese.

Pachomius's next and penultimate illness adds two important elements for making sense of the saint's chronic illness in the Coptic *Life*: the transcendent power of ascetic illness and Pachomius's illness as martyrdom. Once again this episode is unique to the Coptic *Life*, absent from the parallel Greek *Vita Prima*.

This illness narrative begins much like the previous.[66] Pachomius has fallen ill again, suffering horribly. Much as Pachomius's great suffering had prompted the brothers to acclaim Theodore prematurely as his successor in anticipation of his imminent death, in this case the sheer magnitude of his pain (*mkah*) fools the angels into taking his soul to heaven, killing him. It was then up to god to rectify the premature death: "It happened once that he was sick and in so much pain that the messengers who were sent after him took his soul, and he died. He was brought to the other realm ([*p*]*keaiōn*). But when he reached the gate of life, an order came from god that they return him again to his body."[67] God's order that he be returned to his body is not exactly what Pachomius wanted, and he is saddened (*aflupi*=Greek *lupein*) at the prospect. But fortunately a luminous man, later revealed to be the apostle Paul, consoles him by letting him know his bodily fate: martyrdom: "'Go, my son,' [Paul says,] 'return to your body, for you have yet a little martyrdom in the world' (*ountkkekoui mmntmartyros hmpkosmos*). When [Pachomius] heard this word he was very happy, for he greatly desired to be a martyr for the name of the Lord."[68] Pachomius then happily accompanies the angels back to his body, which was well and truly dead; and "when [Pachomius's] soul approached the body, all his members opened up imperceptibly and the soul rested in its place once again, and that [body] came back to life."[69]

Pachomius's death trip to heaven highlights two aspects of the function and meaning of ascetic illness in the Great Coptic *Life* that distinguish it from other monastic sources. First, illness functions as a mode of visionary transcendence. Second, the *Life* interprets Pachomius's illness within the symbolic matrix of martyrology, prefigured in three episodes: the *Life*'s prologue; Pachomius's curious weakness as a young conscript; and Palamon's death.

First, illness as transcendence. The *Life* details a number of Pachomius's visionary experiences, by no means unique in late ancient hagiography. He is endowed with clairvoyance, and he receives visions on a number of occasions. He foresees where and how to organize his first community, glimpses the souls of other monks ascending to heaven, sees in the heavens a frightening vision of future turmoil in his communities (66), and sees the heavens opened up, at the sight of which he nearly dies in convulsions (73). Pachomius even takes another journey to the underworld, witnessing the manifold punishments that await sinful monks in hell (88). But the vision described above is unique in that he journeys to paradise, to the very gates of heaven. It also differs from his previous experiences, significantly, in that Pachomius dies in order to achieve this visionary experience.

According to the Coptic *Life*—again the entire story has no parallel in the Greek *Vita Prima*—other visionary journeys to paradise by Pachomius follow this ascension. The *Life* is circumspect about the mechanism of these later journeys. Did Pachomius, one might ask, die bodily in his other journeys? The *Life* defers answering such a question, echoing Paul's description of his own journey in 2 Corinthians: "After this he was taken up to Paradise on other occasions. How? God knows, as the apostle says, 'Whether in the body, I do not know. Whether outside the body, I do not know. God knows. And in this manner that one was carried up to the third heaven. And he heard hidden words that it is not right to speak of.' In this same manner when our father Pachomius was taken to that place, he saw the cities of the saints, for which there are no words to describe their buildings and crafts, and all the good things that the lord has prepared for those who love him."[70] Pachomius's visit to paradise forms an important component of the Coptic *Life*'s presentation of Pachomius's illness. While visionary journeys frequently figure in the Lives of saints, as they surely do in the violent sufferings of the martyrs, in the Great Coptic *Life* Pachomius's greatest visionary journey—to paradise—is possible only through his illness and death. In addition, while we have seen that illness could be framed as an aid to ascetic practice, cutting off the body from temptations and vices, the Great Coptic *Life* distinctively presents his illness as a mode of charismatic and prophetic transcendence. Furthermore, unlike other saints, and perhaps echoing Lazarus of the Fourth Gospel, Pachomius is blessed with an uncommon cross to bear: he suffers sickness unto death twice.[71] Even the blessed Antony dies only once (being merely mistaken for dead early in his career).

The assertion that Pachomius is returned to his body in order to suffer a martyrdom in the world shows a further aspect of the meaning of ascetic illness in the Great Coptic *Life*. Paul's prediction of Pachomius's future "little martyrdom" echoes both the *Life*'s early assertion of the monastic inheritance of the martyrs' crowns and Palamon's final illness, in which he abandons the doctor's care and returns to his asceticism, inspired by the example of the martyrs. Since, as Palamon notes, his own struggle pales in comparison to the tortures of the martyrs, his own illness is implicitly a little martyrdom. Paul's prediction thus sets up Pachomius's future suffering as another, final imitation of Palamon's illness. In this last illness, however, Pachomius's little martyrdom—like Palamon's—will be perfected. He will die (for the last time) as witness for Christ.[72]

Pachomius's sixth and final illness is detailed in both the Coptic and

Greek versions, although in the Great Coptic *Life* (best preserved in the Sahidic version) the narrative is over four times the length of the Greek version, which gives some indication of the importance that this episode holds in the Coptic tradition. Pachomius's long illness begins with his collapse in the fields: "And it happened again one day that our father Pachomius fell ill. He did not tell any of the brothers that he was sick, nor did he believe in his illness, as was his custom, but because of his determination (*tfmntjōōrei ettajrēu*) he had gone with them to the harvest, for the brothers were reaping in those days. And while he was reaping he fell down on his face among them. The brothers were disturbed, and they ran to him and laid him on the ground. They found that he had a high fever in his body because of the illness."[73] After the brothers bring Pachomius back to the monastery, their entreaties and Pachomius's reactions are now entirely predictable: they plead with him to take off his ascetic garb and to rest on a bed, rather than on the ground or on a reclining seat as is the general rule in the koinonia. Pachomius refuses these accommodations and even being cooled with a fan.

Pachomius was not alone in his illness, as "many succumbed to the illness in those days, for the disease that laid hold of them was a severe and pestilential disease (*oušōne . . . efnašt . . . nloimos*)."[74] Death came quickly for most, taking as many as four victims a day: "When the fever laid hold of them, their countenance changed and their eyes filled with blood, and they became like men being choked until they brought up their spirit."[75] Rodolph Yanney, a physician, argues that the disease that claimed these victims was almost certainly pneumonic plague.[76] In the end the Coptic *Life* places the total dead at about 130, including a number of important leaders: Apa Paphnouti, steward of Phbow; Apa Sourous, leader of Phnoum; Apa Cornelios, leader of Thmoušons; and Pachomius's successor Petronius.

While Pachomius suffers among many, his illness distinguishes him and marks his exceptionality, as had his previous illnesses. Pachomius's symptoms differ markedly from the violent deaths of so many others. Pachomius remained sick for the forty days of Lent and through much of the fifty days of Pentecost. From the perspective of western biomedicine, he could not have been suffering from the same underlying disease of plague that afflicted the other monks. Yanney has suggested that Pachomius's underlying pathology was malaria, a chronic condition in Egypt and the ancient Mediterranean and a possible cause for his repeated illnesses.[77] Whatever may have been plaguing Pachomius, in the hands of the narrator Pachomius's different symptoms point principally not to a different "disease" but to Pachomius's greater status, as his illness stretches out for the ascetic and liturgical season of Lent.[78]

The lengthy narration of Pachomius's final decline reflects little of the commonplaces of hagiography, even undermining narrative norms. For example, Pachomius had no particular predictive powers about his own passing. He even misinterprets one of his visions, an interesting counterpoint to the frequent trope of monks who know exactly when they shall die, such as at the monastery of Isidore described in the *History of the Monks in Egypt*. An angel appears to Pachomius saying, "'Prepare yourself, Pachomius, for the Lord will raise a great sacrifice in your house on the day of celebration.' And he thought to himself, 'Perhaps the Lord will visit me on the Saturday of the Lord's celebration.'"[79] Pachomius spends the following four days fasting, grieving, and weeping in penance, anticipating his death and the inevitable discord that would follow among his disciples. After gathering the community together, he delivers a lengthy farewell address, defending the propriety of his actions in the past (including a special defense of his behavior in times of illness). The *Life* compares his address to the prophet Samuel's farewell speech of 1 Samuel 12 and to King David's farewell speech of 1 Kings 2; Pachomius even begins the speech by quoting David's famous line "I am about to go the way of all the earth" (1 Kings 2:2, NRSV). From the perspective of the *Life*, the comparison is apt. Not only is Pachomius about to die, but also the community, which the *Life* compares to a single person, "a single spirit and a single body," will descend into rivalry after his death.[80]

Pachomius's apologetic goodbye builds to an emotional climax as the brothers break down in tears: "When our father Pachomius was proclaiming all this (read *ntereftauenai* for *nterfnau enai*, per Lefort) to the brothers, he was lying down sick, it being his third day without eating. And they were all weeping, for misery (*oumntebeiēn*) would befall them if the Lord were to visit him."[81] One might expect such a collective catharsis to provide a sufficient "community building" exercise to transition themselves from the loss of their father.

Yet Pachomius did not die. He had misunderstood the vision, presuming himself—perhaps a sign of lingering pride—the subject of the angel's prediction. Instead it was Apa Paphnouti, the steward of the Koinonia and Theodore's brother, whom the angel took to visit god. "Immediately our father Pachomius remembered what the angel had said to him, 'A great sacrifice (read *thusia* for *thesia*) will be raised in your house on the day of the celebration.'"[82] With the prevalence of the topos of monastic foreknowledge of death, the episode is jarring. The *Life* seems to warn against assuming the illness or health of the saint to be straightforwardly meaningful.

According to the Great Coptic *Life*, Pachomius remains ill throughout Lent and Pentecost as well, although the precise number of days is not of clear importance in the text. Throughout he suffers greatly, and yet he accepts no special treatment, even down to the quality of his blanket. Then, in a move that must have been shocking to his followers (the *Lives* certainly present it as such), Pachomius appoints as his successor not his heir apparent Theodore but Petronius, the Father of the monastery of Tsmine. Petronius, like Pachomius (and like Theodore), was a visionary, something clearly valued in a leader. But he was also extremely sick, as Pachomius knew.[83] It is not hard to understand how this choice could fail to inspire a great deal of confidence, especially among the monks who had expected Theodore to take control after Pachomius's death.

Pachomius then instructs Theodore to bury his body in secret. Pachomius says that this is so that relic hunters do not steal it and place it in "a *martyrion* . . . as they do for the holy martyrs.*" As in the heavenly Paul's prediction of Pachomius's "little martyrdom," the mention of Pachomius's grave as a would-be *martyrion* is unique to the Great Coptic *Life*. At last the end comes:

> When he had said this, he gazed in silence, and said nothing to them. Immediately after crossing himself with his hand three times, he opened his mouth (read *nrōf* for *erof*) and gave up his spirit on the fourteenth of the month of Pašons at the tenth hour (May 9, 346), and they had become very afraid at that time because that place shook three times. And many elders who regularly saw visions said, "We saw multitudes of angels, angels upon angels, gazing (*theōrei*) upon him. Then they sang hymns before him very joyfully until he was received into his resting place," with the result that the place where he rested was fragrant for many days.[84]

While Pachomius would stay dead this time, he is not absent from the later portions of the *Life*. He advises Theodore how to govern in a vision (144), and his presence suffuses the later chapters. Theodore claims that Pachomius is an even greater patron and protector for the monastery than before because he is now with god (125). His successor Horsiesi even claims that "our Father Pachomius did not die completely" (*nkotk eptērf*).[85] Regardless of his posthumous presence, his death was controversial, for he died quite young, at least for a holy man. The Great Coptic *Life* gives his age at death as sixty, but even this is probably generous. If born in 292, as other late ancient sources suggest, then Pachomius died at fifty-four.[86]

Now at the end of Pachomius's *Life* (and I will not discuss the illnesses and deaths of Pachomius's followers), a number of important points stand out, especially in the context of other monastic *Lives* from the fourth and fifth centuries. Pachomius's health throughout is presented as mundane, even poor. From his early conscription to his death, Pachomius is characterized as weak and infirm, and his health (in contrast with dominant trends in late ancient hagiography) does not improve with ascetic training. Pachomius does not emerge from the chastising of the body with a stronger constitution; angels do not descend to the infirmary to perform surgery on him; and he certainly does not live a long or healthy life. Pachomius is simply sick—chronically—his whole life.

Illness is for the Coptic *Life* an important terrain for asceticism. While it is tempting to describe it as something of a field of battle on which Pachomius proves his strength, the *Life* does not employ this sort of agonistic, athletic, and martial language when speaking of Pachomius's illness. Given the ubiquity of this sort of trope in monastic (and martyrological) literature, this is noteworthy. While we have seen a well-developed tradition of interpreting illness as a mode of (and model for) asceticism in such authors as Basil, Syncletica, and Joseph of Thebes, this does not seem to have influenced the Coptic author(s) of the *Life of Pachomius*. While illness and death are useful as a gateway to visionary experience, the *Life* does not describe illness behavior as an asceticism in itself. Pachomius, even as far as his own farewell monologue, is described as not lessening his asceticism in the face of illness; any accommodations he may have allowed himself are vaguely described. This is all despite the fact that his endurance does not result in the recovery of prelapsarian health seen in Chapter 3. Pachomius's relentless *askēsis* is further complicated in that this is not the general picture of Pachomian and related coenobitic regulatory literature, which encourages monks to cease ascetic practice in time of illness.[87] For the saint, it is not appropriate to modify one's asceticism in the face of illness.

A further point of contrast (especially with the *Life of Antony*, for example) is that Pachomius's illness is not demonic. The devil and demons are no strangers in the Coptic *Life*; possession and demonic illness are described on a number of occasions in the Coptic *Life*, suffered by monks and outsiders, of which Pachomius is a healer. Yet Pachomius's illness is not described as demonic. An exception might be the mention of demonic temptation in the *Vita Prima*: the demons trick monks into believing they are sick, similar to many descriptions of "acedia" in non-Pachomian sources; but the monks are not possessed, and moreover they are not actually sick. The "cure" is not exorcism but simply to recognize the illness for what it is: an illusion. There are fainter echoes of this kind of illusory demonic illness in the Coptic *Life*, but it is significantly played down compared to its presence in the Greek *Vita Prima*.[88] Aside from this illusory illness, the devil and demons are not identified as agents in Pachomius's diseases. In fact the cause of his disease lies squarely in the saint's own asceticism, for Pachomius as for Palamon. We may note also that Pachomius is not described as torturing himself, as are Simeon and others in both Syrian and Egyptian monasticism. He does not set out to injure himself or make himself sick as an ascetic practice. Furthermore there is little in the way of valuation of illness as a goal or as aesthetic object. Again in comparison to contemporary depictions of monastic illness, such as the *Lives* of Syncletica and Simeon and even Basil's concerns in his *Letters*, Pachomius's illnesses are barely described. They are given just enough detail to provide a sense of their nature and the suffering of the saint. If symptoms are described at all, their descriptions tend toward the plain and understated. There is no reveling in the grotesquery of the saint's disease. The mundane aspects of Pachomius's illnesses stand out in the context of late ancient hagiography. Pachomius does not behave as a saint should behave and does not suffer in the way that a saint should suffer.

Illness and Apologetics

The Great Coptic *Life* is all too aware that Pachomius's life and death break the molds of late ancient hagiography. Three times the Coptic *Life* explicitly defends the illness and comparatively early death of St. Pachomius against the expected critiques of others. It should be no surprise by this point that all of these passages that highlight the centrality of Pachomius's ill health are unique to the Great Coptic *Life*.

The first of the three apologies for the illnesses of Pachomius, or the illnesses of the saints more generally, occurs as Pachomius visits a monk dying in the infirmary of the monastery of Thmoušons, a monk whom the other monks were unable to baptize for want of a priest. While he is investigating the matter with the monastery's leaders, Pachomius sees angels descend from heaven and baptize the sick brother just before his death.

The *Life* then includes a long excursus—claimed to be a vision received by Pachomius at the death of the angelically baptized monk—about the various ways that holy monks are taken to heaven by the angels, in accordance with their sanctity and good works. After the angels explain the various levels of heaven and the various modes of transport for the heaven-bound souls, Pachomius asks what happens to the dying sinners. It is not pretty:

> If it is a soul evil in its actions at the time that they visit it, the two merciless angels fetch it. When the man is about to die, unable to recognize anyone, one of the merciless angels stands by his head and the other by his feet. In this way they stand, whipping him until his miserable soul is about to come out. Then they cast an object bent like a hook into his mouth, and they pull his unhappy soul up from his body. They find it black and very dark. Then they tie it to the tail of a spiritual horse, for it is as a spirit, and in this way they take it away and cast it into torments, and down to hell, according to the merits of his actions.[89]

The angel's description of the deaths of the holy and the sinners conforms fairly straightforwardly to normal expectations about good and bad deaths. Within monastic hagiography as a whole the "good death" is widely seen as reflecting the sanctity of the soul. Gruesome or degrading deaths likewise are commonly understood as signifying that the sufferer is bound for hell. This is intuitive, and such expectations are widely shared in other periods, including our own. But of course such expectations are not predictably realized, as our hagiographer recognizes. In fact, in the Great Coptic *Life*, the symptoms of the plague that takes some 130 brothers fit the angel's description quite closely: change in color and countenance; bloodshot eyes; choking and convulsing until death. The careful reader might wonder, were the monks sinners who were killed by the plague? Were their wretched deaths their just deserts?

I suspect that it is in response to just such questions about meaning and morality that the *Life* follows this fairly straightforward description of good and bad deaths with a caveat that effectively undermines the angel's previous claims. The angel continues,

> In fact, many good people also suffer these things in the illness in which they are visited and at the hour that they give up the spirit. For those of this sort are like a dish that has not been cooked enough, and needs to be cooked a bit longer before it can be eaten. This is how the faithful

are who suffer at their end before they have been perfected, so that they might be free from all their deeds and be holy before the Lord. We find also many of the saints who have suffered at the hour that they died, like Saint Stephen and also all the martyrs and those like them; also Job and David, and multitudes of other saints who have borne many sufferings and afflictions in their life, and others at death. In fact, many sinners also die comfortably, having endured no sufferings in this world, due to the afflictions and punishments that are prepared for them, as it is written, "The impious is kept for an evil day" (Pro 16:4). Therefore, seeing this in this way Ecclesiastes said, "The same chance (*apantēma*) will fall to the just and unjust, the pure and the impure, the good and the evil" (Eccl 9:2) In fact, we see our savior, the Lord of all, raised on the cross with two robbers, one on the right and one on his left, and the Lord in the middle.[90]

The angel's closing remarks—perhaps the mark of a later reviser—undermine the whole purpose of the vision. They show that the peacefulness or pain of death holds no predictive power for the holiness or sinfulness of the dead and dying. Someone who dies in suffering could be headed to hell, or could need further refining in purgatory (the vivid metaphor of the soul as inadequately cooked food), or could be the greatest of saints, such as Stephen, Job, David, or even Jesus Christ. And the person who passes away in peace could just as easily be a wretched sinner as a holy person. Given the predominance of Pachomius's illness in the *Life* and the great suffering that attended his death, this vision clearly functions apologetically, answering questions about the meaning of Pachomius's chronic illness and drawn-out death that might linger in the minds of his followers, not to mention followers of his rivals or opponents.

The *Life* includes a second apology in the narrative of Pachomius's death. On this occasion the controversial point is not the magnitude of Pachomius's suffering but his age at death. Pachomius's death at sixty in the Coptic *Life* has the saint dying prematurely in comparison to those in other monastic hagiographies.[91] His life span is dwarfed by the 105 years of Antony and the many octogenarian and nonagenarian saints described in the *History of the Monks in Egypt*, not to mention Paul of Thebes's 113 or Shenoute's 118 years.[92] The contrast was very much noticed in the *Life*. The burial narrative of Pachomius concludes, "All the days of his life number sixty years. He became a monk when he was twenty-one years old and the other thirty-nine years he spent as a monk. Actually, when the Lord saw that he had crucified his flesh in everything so as to do His will, He wished to give him rest. He took him to Himself and did not allow him to reach such a great age that he would suffer the weakness of the body more than He wanted."[93] Thus according to the Great Coptic *Life* Pachomius's early death signifies his especial holiness. Pachomius had perfected his *askēsis* and condensed so much holiness into his few years that it was his reward to die young (and twice at that) and be spared the weakness (*mntcōb*) of old age. This is notwithstanding the fact that Pachomius had been weak, infirm, and chronically ill for much of his existence. Again the defensiveness about Pachomius's bodily constitution is clear. This appears to be of significant importance to those who had transmitted Pachomius's *Life*; some versions of the Coptic tradition, Pierpont Morgan M.663a (manuscript *S7* in Lefort's numeration) and the Vatican Arabic translation, end the *Life* with this defense.[94]

The Great Coptic *Life* includes still one more apology for the manner and timing of Pachomius's death. Shortly after Pachomius dies, Theodore and some other monks are sent north to Alexandria to purchase supplies needed to care for all those afflicted by the plague. On their way they visit Antony's first monastery at the outer mountain at Pispir or Tiloj, which he had left to establish his more famous community near the Red Sea. This narrative is set during one of Antony's occasional visits to his former residence.[95] Antony's general demeanor near the end of his life is by now familiar. According to the *Life of Antony*, even to the very end Antony retained the full power of his physical and mental faculties. He was not debilitated in any way and did not have to lessen his ascetic practices in any significant way, and the *Life of Antony* does not mention a single episode of illness of any sort in Antony's long life. In the Coptic *Life of Pachomius* the episode in question is set in A.D. 346, ten years before Antony's death, thus making him approximately ninety-five. According to the image conveyed by the *Life of Antony*, Antony should be in the prime of health.

Yet Theodore and his companions find a very different, very sick Antony: "When they reached the mountain of Tiloj, they inquired after the blessed Apa Antony the anchorite, and they were informed that he was in his monastery at the outer mountain, lying down sick (*efnkotk efšōne*)."[96] Antony welcomes the coenobites warmly but cannot stand on his own, needing help from another monk "since he had been sick for a long time (*afōsk hmpšōne*) because of his old age." He was so weak, in fact, that the brothers of Antony's monastery "were surprised" that he even attempted to stand, "and they took hold of him," obviously unsure that he could support himself.[97] According to the Great Coptic *Life*, Antony had not risen to greet visitors for a long time. One of Antony's monks even chastises Antony for having neglected other visitors: "Look, it has been a long time since you have fallen sick (*jinntakšōne*), and as for every one who comes to visit you, whether bishop or tribune, or duke, or noble, you have been simply unable to get up to greet any of us."[98] The story functions in part as a defense, through the mouth of Antony, of his preferential treatment of the Pachomians. The coenobites, says Antony, follow the superior way of monasticism. In fact, had it been possible, Antony would have chosen the coenobitic path, the authentic enactment of apostolic ideals.[99] Furthermore, Antony says, the Pachomians are right to keep themselves doctrinally pure, unlike the anchorites and the followers of Antony himself who willingly consort with Melitian schismatics. The Coptic *Life* presents Antony's arguments as effective, and even his own followers are convinced of the superiority of the Pachomian lifestyle.[100] The episode narrated here is in part an extreme example of the rivalry that existed between monastic lineages.

Far more striking is how radically the Great Coptic *Life* undermines the Athanasian picture of Antony's ascetic health. The *Life of Antony* interprets his health as a sure signifier of his sanctity; his health is a necessary component of the *Life of Antony*'s vision of the ascetic reclamation of humanity's long-lost equilibrium of soul, body, and divine logos. The Antonian model of making meaning out of ascetic health and illness was extraordinarily influential. In fact the *Life of Antony* was known to the author of the Coptic *Life*; he quotes it in this very episode.[101] By transforming Antony from the paradigmatic healthy monk into a sick one, the Great Coptic *Life* defends the sanctity of Pachomius as a sick saint. It moreover complements the *Life*'s radical revision of the meaning and function of health for the saint. In contrast with the Antonian model of the saint who suffers through pain to be rewarded with extraordinary health and strength (which the Coptic *Life* rather baldly presents as false), the Coptic *Life of Pachomius* offers a very different saint who endures the illnesses of the world with patience and humility, embracing illness and weakness (*astheneia*) as the full consummation of the spirit of martyrdom.

Conclusion

The Great Coptic *Life* of Pachomius is a remarkable hagiographical witness to the contentious meaning of illness and health for the Lives of ascetics. The *Life* explicitly sets the career of Pachomius in contrast with earlier hagiographies, especially the *Life of Antony*, whose depiction of the orthodox ascetic as preternaturally healthy and long-lived is undermined in the Great Coptic *Life*. The Great Coptic *Life*, faced with the memory of a holy man who lived a relatively short life for a saintly ascetic and who died in a plague, raises Pachomius's chronic illness as a core component of its protagonist's sanctity. At the hands of the *Life*'s author (or authors) Pachomius's six major episodes of illness—most of which are unique to the Coptic *Life* and not included in the parallel Greek *Vita Prima*—tie together this sprawling narrative. Pachomius's illness becomes an emblematic feature of his sanctity; from his weakness as a youth through a life punctuated by sickness and near-death experiences (he even dies from illness twice!), Pachomius's illness is as fundamental to his identity as a saint as Antony's health is to his. It is through illness that Pachomius gains his visionary experiences, through illness that Pachomius enacts an asceticism that outpaces that of his spiritual children, through illness that Pachomius further displays his characteristic humility, through illness that Pachomius emulates the (fatal) *askēsis* of his spiritual father Palamon, and through illness that Pachomius gains his martyr's crown. While the Great Coptic *Life* may not offer a window into the life of the "historical" Pachomius, it functions as a hagiographical reflection of the persistent concerns among monastics about the meaning and function of illness, as reflected in the range of sources explored in the previous chapters and the Introduction.

Illness and Spiritual Direction in Late Ancient Gaza: The Correspondence of Barsanuphius and John with the Sick Monk Andrew

Spiritual direction is an aspect of late ancient asceticism that has not yet been central to my analysis but is no less fundamental to the monastic project. While I have had the opportunity to delve into the theological elaboration of monastic health and illness in Lives and letters and the controversies that illness among ascetics provoked in regula and practical treatises, much of the life-world experienced by the late ancient monks was conditioned more directly by intense personal relationships with senior monks or spiritual directors. While the reflections of Basil, Evagrius, and Syncletica deal with illness as a component of monastic life more generally and theoretically, their attitudes and approaches were no doubt rooted in their experiences as spiritual directors, in the case of Evagrius and Syncletica with a small-scale ascetic community and in the case of Basil as a bishop and correspondent with a number of communities. Yet the details of their relationships as spiritual directors, whatever they might have been, are filtered through their composition of practical treatises and rules or through the collection of stylized apophthegmata, usually stripped from their original context of spiritual direction.[1]

As a reflection of the role and strategies of the spiritual director to wrestle with the meaning and function of illness in asceticism I turn to a remarkable body of literature that has been relatively little used as a source for late ancient monasticism: the *Letters* of Barsanuphius and John.[2] The collection is organized not chronologically but rather in variously cohesive units of correspondence, sometimes addressed to a single monk and sometimes connected thematically, such as letters to various lay followers.³ Yet within its discrete epistolary units the *Correspondence* appears to be edited in chronological order, which gives an extremely valuable view of the process of spiritual direction.⁴ As much as the spiritual and psychagogic practices of the Great Old Men reflect the sorts of authoritative texts already explored here, such as of Basil, Evagrius, and the desert Abbas and Ammas, the dialogic format of the *Correspondence*, as well as its temporal span, provides a view of the contentiousness and disagreement that were inevitably part of ascetic life.

Concerns with illness and healing recur throughout the *Correspondence*. Barsanuphius was sought for his gifts as a faith healer, and a number of questions address the proper use of "secular" medicine as well as the issues involved in Thavatha's infirmary, at which the famous monk Dorotheus worked.⁵ Yet it was primarily as spiritual healers—guides in making sense out of illness and of ridding the sufferer of anxieties and evil thoughts—that the Great Old Men corresponded.

Part of this sprawling corpus of letters that reflects the Great Old Men's role as spiritual healers is a collection of fifty-two letters to an elderly, sick monk named Andrew (the last two letters included in this collection are addressed to his disciple), to which the questions composed by the sick Andrew are prefaced. Andrew's letters are usually summarized by the anonymous ancient editor of the *Letters*, who also sometimes includes direct quotations (some lengthy) from Andrew's own letters.⁶ Andrew's questions thus do not usually represent his ipsissima verba; even when quoted directly they are the product of an editor's mediation. Yet we should not underestimate the rarity and value of this correspondence as an epistolary dialogue and even a dialectic process, defining terms and analyzing and distinguishing phenomena.⁷ This is a remarkable feature within the context of ancient healing practice, whether of soul or body. Rarely do the voices of patients and the sick survive from antiquity, as is the case in many historical periods.⁸ While there are exceptions, it is the authoritative voices of doctors and healers (or their hagiographers) that dominate the record.⁹

In the correspondence of Barsanuphius and John with Andrew we thus witness a singular process: a dialogue between historically known people about the meaning of illness in ascetic practice. Andrew describes his evolving worries and concerns regarding his illness over the course of several months to Barsanuphius and John, and they in turn counsel the sick monk.¹⁰ Viewed together they offer a rare glimpse at the traditions of ancient psychological healing, "the care of the soul," *hē therapeia tēs psykhēs*.¹¹ Ample discussions of the methods of the "care of the soul" from the point of view of the philosopher or doctor survive from antiquity. Book 4 of Cicero's *Tusculan Disputations* provides a picture of how Romans with a Stoic sensibility might cure the passions (Gk. *pathos*, Lat. *perturbatio*, 4.6); and Galen's *On the Passions and Errors of the Soul* vividly prescribes a method for spiritual (or rather psychic) direction for the Antonine elite.[12] In Christian late antiquity the various collections of wise sayings of late ancient monks describe the care of the soul—often characterized as "spiritual direction"—on the part of senior ascetics.[13] It was indeed predominantly through the language of healing that late ancients described the process of spiritual direction.[14] Such reflections, transmitted in rules, gnomic sayings, treatises, epistles, and Lives, are exceptionally valuable sources for understanding how late ancient Christians made sense, for example, of the meaning and function of illness in the ascetic life. But I know of no ancient source that provides the sort of sustained insight into the (at times contentious) process of psychological care (*therapeia tēs psykhēs*) for the sick that we find in the correspondence between Andrew and the Great Old Men. As a prominent scholar of Christian monasticism has put it more generally, "What the *Sayings of the Desert Fathers* let us glimpse only in the form of transitory flashes, is here played out before our very eyes like a film."[15]

The correspondence of Barsanuphius and John with the sick monk Andrew draws on the theological, social, and rhetorical themes relating to the illness of ascetics seen in previous chapters. In particular the various reflections of Basil, Evagrius, and Syncletica analyzed in Chapter 4 are fundamental to the approach of the Great Old Men. In their *Letters* we see the development of illness as a mode of spiritual exercise, as a type of asceticism. Even more interesting, the letters between Andrew and the Great Old Men reveal the difficulties that such a theological, rhetorical, and psychological approach entailed. This late and intimate corpus of letters shows that debates about the meaning and function of illness as a part of ascetic practice that I have noted in early monastic literature were not the limited purview of monastic theorists; nor did they exist only in the idealized world of monasticism as constructed by literary sources. Rather such questions posed deeply personal problems for monks through the very end of late antiquity. The persistence of these problems into the third century of Christian monasticism shows that there were no easy answers to the questions of meaning that illness posed for the monk.

Thavatha and Gazan Monasticism

At the turn of the fifth century monasticism was transplanted to Roman Palestine, including the areas of Gaza and Jerusalem, where it became the center of a booming enterprise, with communities of various types adorning the Mount of Olives and the desert cliffs of Judea. The communities of Gaza maintained close connections to Egyptian monasticism, far more than was the case in the monasteries of Jerusalem and the Judean desert. Tradition identifies Hilarion (d. 291), a disciple of Antony, as the first to bring monasticism to Gaza, detailed in yet another of Jerome's hagiographies. Whatever the historicity of this traditional narrative, monasticism would continue to have a close relationship with Egypt in both theology and practice. In the aftermath of the destruction of much of Lower Egyptian monasticism during bishop Theophilus's purge of Origenist monks, the refugees found safe harbor in the communities of Gaza. It is plausible that this exile from Egypt prompted the process of collecting and editing the oral traditions of Egyptian eremitism into what now are known as the *Sayings of the Desert Fathers*. Gaza's monks would later fall in line with their predominantly anti-Chalcedonian Egyptian brothers in the disputes following the Council of Chalcedon in 451, in contrast to the Judean monasteries that more reliably supported the imperial position. It is surely no coincidence that some of the spiritual leaders of Gazan monasticism came from Egypt, including Isaiah of Scetis (d. 489) and Barsanuphius, a Copt.[16]

The letters between Andrew and the two "Great Old Men" are thus the products of an established and institutionalized monasticism that was considerably later than the sources drawn on in earlier chapters. The monastery of Thavatha (or Thabatha) reflects this later period of monastic development, structured idiorhythmically along lines similar to some Egyptian monasteries and in contrast to the generally semi-eremitical organization of the nearby monasteries of the Judean desert. Bitton-Ashkelony and Kofsky compare it to the monastery of Shenoute of Atripe (near Sohag, Middle Egypt), among others.[17] Thavatha was built around a core coenobium with a common rule, an abbot (named Seridus in the time of the *Correspondence*), and common institutions, such as a church, a refectory, and an infirmary.[18] But affiliated with the coenobium were hermits who did not share the community rule and interacted with the other monks infrequently and indirectly; the two most famous of these hermits, Barsanuphius and John, lived in complete isolation, except, of course, for their voluminous correspondence with suppliants within the monastery and without. Yet for all their charismatic power, the Great Old

Men placed themselves clearly under the authority of the community's abbot. All correspondence to and from the Great Old Men was addressed through (and read by) the abbot Seridus, who apparently transcribed the responses dictated by the hermits. For this reason the Egyptian Barsanuphius refused to write in Coptic, even when faced with the entreaties of a native Egyptian pilgrim; all was to remain transparent to the (Greek-speaking) abbot.[19]

It is within this general structure that the correspondence between Andrew and the two Great Old Men is situated. Andrew, whom we will get to know in some detail, lives among the coenobitic monks, sharing a cell with another, more junior monk, and living in community with the other monks (and under their observation). His letters to Barsanuphius and John are sent via Seridus, as are the hermits' replies.

Framework for Interpretation

Late ancients characterize the process of spiritual direction in the language of healing (for example, "the cure of souls"), and not inappropriately.[20] The correspondence between Barsanuphius and John and the sick monk Andrew reflects the process that anthropologists refer to as symbolic healing, in contrast to the types of faith healing or medical healing familiar from late ancient monastic literature.

The basic term "healing" and the specific process of "symbolic healing" may need some definition. From the perspective of medical anthropology, the process of "healing of illness" that takes place in the correspondence between Andrew and the Great Old Men of Thavatha should be distinguished from "curing of disease." While the distinction between curing of disease and healing of illness is in some sense a heuristic one and not necessarily consistent with colloquial English (they both fall under the umbrella term of "healing" in many cultures), the distinction is a useful one in many contexts, including the correspondence between Andrew and the Great Old Men.[21]

From the perspective of contemporary medical anthropology, curing denotes the removal or elimination of the threat caused by a "disease," an ontological entity (rather than a subjective state) as defined by the culture. In a specifically biomedical context, such threats include bacterial and viral infections, injuries and wounds, cancers, and a host of other ailments classifiable by western nosology. "Curing" in a nonwestern, nonbiomedically based, or premodern society, such as that of late ancient Gaza, will necessarily look different, since the disease taxonomy or nosology on the base of which the healer and patient operate is very different. Given the different nosologies that predominated in antiquity—disease was more often understood as a physiological process of imbalance to be managed than an ontological entity to be identified and eliminated—it is harder to speak of "curing" in the ancient world from this perspective.[22]

Healing (of illness), on the other hand, involves the transformation of meaning, generally through the interaction of a healer and the patient as well as a variety of tertiary parties. Arthur Kleinman defines "healing of illness" as "the provision of personal and social meaning for the life problems created by sickness."[23] Healing in this sense can include training and manipulating the body but usually comprises an important symbolic component, and indeed may be entirely symbolic. Through the healing process, the healer may not necessarily change, eliminate, or neutralize any independent "disease" lurking within the body—and indeed in many cases the healer and patient may not have any such conception of an independent reified force working within the body. But through the mediation of symbols and other interventions the sufferer makes sense of his or her affliction and may experience "some degree of satisfaction through the reduction, or even the elimination of the psychological, sensory, and experiential oppressiveness engendered by a person's medical circumstances."[24]

What do anthropologists mean by *symbolic* healing? Symbolic healing includes modern professionalized talk therapies or psychotherapy as well as religious counseling of all types and practices of witch doctors, magicians, and other folk healers. As different as such therapeutic practices might seem on the surface, a generalized structure of symbolic healing has been observed cross-culturally.[25] The anthropologist James Dow's version of this general structure is as follows:

1. The experiences of healers and healed are generalized with culture-specific symbols in cultural myth.
2. A suffering patient comes to a healer who persuades the patient that the problem can be defined in terms of the myth.
3. The healer attaches the patient's emotions to transactional symbols particularized from the general myth.
4. The healer manipulates the transactional symbols to help the patient transact his or her own emotions.[26]

A few points should be noted here. First, the importance of myth, culturally shared, and archetypal narratives are central to the healing process. Symbolic healing functions to make meaning of, to understand, and to narrativize the sufferer's illness in accordance with the mythic narratives of the sufferer's culture. Second, the object of symbolic healing is the emotions or passions, rather than the body. In the *Letters* of Barsanuphius and John it is not surprising to find that the general myth and mythic figures of Christian sacred history (reflected throughout the previous chapters) play an important role in healing. Furthermore the object of interest for the healing monks is primarily Andrew's emotions or the passions (Greek *pathos/pathē*).

I give this theoretical background for orientation. Given the vicissitudes of time and the fact that ancient sources rarely provide the same types and quantity of information that an anthropologist could elicit from a living source, I wish to be wary of attempting to force the epistolary conversations of the Gazan monks into a rigid structure. Nonetheless anthropological insights into the basic and shared structure of symbolic healing have the great benefit of clarifying the healing processes at work in the letters of Barsanuphius and John, healing processes that are usually left implicit in the monks' consolatory letters.

Reading the Illness Narrative of Andrew

The correspondence between Andrew and the Great Old Men, when read in its entirety, forms a sort of "illness narrative." It is the type of illness narrative one would expect to find in "real life" rather than in literary sources: in fragments, with holes and lacunas, questions left unanswered, and answers to questions that have not been asked.[27] In addition, as with so many stories, the ending never comes to a satisfying resolution. Instead of presenting the entire narrative from beginning to end, I focus on two recurring themes in the correspondence. These themes echo the persistent concerns raised in previous chapters, now recontextualized in spiritual direction and symbolic healing:

1. *The meaning and function of illness.* Why me? Is this a punishment for sin? Is it from god or from the devil? Since illness is a relative category, only meaningful in its relation to health, the obverse is also important: the personal meaning of health and recovery. Furthermore should the monk alter his ascetic practices when sick? Is the monk still a monk if he no longer does what a monk does? And does it not put the monk's salvation at risk if he neglects this asceticism?

2. *Illness and social discord.* Illness is neither purely individual nor binary (between patient and healer) but social, affecting the people around the sick, especially the family and significant others expected to be caregivers. An integral part of many symbolic healing practices is to restore the social relationships that are damaged or strained by illness. The breakdown in social relationships, caused or at least brought to a crisis by illness, is actually the most common problem that Andrew refers to in his letters.

The Meaning and Function of Illness

The correspondence between the sick monk Andrew and the two Great Old Men begins with *Letter 72*. Barsanuphius's letter is prefaced by the ancient editor's summary of Andrew's letter to the Great Old Man, a format that is repeated through much of the correspondence. "An old man who was ill (*asthenēs*), named Andrew, who was living in stillness in the monastic community, declared some of his secret faults to the same Great Old Man (Barsanuphius), while at the same time giving thanks for the fact that he had been counted worthy to dwell near such a person; and about his bodily illness (*peri astheneia sōmatikēs*). Response by Barsanuphius."[28] Two elements will endure through the lengthy correspondence. First, Andrew confides in Barsanuphius (and John) as his confessor. Second, his concern is not only his bodily illness but also his secret moral failings (errors or missteps, *sphalmatōn*). These two components of Andrew's concern, his bodily illness and his moral faults, which Barsanuphius characterizes as "passions of the soul" (*psykhikōn pathōn*) in this response and elsewhere, will be inseparable. In fact Barsanuphius will argue that the process of illness (*astheneia*) and convalescence (or even the failure to recover) is fundamentally about controlling the passions or thoughts (*logismoi*)—the process of spiritual direction and symbolic healing—rather than treating a "disease" (*nosos*), a term that, tellingly, Barsanuphius and John never use. The editor's summary does not reveal precisely what Andrew wished to know "about his bodily illness," but Barsanuphius's response and the responses that follow it suggest that Andrew was primarily interested in questions of meaning and ascetic practice rather than a request for healing.[29]

Barsanuphius responds first by emphasizing that Andrew must entrust all his cares to god and trust that all will happen as god wills it. The monk who fails to entrust all concerns to god, "whether about bodily illness or the passions of the soul," or suffers doubt (*hē dipsykhia*) will be left to answer his own thoughts and anxieties about the source and meaning of his illness. A prime anxiety: is it due to his asceticism that he has fallen sick? "If perhaps I had taken care of my body," Andrew wonders, "I would not have to be afflicted in this way," a concern that he had likely betrayed in his letter. But to rid himself of such thoughts, Barsanuphius writes, the monk must put all concerns on god, echoing the characterization (compare Palladius's Stephen) of suffering of illness as a form of penance far preferable to the punishments that would otherwise come after death: "And to the degree that he allows you to be afflicted in the body, he accordingly lightens the burden of your sins."[30]

As a symbolic healer, Barsanuphius displays his empathy, offering to "bear half of your burden."[31] While his words echo Galatians 6:2, a passage that Barsanuphius returns to repeatedly as a core mandate for his community, as well as a common precept of late ancient spiritual direction, they are actually a direct quote of an Antonian apophthegm from the *Sayings of the Desert Fathers*, a reference that Andrew, interestingly, does not understand and which only provokes more anxiety.[32] Barsanuphius draws on paradox, a common feature of symbolic healing, such as the classic model of paradox in interpersonal communication of the "leader who intimates to the group that he is not going to direct it," or in an ancient context, the holy father who declares himself a sinner or the sage who declares himself a fool.[33] Barsanuphius promises to bear half of Andrew's burden, while acknowledging that he, strictly speaking, lacks the strength to do so. He has spoken senselessly (*hōs paraphronōn elalēsa*), for he too is "weak and incapable and naked of every good work" (*asthenē kai adunaton kai gumnon apo pantos ergou agathou*).[34] Barsanuphius describes himself pointedly in the terminology of illness: "weak and incapable" could in another context be rendered "sick and disabled." Barsanuphius makes plain his empathy: he suffers like Andrew and feels his pain, so to speak.[35] It is clear from later correspondence, however, that Barsanuphius uses this weighted illness language not to refer to any bodily illness on his part, since he has not been sick in some time (*Letter* 74), but in a spiritual or psychic sense.[36] Whether spiritual or bodily, Barsanuphius regardless says that his own "shamelessness" (*anaiskhuntia*) "does not allow [him] to despair (*apelpisai*)."[37] The importance of avoiding despair will recur repeatedly in the correspondence.

It is the challenge of making meaning of illness, rather than requests and prayers for bodily healing, that in fact dominates Andrew's thoughts throughout the correspondence. Does the disease come from god or the demons? Is it a punishment for Andrew's sins or a sign of his virtue? Andrew asks not for healing but for meaning, as in *Letter* 88: "So I implore you, father, for the sake of the Lord: pray for me, and declare to me what this means."[38]

Barsanuphius uses a number of techniques to guide Andrew to make sense of his illness. One technique is to guide Andrew in interpreting his illness within their shared symbolic system. This typifies what Arthur Kleinman describes as the third stage in symbolic healing, in which "the healer skillfully guides therapeutic change in the patient's emotional reactions . . . through mediating symbols that are particularized from the general meaning system."[39] Another way that anthropologists describe this process is as the manipulation of "master narratives" or "cultural (or cognitive) models." That is, when a sufferer makes meaning out of illness or creates a provisional "illness narrative," the sufferer does not begin de novo but is constrained by a sort of grammar of shared symbols, what Kleinman calls the "general meaning system."[40] Anthropologists have analyzed illness narratives by isolating the cultural or cognitive model (symbols, effectively) with which individuals construct their narratives of self. These narrative types and cultural models vary significantly among cultures.[41]

Barsanuphius adduces a number of such "cultural models of affliction" by which Andrew might interpret his own suffering.[42] Barsanuphius responds to Andrew's question "What does this mean?" by arguing that god frequently brings illness (*astheneian*) upon his beloved as a form of testing, of which he cites the biblical models of Job, who suffered illness and worse though he was righteous, and the apostle Paul, sufferer of the famous thorn in his flesh. Barsanuphius, like Palamon in Chapter 5, also adduces the martyrs as models for Andrew's suffering: "How shall we call the holy martyrs blessed on account of the sufferings they endured for the sake of God, if we are unable to bear a simple fever (*pureton*)?" He then evokes the prospect of future suffering to put his present afflictions in perspective: "the fever [is] better for you than [the fire of] hell." Yet god never imposes a greater test than can be borne, for he knows the illness far better than any human. Thus it is imperative that Andrew "not grow despondent or weary" in illness (*mē oligōrēsēte mē ekkakēsēte*).[43] Furthermore, Barsanuphius notes that illness should not be considered as affecting the individual alone; it affects those who must care for the patient as well, "and both these tasks will be for the glory of God."[44]

It may seem simply intuitive for a healer like Barsanuphius to adduce role models for someone like Andrew, to recall stories of others who had suffered as he did or far worse than he. Yet from the perspective of medical anthropology, it is an integral component of healing. Barsanuphius as a symbolic healer draws on shared symbols from the world of meaning of healer and patient, and he manipulates or applies the symbols. "Manipulation" is important, since symbols, such as Job, Paul, or the martyrs, are polysemic: they have more than one meaning or may be made meaningful in more than one way. In the process of symbolic healing the goal of such symbolic manipulation is for the sufferer Andrew to reevaluate and make a different—hopefully positive— meaning out of his illness by recalling the cultural models of affliction and experiencing (and reexperiencing in narrativization) his illness through them.

Andrew is not concerned with merely understanding his illness as a whole but with interpreting the meaning of his symptoms. In *Letter* 78 Andrew fears that his arthritis is caused by demons. Further distressing are the visions of wild animals (perhaps evoking Antony's temptations) that haunt his dreams.

Barsanuphius counsels Andrew, first and foremost, not to be sad (*lupētheis*), perhaps reflecting the categorization of sadness or despair as an evil thought in late ancient—especially Evagrian—Christianity or even the more general critique of *lupē* in Stoic thought. Barsanuphius furthermore assures the arthritic Andrew that his bodily affliction is not from the demons, "but it is an influx of God's training (or education, *paideia*) for our improvement, in order that we may give thanks to God."[45] Barsanuphius echoes here another of Christianity's cultural models of affliction as identified by Garrett, the paideia model, of which Barsanuphius adduces Job yet again as the proper comparison for Andrew's condition, as Job's "patience led him to incomparable glory."[46] Barsanuphius's use of Job is another useful case in point of the "manipulation" of symbols, since in the biblical narrative Job's illness and various other misfortunes are least arguably caused by the devil and only allowed by god. This detail apparently was not as important in Barsanuphius's mind as Job's behavior in the face of disease. Barsanuphius consoles Andrew with the prospect of hope, the cure for despair and sadness: "Therefore, you also should be a little patient, and 'you will see the glory of God,'" citing John's Gospel.[47] Yet Andrew has a tendency to pick out the glimmer of despair in Barsanuphius's consolations.

The dreams about wild beasts, however, *are* from the demons, who want to trick Andrew into thinking that they have also caused his arthritis. There is hope for this too, for the demons can be dispatched through prayer, especially the powerful prayers of the saints on Andrew's behalf. Again Barsanuphius urges, "do not be sad" (*mē lupētheis*). . . . Yet I believe in regard to this bodily suffering that God will do with you as his mercy wills." Barsanuphius also sends, as Andrew requested, holy water and "a small blessing" from his own food, which Barsanuphius humbly says is "so that you may bless my food [also]."[48]

When Andrew asks again about his specific symptoms later in the correspondence, Barsanuphius's diagnosis is similar. Andrew reports that he feels pain in the stomach, dryness in his extremities, tremors when waking, unshakable fatigue, and sleepiness. Barsanuphius claims that the stomach ailment is "a minor illness" (*mikran astheneian*), that is, purely physiological and at the same time nothing to worry about.[49] But his condition is "also heavily involved with the activity of the demons."[50] Barsanuphius does not specify which demons, but given commonalities in late ancient description of demonic thoughts, the demons of acedia and related thoughts are likely culprits.[51] The proper response to both the physiological and demonic illnesses is the same: "despise" (*kataphronēson*) them. Barsanuphius closes by offering hope to Andrew again: "Therefore, brother, do not become weary. For Jesus has begun to work his great mercy within you."[52] Again symbolic healing is effected through manipulating emotions.

Yet Andrew's struggles to understand his affliction do not abate. In *Letter* 102 he writes, "Pray for me, father; for I have fallen into fantasies (*phantasias*)."[53] Barsanuphius recognizes in this request two interrelated concerns on the part of Andrew: first, are these visions from the demons; and second, has god abandoned him? Barsanuphius first assures him that whatever the proximal cause of these fantasies may be—an issue that Barsanuphius simply does not address—god allows Andrew (and others, he notes empathetically) to fall into these visions and passions (*empesein eis phantasias kai eis alla pathē*) because of "our negligence," referring to the fall.[54]

But passions and fantasies, like the created world as a whole, are pedagogical: they are tools for the ascetic to know his true nature; as the famous Greek axiom has it, "Know thyself" (*gnōthi seauton*). In this sense Andrew's illness functions as a spiritual exercise or technology of the self, as Hadot or Foucault might put it, or at least as a special matrix in which spiritual exercises might flourish. Equating the experience of illness with the universal postlapsarian weakness of humanity, Barsanuphius explains that passions afflict us "so that we may come to know our illness/weakness and where we still are (*hina gnōmen hēmōn tēn astheneian, kai hopou akmēn esmen*). Out of his goodness, he allows this for our benefit, in order that the conviction of our hope may be from God and not from ourselves."[55] Yet the passions and fantasies are not caused by god and are themselves not the cause of our salvation. Barsanuphius again adduces cultural models of Christian affliction, manipulating symbols of the Christian myth: even the saints Paul and Peter suffered afflictions of their passions and fantasies (cowardice in their cases, as Peter denied Jesus and Paul fled Antioch). But their passions served to teach them to put all their hope in god. Andrew's fantasies and passions too function as tools of self-knowledge, a basic goal of ancient spiritual exercise. "You," Barsanuphius advises, "should learn what you are and where you are."[56]

Barsanuphius's emphasis on interpreting illness within the context of passions (*pathē*) or "thoughts" (*logismoi*) is an important aspect of his approach to symbolic healing, which draws on the psychological theories developed by Isaiah of Scetis and (more controversially) Evagrius of Pontus. Isaiah of Scetis was among the Egyptian monks who fled from Scetis in the aftermath of the repression of Origenist monasticism in Lower Egypt.[57] His teachings as an eremitic leader of monks and laity are collected in *Logoi* (*Discourses*), which were transmitted in Gaza and in Thavatha. Barsanuphius and John refer to Isaiah on a number of occasions and "clearly imply or else echo Isaian doctrine on numerous other occasions."[58] Isaiah embraces the restorative theology of ascetic healthiness witnessed by Antony's *Letters* (discussed in Chapter 2) in his *Discourse* "On the Natural State of the Intellect."[59] "[W]hen Adam was created," Isaiah writes, "God placed him in Paradise with healthy senses (*regšē ḥlimē*) that were established according to nature (*bikyānāyutā*)," senses that were perverted (*ethpek*) by Satan. As in Antony's explication of Christian salvation history, god in his mercy could not abide such disease to fester and sent his son "that we may stay in the natural state in which God created us."[60] The means of this reclamation of humanity's natural state is through asceticism, described in terms that Foucault identifies as central to ancient "care of the self": "Let us, then, take care of ourselves (*nēṣp hakil dnāpšan*)."[61] Again echoing Antony's *Letter* I, we Christians may take care of our selves by "taking control of all our [bodily] members (*hadāmē*) until they are established in the state that is according to nature."[62] Yet in other ways Isaiah diverges from the psychic healing advocated by Antony. Isaiah does not guide his readers to any extirpation of the passions (in Stoic terms, *apatheia*). Rather the passions or desires (*regtā*), such as ambition, hatred, anger, and pride, exist as the natural (and thus desirable) state of humanity.[63] The goal is not to eliminate the passions but to straighten them back into their original shape before the fall.[64]

Closer to the approach of Barsanuphius and John in their *Letters* to Andrew is that of Evagrius, discussed in Chapter 4. The writings of Evagrius were transmitted, although contested, in the monasteries of Palestine, including Thavatha.[65] Barsanuphius fielded a series of questions about the appropriateness of reading the works of Origen and the later Origenists Didymus the Blind and Evagrius, particularly the latter's *Gnostic Chapters* (*Letters* 600–607). Barsanuphius criticizes certain Origenist doctrines, such as the final and inevitable salvation of all creation, including the devil (the *apokatastasis*), but still encourages his monks to read the works of Evagrius and the other theologians as long as they know to discount their speculative and potentially heretical theories.[66]

Whatever his concerns about Evagrius's orthodoxy, Barsanuphius's interest in identifying the evil thoughts at work in the mind of the monk, whether himself or Andrew, betrays the influence of Evagrius, especially the popular and practical writings on spiritual direction and discernment, such as the *Praktikos*, *On Thoughts*, and *On the Eight Thoughts*, which are all works preserved in Greek, unlike his more controversial theological treatises such as the *Gnostic Chapters*. The underlying Evagrian orientation—reflecting a later elaboration of the monastic Origenism of Antony in his *Letters*—is clear: the monks' primary battle is with demons, and the primary mode of demonic opposition is through thoughts (*logismoi*) that distract, confuse, and corrupt the monk. The proper response to such demonic temptations is to recognize the thoughts for what they are and to repel them, for example, by contradicting them (*antirhēsis*, *antilegōn*, *Letter* 92) or applying quasi-medically the principle of opposites (*Letter* 86). Whether in a more Evagrian or Isaian mode or even a more basic Stoic common sense, the *Letters* of Barsanuphius and John reflect the reception of centuries-old ascetic traditions of illness and the passions within the context of spiritual direction and symbolic healing.

The correspondence is especially valuable in that it shows how difficult the process of symbolic healing could be. Here we see renowned, even miraculous, healers counseling an eager sufferer who, being a Christian and a monk in the very same monastery, shares the same symbolic world. Yet Barsanuphius's attempts to care for Andrew's soul appear largely ineffective. Much later in the correspondence, *Letter* 106, Andrew still struggles to make any sort of sense out of his continued illness, having fallen into "deep depression" (*pollēn athumian*).[67] For Barnanuphius, as we have seen, sadness and depression (*lupē* and *athumia*) are disastrous reactions to illness. While the illness may be a testing from god (and thus not evil in and of itself), sadness and depression are evil thoughts sown by the devil. He again applies symbols, cultural models of affliction, to the problem, including Abraham, Job, and the tortured and crucified messiah, and urges Andrew to evaluate his own illness not through the depressive thoughts of the devil but through these cultural models. Andrew should envision the sufferings of Jesus "and endur[e] with him the shame, the stigma, the humiliation, the contempt of the spitting, the insult of the cloak . . . the pain of the fixing of the nails, the piercing of the spear."[68] Underlying Barsanuphius's mimetic instructions is the familiar refrain "Do not be sad."[69]

Even when Andrew does recover for a time, he returns to the question of the meaning of his "thoughts." After a series of letters to the Great Old Men, which are only briefly summarized by the ancient editor, Barsanuphius at last tells Andrew via the abbot Seridus the good news, that through the intercessions of the saints god will soon heal him. Andrew was healed (*hygiane*) that very day.[70] When Andrew expresses his thanks to the Great Old Men, Barsanuphius reminds him that passions, not his bodily illness, were the truly important affliction. He should be more focused on the joy we will feel when we "receive complete purification from all the passions of our soul through his fearful, glorious name."[71] Over the course of the next five letters (*Letters* 83–87), the thoughts or passions form the focus of the correspondence. Andrew asks, "Father, when I am relieved of illness (*arrhōstias*), how should I spend each day?"—an interesting question, for just as Andrew seeks counsel for how to spend his days in illness, the question is no less pressing during health.[72] The advice given by John and Barsanuphius is in keeping with the Christian spiritual traditions influenced by Evagrius of Pontus. A goal of ascetic practice is to achieve unceasing prayer (*to adialeiptōs proseukhesthai*; compare 1 Thess. 5:17), which is a function of the mental or psychological state of "freedom from passions" or "dispassion," the aforementioned *apatheia*, traced at least to the Stoics but a core of Evagrius's spiritual theology.[73] This state of freedom from negative thoughts, such as lust, anger, and pride, allows the ascetic to focus on contemplation of divine and natural matters and to glorify god through unceasing prayer. To attain the state of apatheia is a lifelong struggle for the Christian ascetic and in large part hinges on the monk's ability to recognize the demonic nature of the thoughts (*tous logismous*) that attempt to capture the monk.[74]

Unexpectedly the demons use Andrew's miraculous recovery as an opportunity to tempt him. The summary prefaced to *Letter* 83 states, "A certain brother said to this old man (Andrew): 'Behold, old man, you have been restored [to health] through the prayers of the saints.' And he answered, saying, 'Whenever you have spoken this word to me, and this is now the fourth time, I have observed that demons wear down (*suntribousin*) my body.' So the Other Old Man was asked about this."[75] John explains that such illnesses (*astheneia*) are indeed demonic. The demons sow them so that the convalescent monk may become "doubtful in his heart" (*distasēi tēi kardiai*) and lose his faith in god (*apistian*). As seen in the *Letters* of Antony, demons were considered to be driven by envy (*phthonos*) more than any other passion; in their utterly fallen and forsaken state they want nothing more than to prevent humanity from being saved. John writes in this tradition that "the demons are not happy that a person should benefit," and thus they "sow lack of faith through their envy."[76] It is possibly in suspicion of the envious "evil eye" (*baskanos*), a fear widespread in antiquity, that Andrew is so fixated on the ostensible complements and well-wishes of his companion: they actually bespeak of envy and invite demonic nemesis.[77] Regardless, whether in illness or in health, Barsanuphius identifies not the body but the soul as the most meaningful area for interpretation, in particular the thoughts or passions that demons inflict on the monk.

For all of Barsanuphius's and John's interventions, Andrew is dragged down in a tide of anxiety and sadness over his bodily afflictions. Andrew's anxieties involve most poignantly his inability to carry out his ascetic practices. He frets that he is consuming what he considers an unacceptable amount (and perhaps quality, but this is not stated) of food.[78] These concerns echo the late ancient sources examined in previous chapters. In Andrew's personal, and hardly hagiographical or idealized, account, the problem is especially pressing. While most details of his biography are opaque, we can at least deduce that Andrew had dedicated a significant portion of his life, long enough to become an old man (*gerōn*), cultivating the monastic "way of life," or *politeia*. His monastic life-world had been formed by a set of enduring practices or performances, fasting, prayer, vigils, and labors, through which he engages in the religious experience.[79] These have altered his body (although we cannot know how); but more fundamentally such positive ascetic practices (rather than mere negative renunciations) have inaugurated a new self. We may recall Richard Valantasis's definition of asceticism as "performances within a dominant social environment intended to inaugurate a new subjectivity, different social relations, and an alternative symbolic universe."[80] This discussion of the epistolary interactions between Andrew and the Great Old Men has already pointed to one element of the new subjectivity: the symbolic universe that Andrew inhabits. Another part of this new subjectivity or self as a senior monk is the training of a junior brother (discussed below). Valantasis's definition of asceticism as a set of performances that inaugurate a new subjectivity pinpoints a third significant problem posed by ascetic illness (already encountered in other contexts and discussed presently): the monk's inability to carry out his usual spiritual exercises. Now that he is sick, Andrew finds himself unable to carry out the practices that had been central to his monastic self and formed the foundation of his life-world and that set him apart from the secular and worldly.[81] In this light it should be no surprise that illness could precipitate such a crisis of meaning.[82] It is of course not specific to asceticism that illness can provoke such a crisis. But for the ascetic, whose very life comprises a complex of practices designed to inaugurate and maintain this new subjectivity, a self that is apart, withdrawn from (and even at cross-purposes with) the dominant society, the crisis posed by asceticism is especially acute.

In reflecting such concerns Barsanuphius clarifies what god expects from the sick and elderly monk. He writes early in the correspondence (*Letter* 74) that god does not test anyone more than they can bear and that illness and the care of the sick are both "for the glory of God." While he is not yet explicit in this point (he will make the equation clear later), this points to the potential of illness (and also care for the sick) as a form of asceticism, a spiritual exercise. Yet it is a fact of which Barsanuphius and Andrew are well aware that the holy were widely expected to achieve a level of health that surpassed that of their secular counterparts (reminiscent of the hagiographical Antony, Paul, and Paphnutius's hermits). In fact Barsanuphius admits that he no longer gets sick himself, perhaps anticipating that Andrew has heard this already and thus contemns himself for his utterly mundane illness. Yet even in his preternatural health—gained from a life of strict asceticism—Barsanuphius is still subject to demonic thoughts. Typical of advanced ascetics, his weakness is vainglory (*hē kenodoxia*). Whenever he has been sick, he has not lessened his asceticism or labors, and "yet great illnesses (*megalai . . . astheneiai*)" befell him.[83] This directly contradicts the advice that Barsanuphius and John give to Andrew later in the correspondence, which of course Barsanuphius acknowledges when he characterizes it as due to vainglory. The saint too is a sinner, sinning through his sickness.

Yet his current health is no blessing for Barsanuphius. The demon thought of vainglory—that thorn in the side of the senior monk—afflicts Barsanuphius by preventing him from falling ill (*astheneian*). Barsanuphius is grieved (*lupoumai*) at this unwanted health, for it deprives him of practice in the virtue of patience (*tēn hupomenēn*).[84] Barsanuphius's consolation is again paradoxical. While Andrew's illness is a test from god for his greater glory, Barsanuphius's health is a temptation from the demons who hope to bring him down to their forsaken level. As Andrew is prone to fall into despair and sadness (*lupē*) because of his illness, Barsanuphius is beset by the evil thought of sadness (*lupoumai*) because of his continued health. It is not hard to hear in Barsanuphius's lament an echo of Syncletica's (and Joseph of Thebes's) praise of thankful perseverance in illness as a great asceticism: his unwanted health has cut him off from the great asceticism. The use of this paradox, lamenting the misfortune and affliction of good health, is rare in ascetic literature.[85] This equation levels health and illness: both pose their own tests and challenges; in each case the fundamental concern is to control the thoughts (here primarily sadness) that assail the monk. I am skeptical that such a paradoxical reversal of health as affliction would have been any more convincing in a late ancient context than it would be today. But the rhetorical intent of empathy and paradox is clear: Barsanuphius, though a senior monk and a healthy one at that, is presented with the same temptations and challenges as is the sick Andrew, the temptations of demonic thoughts and the challenge to endure through affliction for the glory of god. Whether Andrew practices his former asceticism is not the important issue; his thoughts pose the greater challenge for his spiritual progress.

The anxieties about his (perceived) ascetic failure continue to haunt Andrew through most of his correspondence. It appears that Barsanuphius's words of healing did not hit the mark. Quite to the contrary, Andrew feels the demon or thought of despair (*apognōsin*) at his back, since he can no longer practice the asceticism that made him who he is: "Since my thought (*logismos*) tells me that I cannot be saved, pray for me, merciful father, and tell me what I should do when I am prevented from fasting."[86] Apart from the now-familiar advice that Andrew not fall into despair, Barsanuphius answers his concern dialectically, distinguishing between material (or bodily) fasting and spiritual fasting (*tēs pneumatikēs*), without which mere bodily fasting "is nothing" (*ouden*).[87] Echoing earlier advice of Evagrius and others, Barsanuphius assures Andrew, "God does not require asceticism from those who are physically ill (*para tōn oun asthenountōn tōi sōmati*), but only from those who are able and healthy in body. Condescend a little (*mikron*) to your body, and it is not a sin. For God does not require this of you. He knows the illness that he sent you."[88] Barsanuphius explicitly frames Andrew's behavior in illness in the terms of ascetic spiritual exercises and the creation of a new subjectivity, citing Paul's admonition to "put away the old self with its lusts, and put on the new self, created according to the likeness of God" (Eph. 4:22–24, Col. 3:9). Barsanuphius's point in quoting Paul here is that the new self of the monk is formed not by fasting or vigils or prayers but by the fight against thoughts, such as lust (*epithumia*).[89] Thus, while certain famous saints of hagiography—and Barsanuphius himself—may be freed from disease, it is the battle against thoughts that is significant.

In the next letter Barsanuphius responds to Andrew's despair in stronger terms; as a skilled healer, Barsanuphius first applies a little consolation, and when that fails, he applies a stronger dose.[90] In this letter, citing Paul's familiar refrain from 2 Corinthians 12:10, Barsanuphius encourages Andrew to think of his illness as a type of asceticism, even a higher form of asceticism than he practiced in health: "What else is fasting but discipline of the body (*paideia tōi sōmati*), in order to enslave a healthy body (*hygies sōma*) and weaken (*asthenopoiēsēi*) it on account of the passions (*dia ta pathē*)?"[91] Barsanuphius's choice of words is significant. Asceticism or discipline (*paideia*) has the same effect on the healthy body as disease: it renders it *asthenēs*, weak or sick. This weakness/sickness has a positive effect: it limits the influence of the passions, thoughts, or demons. Illness, therefore, *is* asceticism.

He expands on this point in a passage worth quoting at some length:

> Illness, however, is greater than mere discipline (*hē de astheneia perissotera paideias esti*), being reckoned as a substitute for the regular [ascetic] way (*anti politeias*); and it is even of greater value (*perissoteron*) [than asceticism] for the person who endures it with patience and gives thanks to God. That person reaps the fruit of salvation from such patience. Therefore, instead of the body being weakened (*asthenopoiēsai*) through fasting, it is weakened in and of itself (*aph'heautou asthenei*). Give thanks that you have been exempted from the toil of regular [ascetic] behavior (*kopou politeias*). So even if you eat ten times, do not grieve, for you are not condemned. For this is a result neither of demonic action (*kat'energeian daimonōn*) nor of slack thought (*kata khaunotēta logismou*).[92]

Illness both substitutes for regular asceticism and surpasses it in value. While fasting (and presumably other disciplines) has the side effect of weakening the body (or making it sick, *asthenopoiēsai*), illness weakens it as an inherent quality (*aph'heautou asthenei*); it accomplishes the goals of asceticism even more effectively than mere discipline. All regular ascetic practices are therefore superfluous for Andrew, save to endure his illness patiently with thanksgiving.

Here Lucien Regnault's observation that the *Letters* of Barsanuphius and John are like a film in comparison to the short bursts of light from the aphoristic literature of the desert is especially apt. In the *Life of Syncletica*, Basil's *Rules*, and the single apophthegm attributed to Joseph of Thebes, for example, we see glimpses of this understanding of asceticism in the form of short, gnomic sayings. But in the *Letters* we see the same advice in the context of a dialogue between suffering monk and healer, as the healer empathizes with the sufferer's emotions and manipulates the appropriate "transactional symbols" to enable the sufferer to "transact his . . . own emotions," in anthropological terms.[93] We see how the sayings of Syncletica and Joseph about illness as a "great asceticism" or about the benefit of "choosing illness" function in the context of spiritual direction.

But for all Barsanuphius's skills as a healer, amply attested in the hundreds of letters to and from his hermitage, Andrew did not apparently find the answers he was seeking. In some of the last letters of the correspondence, written several months after the letter just discussed, Andrew betrays that he is still suffering. He despairs at his continuing struggle with demons, thoughts, and passions, weighed down with the same anxiety over his abandoned asceticism. Barsanuphius assures him that the "throng of demonic passions and fantasies . . . accomplish nothing . . . except to multiply virtue." The greater the temptations, the brighter (*lamproteron*) the righteous will shine.[94] When Andrew continues to worry about his inability to fast, which he feared "was preventing him from reaching what had been promised him," Barsanuphius responds in exasperation, "It is not because I wish to abolish abstinence and the monastic discipline (*tēn enkrateian kai tēn politeian*) that I am always (*aei*) telling your love to perform the needs of your body as necessary—far be it from me! Rather, I am saying that, if the inner work does not come to our assistance after God, then one is laboring in vain on the outward self."[95] Barsanuphius assures Andrew, as he has "always" been doing, that as long as he is focused on his inner dispositions, no "bodily foods" can harm him, as Christ said (Matt. 15:11). The problem is not food but thought: "Therefore, when you carry out your bodily needs (*tēn khreian tou sōmatos*), do not have any doubts, but do whatever your inner nature can do to labor (*tou ponesai*) and humble its thoughts (*tapeinōsai tous logismous autou*). Then God will open the eyes of your heart in order to see 'the true light' and to understand the words: 'I am saved by grace' in Christ Jesus our Lord. Amen."[96] Barsanuphius could hardly be clearer or more consoling. Andrew's illness does not mean a failure of discipline. It is a discipline in and of itself, a tool of "spiritual progress" (*prokopēs*, Letter 89) that can carry the sick monk to spiritual transcendence, to achieve *gnōsis*, true knowledge of the self and of god.

Illness and Social Discord

The second theme that runs through the correspondence is the conflict between Andrew and fellow monks, especially his unnamed "brother." In fact
it is his damaged social relations that concern Andrew most in his letters,
outnumbering the questions focused on the meaning of illness or questions
about illness and ascetic practice. This is not entirely unexpected, as illness
commonly manifests in troubled relations among significant others, especially
family members. Kleinman and others have noted that a significant component of many symbolic healing systems is to heal interpersonal relations, even
in those systems that do not link disease etiologically with social discord.[97]

One issue that Andrew raises in his questions is the effect that his inability
to carry out the ascetic practices normally expected of him will have on others.
After Barsanuphius has written several letters to Andrew assuring him that he
has no need of fasting or other ascetic exercises (*Letters* 74, 77, 78), Andrew
writes to the Other Old Man, John, this time about the social repercussions
of his lack of fasting: "Pray for my most unbearable illness, father, and declare
to me about diet, whether it does not perhaps cause a scandal (*skandalon*)
that I readily and continually eat."[98] John chides Andrew for having, perhaps,
tried to get a second opinion apart from Barsanuphius and assures him that
he agrees with everything Barsanuphius has said. Furthermore why should
Andrew want the "very watery milk" of John when he has the "solid food of
spiritual bread" of Barsanuphius, especially when John's advice is the same?[99]

Yet the thoughts persist. Andrew writes back to Barsanuphius with a new
concern: his illness is excessively burdening the other brothers. We have no
way of knowing whether this was only a *phantasia*, a temptation from demons, or whether his brothers indeed let it be known that they had grown
tired of caring for his special needs. It is certainly to be expected that caregivers
might come to resent the burdens placed on them and the impositions of the
sick, and indeed other monastic sources reflect that monks were prone to such
base feelings.[100] In the face of this perceived resentment, Andrew asks not for
healing but for the ability "to perform my needs by myself, so that the brothers
will not carry my burdens."[101]

Barsanuphius assures him that this is of course possible with Christ, who
has the power to raise from the dead, cast out demons, abolish wars, and open
up the heavens. Even in his very community, he says coyly, there is a monk
who can raise the dead through Christ (he insists it is not himself). If Christ
can provide blessings in heaven, then it is but a small matter "not to be sick or

afflicted (*to mē asthenēsai se ē thlibēnai*) even for a single day" through his help. But Andrew should ask for no such thing, since Jesus knows what is best for us. Illness may profit (*sumpherei*) or benefit (*ōphelei*) us. This may be through the patient and thankful suffering of illness, of which Job is again adduced as a model. But illness may benefit the soul also by the endurance of "the reward of service." The narrative model for this comes not from the Bible but from the *Lausiac History* of Palladius. Barsanuphius cites—but does not tell—the story of Eulogius, which relates not only to the challenges of caring for the ill or disabled but also to the difficulties in being cared for. Eulogius, a lawyer in the city of Alexandria, had abandoned the bar and converted to the ascetic life, but he did not wish to settle in a traditional community. When he came across a cripple in the street without hands or feet and living on alms, Eulogius decided to make his asceticism the care of this cripple. The cripple accepted his offer of service, and for years Eulogius and the unnamed cripple lived in harmony in a cell, as Eulogius devoted his time to caring for this outcast. Eventually, however, the cripple came to miss the former autonomy of his begging days. A demon made the cripple resentful of Eulogius's care, and he berated Eulogius mercilessly, demanding to return to his life on the streets. Tempted to cast him out, Eulogius took the cripple to meet Antony in his mountain retreat for advice. Antony apprised the situation, criticized Eulogius for wishing to cast him out, and berated the cripple harshly for not recognizing that it was Christ who cared for him through Eulogius. Conflict resolved, they returned to their cell. Whether Andrew would have recognized this allusion to Eulogius is not certain; he previously misunderstood Barsanuphius's quotation of a familiar saying of Antony. But the point is clear: the problem here lies not with his caretakers but with Andrew himself. His concerns with burdening his brothers is but pretext for his own resentment of the care provided for him and his nostalgia for his earlier life of relative self-reliance. In his professed concern not to burden his brothers, he rejects the care of Christ. Yet much as patiently suffering illness (like Job) may benefit the monk as an ascetic discipline, so does patiently receiving help from others (like the cripple). Therefore, says Barsanuphius, "ask nothing else of God or through his servants, except assistance and patience" (*boētheian kai hupomonēn*).[102]

The remainder of Andrew's social problems involve his disciple (or "brother"). Andrew's unnamed disciple is introduced early in the corpus, for he falls ill along with Andrew, and Andrew requests the Other Old Man John to pray for them.[103] Presumably, unlike Andrew, the brother recovered. The relationship between Andrew and his brother was fraught, yet this was by no means unique to Andrew's domestic situation. The *Letters* of Barsanuphius and John as well as the *Asceticon* of Abba Isaiah, which comes from the same community, document a number of troublesome aspects of the relationship between master and disciple in the Monastery of Thavatha. While the literature of semi-eremitic monasticism generally characterizes the matching of disciple and master as one of mutual consent, in Thavatha this matching followed a different pattern, one that may have exacerbated the potential conflicts between the two. Thavatha, as a self-described coenobium, was a community that valued the virtue of absolute obedience and complete neglect of the will. Thus, Thavatha's abbot made the matches. One would hope that an abbot would possess the virtue of discernment to match appropriately disciple with master, but such matches might not work out, and in any case an abbot might not think it his duty to minimize conflicts. At any rate a number of letters reflect the complaints of novices to the Great Old Men about being exploited by their masters or that their master cannot answer their spiritual questions.[104]

Problems between the brothers emerge after Andrew has recovered briefly from his illness but has fallen ill yet again with stomach pain and other complaints. Andrew's *Letters* from 92 to 109 focus on his brother's treatment of him. The summaries of Andrew's letters fail to provide precise details, but the brother, in Andrew's words, "afflicts" (*thlibei*) him. Andrew furthermore is conflicted because he finds it impossible to guide or discipline the younger brother, who apparently disregards Andrew's authority over him. Expressing his concern first in *Letter* 92, he asks for a demotion, as it were, since he feels incapable of carrying out his duties as a senior monk, much as he has been relieved of his ascetic obligations due to illness: "Father, give me the rule of a beginner, who has not yet received the habit. And pray for me, because my brother afflicts me, while nevertheless at the same time comforting (*anapauei*) another person."[105] Barsanuphius empathizes with Andrew's difficulties, though he and John will grow less patient with Andrew's complaints as the letters continue. He recognizes that Andrew is having difficulties with his brother due to his bodily illness (*tēn astheneian tou sōmatos*) and his old age (*ephtakenai se eis to gēras*). Barsanuphius tells him that he will put upon him the simplest, most basic rule: "[r]egard your brother as your child . . . as indeed you do regard him in this way," and endure whatever affliction he may cause, also realizing that perhaps it is Jesus who wills it, "for it is by endurance of afflictions that we gain our souls."[106]

Here and elsewhere Barsanuphius (and later John) disregards Andrew's complaints about his brother and instead focuses on Andrew, especially his thoughts, to which he urges Andrew to "pay attention" (*prosekhonta tois logismois*), drawing on the common ancient terminology of spiritual exercises.[107] Drawing on the shared tradition of Evagrian spirituality, Barsanuphius identifies the demonic thoughts afflicting the monk as anger and envy. He advises Andrew to spend the rest of his days, which he implies may not be many, "in the search of your thoughts" and to "contradict (*antilegōn*) those thoughts that bring you turmoil." In counseling Andrew to contradict or "talk back" to the thoughts, Barsanuphius draws on another popular aspect of Evagrian spiritual direction.[108] For each of the eight evil thoughts, Evagrius lists samples of the tempting thoughts, each accompanied by a biblical verse to "contradict" the demon. Book 5, *On Anger*, has much of relevance to Andrew:

9. Against the soul that has neglected humility but longs to learn the ways of the Lord:

    He will guide the meek in judgment; he will teach the meek his ways (Ps. 24:9).

10. Against the soul that accepts thoughts of anger and collects against the brothers wicked pretexts and false suspicions:

    Cease from anger, and forsake wrath; do not be anxious, so that you do evil. For the evildoers shall be destroyed, but those who wait for the Lord, they shall inherit the earth (Ps. 36:8–9).

11. Against the thought that is set in motion by slander of the brothers and that obscures the soul with a cloud of rage:

    Sitting, you slander your brother, and against your mother's son you have placed a stumbling block (Ps. 49:20).[109]

In the common Evagrian tradition of paying attention to thoughts, Andrew should have examined his thoughts, searched out the demons of anger and envy, banished those thoughts, and then, as Barsanuphius advised, treated his brother as his own child, counting as nothing whatever afflictions he might cause.

This was not to be. In the next letter Andrew is distraught. He has tried to discipline the brother "once, and even ten times" but to no avail. Now his thought (*ho logismos*) tells him to "leave him alone . . . and be carefree."[110] Barsanuphius responds more strongly here. At stake is not merely Andrew's salvation but also that of the brother. While in the previous letter Barsanuphius spoke of thoughts and left the work of the devil implicit, now he specifies the diabolical threat: "The devil is moving on every side to trouble you, whether by envy or by anger (*dia phthonou, di'orgēs*), but he has found no place." While there is still hope, the devil, through Andrew, is also troubling the brother. Here as elsewhere Barsanuphius and John are much more concerned with the trouble that Andrew is causing the brother than any trouble the brother is causing Andrew.[111] A harshness of tone is clear in Barsanuphius's words: "Nevertheless, what I wrote to you in previous letters, to tell your brother of his mistakes and to admonish him, either I did not say it clearly enough and you did not take it seriously, or else I did say it clearly but you were defeated in the struggle."[112] By not disciplining his brother continually, Barsanuphius argues, Andrew does him no good and certainly does not manifest godly patience. Rather his ostensible long-suffering and silence will erupt in spiritual violence: "[Y]ou are long-suffering for many days, but then afterwards you give him a single blow on the back and take his life."[113]

Andrew writes to the Other Old Man John for a second opinion: he wants to leave his cell for another. John is no less harsh in his response. John notes that Andrew's letters about his brother's alleged faults have been going on for three weeks. He makes it painfully clear that it is Andrew's failure for focusing so relentlessly on his brother's faults: "Do you not know that you are casting yourself into great condemnation? For indeed, if you call your brother to account for these trespasses, God will call you to account for your own sins from your youth to this day. What happened to: 'Do not let the sun go down on your anger'? Where is: 'Bear one another's burdens'? Where is the letter from the [Great] Old Man, which could serve as your rule? Instead of giving thanks, you offer this?"[114] John points out what is at stake. Andrew, says John, is going to die soon, and as it stands, his eternal soul is at risk. He must bring his entire being to bear against the demonic thoughts if he wishes to "find rest (*anapauēi*)," rather than worrying about whether or not his brother "comforts" (*anapauei*) him.[115]

The letters from the distraught Andrew continue. In *Letter* 95 he has admonished his brother, who disregarded him, and Andrew is troubled. In *Letter* 96 Andrew feels afflicted and wishes to leave the cell: "My thought tells me that if I were alone, I would not have affliction, but rather find salvation." In the latter it is worth noting that John takes a more gentle tone than his fire and brimstone talk of the end in *Letter* 94. Here he at length argues that the tribulations are from the lord, or at least allowed by him, for the benefit of his soul. Regarding changing cells and taking a different brother, John says that it is easy to do and well within the power for the abbot but that it would make no difference, for new troubles would emerge. He insists that he does not forbid

Andrew from taking a new brother but urges him simply "to 'test everything, and hold fast to what is good'" (1 Thess. 5:21). He encourages Andrew to see the benefit in affliction, for "it is God's will for us that we should be a little troubled. For without tribulation, there is no progress in the fear of God."[116]

Yet the complaints continue. Whether Barsanuphius's *Letter* 98 responds to Andrew's own letter or that of one of his brothers or to something that he has simply heard is not clear. Regardless he rebukes Andrew harshly: "I am . . . astonished at how those who have spent a long time in the monastic life, and ought to be able to discern the deeper thoughts of others, are nevertheless still besieged by the warfare of novices. You ought to be guiding into the straight way those who have gone astray, as if you were perfected; and yet, instead of bearing the burdens of the weak, you burden them to the point of drowning on account of sorrow. . . . I wonder, does this not inflict harm on your soul at all, that you trouble the thought of your neighbor?"[117] Barsanuphius is aware that his words will sting, and he draws on the common analogy of the cure of souls with that of the body; even though the physician's treatment may hurt, it is necessary to heal. So though his words may burn, Barsanuphius says, "I am writing these things because I desire to remove from you every bit of rot (*sēpedona*)." It is important to do that quickly, for yet again Barsanuphius predicts, "you do not have very long to live in the body."[118]

Andrew's afflictions would continue until in *Letter* 109 he writes to Barsanuphius full of thanks that he has at last been "delivered from temptation." Although the temptations are not described explicitly, Barsanuphius's quotation of Proverbs 18:19 in the response ("A brother assisted by a brother is like a city fortified with ramparts") makes it clear that the temptations were his dejection at his brother's lack of compassion and his own desire to leave the cell. Barsanuphius characterizes this turn of events as a type of healing due to the interventions of Christ, "a physician who can heal our passions" (*iatron hina therapeusēi hēmōn ta pathē*) and "a nurse who can nurture us with spiritual food."[119] The letters that follow suggest that this healing was indeed of Andrew's own passions, rather than due to any dramatic change in behavior on the part of the brother. At any rate Andrew's worries did not entirely abate. In *Letter* 121, the final letter preserved from the sick monk, Andrew yet again writes in words that echo throughout his correspondence: How should I treat my brother?

The correspondence between Barsanuphius and John and the sick monk Andrew ends with two responses not to Andrew but to the troublesome brother. The ancient editor summarizes his letter in the preface to *Letter* 122:

"The brother who lived near this elder, who was unwell (*asthenountos*), had compassion on his illness (*astheneiai*) and asked the Great Old Man to pray for him."[120] From Barsanuphius's responses it is clear that the "trouble-rousing brother"—as Barsanuphius calls him—was asking why Andrew was sick and perhaps why Barsanuphius and the saints in heaven have not "ha[d] compassion on him."[121] The explanations that Barsanuphius offers echo those offered to Andrew some fifty letters, and several months, before. These were persistent questions.

The last we hear from the monks is again from the trouble-rousing brother, who now is facing some social conflicts of his own. Now that he is attempting to serve the sick monk, Andrew has refused the help, appealing to the model of a famous monk from the *Sayings of the Desert Fathers*, Theodore of Pherme, who refused even to "command his own disciple." The brother is wondering about the rule of asceticism in illness. Barsanuphius answers with familiar advice: Theodore of Pherme is not appropriate as a model for Andrew's behavior since Andrew is sick. Barsanuphius adds, "As he has often heard, God does not require anything from the ill person except thanksgiving and patience."[122] If the letters of Andrew's correspondence are indeed ordered chronologically by the ancient editor—the most likely scenario—it appears that the lessons taught by Barsanuphius were difficult ones for Andrew to accept.

Here the correspondence between Andrew and the Great Old Men ends, and the collection of *Letters* moves on to other topics. We cannot know whether Andrew recovered from his bodily illness, suffered for a long time, or died shortly thereafter, though the fact that his voluminous correspondence ends here suggests the likelihood that he died suddenly without writing or dictating any final missive to the Great Old Men. We cannot know whether Andrew was "healed," whether he found meaning in his suffering and came to be at peace with it; nor do we know whether he and his brother were ultimately reconciled.

Conclusion

The correspondence between the two Great Old Men of Thavatha and the sick monk Andrew constitutes a remarkable document from the end of antiquity, in the period of literary efflorescence of Palestinian monasticism in the century prior to the Muslim conquest of the Levant. Long overshadowed by other more literary accounts of monasticism, such as the Lives of the saints and the

Sayings of the Desert Fathers, the *Letters* of Barsanuphius and John reveal the contentious discussion of illness and its function and meaning within ascetic practice played out in the process of spiritual direction, a dialogue that reflects the conflicting points of view of both the sufferer and the healer. Interestingly, Barsanuphius himself underscores the dialogic nature of this healing process. It is not a one-sided intervention by the healer. Rather, Barsanuphius and Andrew are both agents of the healing process. So Barsanuphius explains that his offer to bear half of Andrew's burden was to make him "a partner in this good conversation" (*sunkoinōnon . . . tēs kalēs epistrophēs*).[123] The conversation would last for months through Andrew's declining fortunes, and the fifty-two letters to Andrew and his ascetic brother reveal a persistent crisis of meaning on the part of Andrew. The previous chapters in this book observed the frequency with which ascetic literature from the fourth and fifth centuries has dealt with such questions of meaning—in frequently diverging or contradictory ways. Andrew's letters show that in the height of a fully developed monasticism in mid-sixth-century Palestine, these questions still cut to the heart of individual ascetics: Why am I sick? Has god abandoned me? Have I failed as a monk? Am I to burden my fellow monks? The *Letters* of Barsanuphius and John show that the responses to these questions elaborated by early monastic writers continued to be important to later generations. They also show that, for all the charisma of holy men such as Barsanuphius and John, monks did not always find these explanations convincing.

Conclusion

Like other core aspects of the human experience such as eating, sex, sociality, and even writing, illness posed significant problems of meaning and practice for late ancient ascetics and their audiences.[1] To a certain extent the challenges posed by illness are intuitive and universal: illness disrupts the life-world; illness, for those spared fatal accidents or murder, will kill all of us. Illness nearly demands explanation and interpretation. Thus late ancient ascetic discourse (from the mid-fourth to the mid-sixth centuries) reflects a sustained and contentious interest in making meaning of illness. If writers such as Basil the Great felt the need to develop a theodicy that explained the meaning and origin of illness and decrepitude among humanity as a whole, it is no surprise that illness among ascetics and saints, who functioned as something more than ordinary humans, as "symbols" and "exemplars," called even more urgently and ambiguously for explanation.

The literature produced by, for, and about the emergent communities of Christian ascetics—the primary focus of this book—shows that ascetic practitioners and their followers were indeed conflicted about how to make meaning of the illness and suffering of ascetics. Such debates and controversies were rooted partly in tensions observable in Christianity's scriptural heritage, which ambiguously reads illness in dialectical tension between two poles, as both an unmistakable sign of the sufferer's sin and as the mark of the sufferer's special holiness and steadfastness in the eyes of god (and in between, the sufferer could just be unlucky). Such controversies were also rooted in elements of the experience of illness observable cross-culturally. Illness has the potential to destroy and to transform the self: to lead painfully and inconsolably to the unmaking of the self, yet also to open up new realms of experience and to create a new self, or at least to create the space for the sufferer to do so.

Monastic thinkers as early as Antony saw in the ascetic project an opportunity to reclaim the primordial health of Adam and Eve, a unity between body and soul. Some, such as Antony and later Isaiah of Scetis and others, described this health in predominantly psychic terms: righting the sickened soul and resisting the infecting agents of demonic thoughts. Yet the association of prelapsarian health with monastic asceticism would be radically expanded upon in influential hagiographies—among the most influential, of course, was the *Life of Antony*—to promote an ideology of monastic health: by proper ascetic practice (and presumably adherence to orthodoxy) monks were expected to achieve preternatural health in body and soul, manifested in a healthy longevity. As influential as such an ideology of monastic health was (and continues to be), it was not free from controversy. The relative health or illness of the saint could be used to establish or displace ascetic authority (as in Jerome's *Life of Paul*). An influential hagiography (Paphnutius's *Life of Onnophrius*) in the generation after Athanasius could even criticize the model of Antony's health as a practical impossibility for flesh-and-blood monks, all the while accepting the preternaturally healthy monk as the basic template for the hagiographical Life.

The ascetic literature of the late fourth and fifth centuries reflects widespread concern about the meaning and function of illness in ascetic practice. Sometimes the deleterious influence of Lives such as Antony's is explicit; other times the inspiration for the controversies is less clear. Regardless illness posed a number of interpretive and practical challenges. Some monks attempted to surpass human limits of asceticism and thus injured or sickened themselves. But given the incontrovertible (yet for some, scandalous) fact that ascetics, even the saintly, fall ill regardless of the models that hagiographies had established for monks to emulate, ascetic writers—Basil the Great and Syncletica are two paradigmatic examples analyzed in this book—variously promoted the proper experience of illness not as a threat to ascetic self-control but as a model or type of ascetic progress, even a mode of asceticism in and of itself, with the potential for self-mastery that surpasses traditional modes of spiritual exercise.

In the generations that followed, ascetic writers continued to grapple with issues of meaning, practice, and sanctity. The Great Coptic *Life of Pachomius* shows how an important hagiography crafted a role for the chronically sick saint in direct dialogue and competition with the *Life of Antony* and indirectly with the types of arguments over illness and asceticism reflected in other earlier and contemporary sources. The *Letters* of Barsanuphius and John, among the best evidence for spiritual direction in the late ancient Mediterranean world, show how deeply the issues reflected on by Basil, Evagrius, the Desert Fathers, Syncletica, John Cassian, Palladius, and others continued to vex monks and their spiritual advisers into the sixth century.

Some of the texts engaged here are familiar, some quite a bit less so; yet they are not only connected thematically but also frequently in dialogue with one another. This set of interrelated texts sheds light on an important aspect of late ancient ascetic discourse (and asceticism) that has been largely unrecognized. The texts that I have chosen to focus on in this volume are more representative—even paradigmatic—than exhaustive, for the contentious issues that the texts grapple with in this volume may be widely seen in other texts as well. By way of conclusion, I present the narrative of Jacob of Cyrrhestica in Theodoret's *Religious History*. Theodoret's *History* has been referred to already, specifically his justifiably famous *bios* of Simeon the Stylite. His life of Simeon holds a prominent place in scholarly studies and undergraduate curricula, for good reason.[2] It is a very good tale and is arguably the highlight of Theodoret's *History*, a classic example of the distinctive Syrian mode of Christian *askēsis*. Theodoret's description of Jacob, however, although it is the longest chapter in the book, has received comparatively less interest.[3] This story shows how important the kind of readings engaged in here are for recognizing the contentious diversity of ancient monastic interpretation of illness in asceticism, and even human embodiment in general.

Jacob's ascetic practice is typical of the general picture of Syrian monasticism familiar from the descriptions of Theodoret and others. His asceticism is publicly performative, not just in the eyes of god but also in the public round. He practices "philosophy" exposed to the elements in a courtyard, with no shade, no shelter, no privacy. He also embraces the weighty self-mortifications so typical of Syrian monks, wearing iron bands and chains under his clothing to abet his suffering.

Despite the brutality of Jacob's mortifications, in this narrative (*diēgēma*) Theodoret reflects an attitude toward illness very much in keeping with the teachings of Basil, Syncletica, Barsanuphius, and others. Theodoret emphasizes that he had witnessed Jacob's illness fourteen years before writing the *Religious History* (thus around 426). The specificity of his eyewitness testimony is telling. "[A] grave illness," Theodoret says, "came upon him which caused him a condition to be expected in one with a mortal body." In the unforgiving summer sun Jacob was afflicted with fever and, most distressing, diarrhea, "a flux of bile moving downwards, hurting the guts, causing pressure and forcing one to run outside." In a description that might catch the interest of those inclined toward Freudian analysis, Jacob's ascetic prowess is manifested in his resistance to involuntary defecation: "[H]e sat there torn by contrary impulses: while nature pressed him to go and evacuate, shame before the attendant crowd compelled him to stay in the same position. . . . [T]he man of God was not defeated by nature, but maintained his endurance until the dead of night set in and compelled everyone to go home."[4]

The point of Theodoret's story is not only to praise the monk's remarkable ascetic bowel control (though it is indeed a remarkable *askēsis*). More fundamental to Theodoret's tale is to emphasize the need for Jacob to lessen his asceticism in the face of illness. The following day Theodoret visits Jacob again and, by feigning illness himself, gradually persuades the athlete of god to take some comfort and abandon his austerities: to move into the shade and sit down (as a start), to accept the comforting touch of the bishop on his back, and to remove the heavy chains strapped to his torso. Theodoret the bishop puts himself in the position of spiritual director in words that could easily come from Syncletica or Barsanuphius: "I begged him to assist his sick body, which could not bear at the same time both the voluntary (*ethelousia*) load and the involuntary infirmity (*tēn akousion arrhōstian*). 'At the moment, father,' I said, 'the fever is doing the work of the iron; when it abates, let us at that stage impose on the body again the labor from the iron.'"[5] While Jacob relents to Theodoret here, he later falls even more grievously ill. Not unlike the sick monk Andrew, who found it so difficult to abandon his austerities, Jacob again resists any rest from his practice. Theodoret beseeches him, echoing the arguments in earlier chapters of this volume, even the concerns of the early suppliants of the Melitian monks of Hathor with their own precarious health, discussed in Chapter 2: "Show consideration, father, for all of us, for we think your health to be a preservation for all (*koinēn gar sōtērian tēn sēn hygieian*). For not only are you set before us as a model that is of benefit, but you also help by your prayers and procure us God's favor. If the disruption of your habits torments you, father (I continued), endure this as well, for this too is a form of philosophy. Just as when in health and desiring food you overcame appetite by endurance, so now when you have no appetite show endurance by taking food (*tēn tēs metalēpseōs karterian*)."[6] Thus within a volume familiar for its tales of a public and extreme spiritual athleticism—monks in chains and cages, immured in tombs, or exposed to the elements like beasts—we see a rather contrary attitude toward the monk's illness, one that is by now familiar from the range of texts engaged in the previous six chapters. Theodoret's counsel reflects that monastic illness is a danger both to the monk and to his suppliants. Yet illness is also a form of asceticism in itself, doing the work of the iron. This is not to suggest that one attitude toward ascetic illness—reflected in the stories of Simeon or Jacob—is more real or privileged than the other. They exist in dialectical tension, a tension that was part of the culturally creative and influential place of Christian monasticism in the later Roman Empire. Theodoret did not resolve them any more than Basil did before him or Barsanuphius did after him.

The issues implicated in the late ancient elaboration of ascetic ideals and practices would create a space for Christian interpretation of illness as an aspect of the human experience, as a site for theological reflection and ascetic spiritual exercise. The questions that early Christian ascetics raised, and their various answers, about the meaning of illness and its potentials and risks for spiritual and ascetic progress would have a long afterlife in Christianity, to discuss which would be far too much for this volume. Suffice it to say that John Donne's meditations on his own illness, which would have an influential place in modern theological reflection on illness, or Robert Burton's musings on the existential quandary of human illness did not spring de novo from the seventeenth century. Illness's threat to our individual autonomy, productivity, and self-control is still a problem that we in postmodernity grapple with, as we still do with the most fundamental need for compassion with the weak and suffering, balanced with our almost inalienable desire to read a just and moral causality into the illness of others, to see illness (certain illnesses more than others) as proper and deserved recompense for sin and dissolution. Of course the specific concerns and perspectives of the late ancient texts discussed in this volume differ in manifold ways from those of modernity. However, drawing out these persistent and contentious debates from the ascetic literatures of late antiquity has shown how late ancient ascetics and their observers grappled with fundamental problems in embodiment, asceticism, theodicy, and religious authority.

Abbreviations

AAR	American Academy of Religion
ACW	Ancient Christian Writers
ANRW	*Aufstieg und Niedergang der Römischen Welt*
Apoph. pat. (alph.)	*Apophthegmata patrum*, alphabetic series
CS	Cistercian Studies
CSCO	Corpus scriptorum christianorum orientalium
CSEL	Corpus scriptorium ecclesiasticorum latinorum
Hist. mon.	*Historia monachorum in Aegypto*
HR	Theodoret of Cyrrhus, *Historia religiosa*
JAAR	*Journal of the American Academy of Religion*
JECS	*Journal of Early Christian Studies*
LSJ[9]	Liddell, Scott, Jones, *A Greek-English Lexicon*, 9th ed.
NHC	Nag Hammadi Codices
NPNF	Nicene and Post-Nicene Fathers
NRSV	New Revised Standard Version
OED	*Oxford English Dictionary* Online
PG	*Patrologia graeca*
PL	*Patrologia latina*
P.Lond.VI	Bell, ed., *Jews and Christians in Egypt*
P.Neph.	Kramer and Shelton, eds., *Das Archiv des Nepheros*
PO	*Patrologia orientalis*
Reg. brev.	Basil of Caesarea, *Regulae brevior tractatae*
Reg. fus.	Basil of Caesarea, *Regulae fusius tractatae*
SC	Sources chrétiennes
SBL	Society of Biblical Literature
TU	Texte und Untersuchungen
V.Ant.	Athanasius, *Vita Antonii* (*Life of Antony*)
VB	L.-Th. Lefort, ed., *S. Pachomii vita bohairice scripta*
V.Onn.	Paphnutius, *Vita Onnophrii* (*Life of Onnophrius*)

V.Pach. G1	First Greek *Life of Pachomius*
V.Pach. SBo	Sahidic-Bohairic (i.e., Great Coptic) *Life of Pachomius*
V.Pauli	Jerome, *Vita Pauli* (*Life of Paul, the First Hermit*)
VS	L.-Th. Lefort, *S. Pachomii vitae sahidice scriptae*
V.Syn.	Pseudo-Athanasius, *Vita Syncleticae (Life of Syncletica)*

Notes

1. Noted by Wayne C. Booth in his introduction to France, *Thaïs*, trans. Gulati. France's astounding popularity and precipitous decline in prestige are discussed by Booth (8–11); he speculates about his influence on twentieth-century literature at 16n6.

2. France, *Thaïs*, 27, citing Is. 35:1. Booth describes *Thaïs* as France's most popular book (9).

3. *V.Ant.* 14, 87, trans. Robert C. Gregg, *Athanasius: The Life of Antony and the Letter to Marcellinus*, Classics of Western Spirituality (Mahwah, N.J.: Paulist Press, 1980), ed. G. J. M. Bartelink, Athanase d'Alexandrie, *Vie d'Antoine*, SC 400 (Paris: Cerf, 1994), 174, 358. I will return to Athanasius (that is, if we accept his authorship of the *Life of Antony* as secure) and the *Life* in Chapter 3.

4. Cioran, *Tears and Saints*, trans. Zarifopol-Johnston, 42–43; Nietzsche, *Genealogy of Morals*, trans. Samuel, 94–178, e.g., 126–27, 159. On Cioran's conflicted relationship with the works of Nietzsche, see Regier, "Cioran's Nietzsche."

5. Cioran, *Tears and Saints*, 22.

6. Jacob of Serug, *Homily on Simeon the Stylite*, trans. Susan Ashbrook Harvey, in *Ascetic Behavior in Greco-Roman Antiquity*, ed. Vincent L. Wimbush, Studies in Antiquity and Christianity (Minneapolis: Fortress Press, 1990), 22.

7. Harpham, *Ascetic Imperative*, 27.

8. "Illness takes on meaning as suffering because of the way this relationship between body and self is mediated by cultural symbols of a religious, moral, or spiritual kind," according to Kleinman, *Illness Narratives*, 27.

9. Kleinman, *Illness Narratives*, 26; also cf. the classic study on stigma and social meaning by Goffman, *Stigma*.

10. For useful surveys of the methodological shifts in contemporary medical anthropology, see Garro, "Cognitive Medical Anthropology"; and Loewe, "Illness Narratives." The relevance of cognitive anthropology for the study of early Christianity is surveyed in Garrett, "Sociology (Early Christianity)."

11. Scarry, *Body in Pain*, 209. See the further elaboration in Shaw, *Burden of the Flesh*, 173–74.

12. *Life of Adam and Eve*, trans. Johnson, in *Old Testament Pseudepigrapha*, ed. Charlesworth. I have consulted the Greek version, the *Apocalypse of Moses*, and the Latin *Life of Adam and Eve*. The extensive manuscript traditions in the Greek, Latin, Oriental and Slavonic versions reflect the widespread popularity of the *Life*, trans. Johnson, 249–52. I have also consulted the synoptic edition of Gary A. Anderson and Michael E. Stone, eds., *A Synopsis of the Books of Adam and Eve*, SBL Early Judaism and Its Literature 5 (Atlanta: Scholars Press, 1994); and Johannes Tromp, ed., *The Life of Adam and Eve in Greek: A Critical Edition*, Pseudepigrapha Veteris Testamenti Graece 16 (Leiden: Brill, 2005).

13. *Apocalypse of Moses* 5, trans. Johnson. In the Greek *Life* all the sons ask, "What is it, Father, to be sick with pains?" and Seth continues, "What is pain, O lord Father? I do not know." See *Life of Adam and Eve* 30, 31, trans. Johnson. This is touched on briefly in Eldridge, *Dying Adam*, 1, 151.

14. *Life of Adam and Eve* 34, trans. Johnson; Anderson and Stone, *Synopsis*, 28.

15. Hesiod, *Works and Days*, 69–105, cf. *Theogony*, 561–612. On envy as motivator of divine-human conflict, see van Unnik, "Der Neid in der Paradiesgeschichte"; Walcot, *Envy and the Greeks*; and more generally Milobenski, *Der Neid in der Griechischen Philosophie*.

16. For ancient "care of the self" and its modern interpretation, cf. Galen, *De sanitate tuenda*; Robert Montraville Green, trans., *A Translation of Galen's Hygiene (De sanitate tuenda)* (Springfield, Ill.: Thomas, 1951); Foucault, "Technologies of the Self"; and Foucault, *History of Sexuality*, trans. Hurley, esp. 39–144.

17. Adolf Harnack, *Die Mission und Ausbreitung des Christentums in den ersten drei Jahrhunderten* (Leipzig: J. C. Hinrichs, 1908), 78; trans. Moffatt, *Mission and Expansion*, 109. Harnack's use of "disability" reflects a period before disability came to indicate a specific ideological category. I have surely profited from the recent surge of disability studies of the biblical and classical worlds, although the questions and interests that drive many such studies differ from my own. A fair representation of the methodological and ideological interest in disability studies among biblical studies scholars (and the title reveals much) is Avalos, Melcher, and Schipper, eds., *This Abled Body*. A useful perspective on disability in the ancient world, and the porous boundaries between illness, disease, and disability, is in Vlahogiannis, "'Curing' Disability"; and the recent volume edited by Moss and Schipper, *Disability*.

18. Harnack, *Mission and Expansion*, trans. Moffatt, 109.

19. On the rarity of healing (particularly miraculous) in the first three Christian centuries, see Ferngren, *Medicine and Health Care*, 64–76; and Ferngren and Amundsen, "Medicine and Christianity." Also cf. Barrett-Lennard, *Christian Healing*. Ferngren and Amundsen note the rarity of supernatural healing in Christian sources from the apostolic period and the second century, and they argue that sources increasingly represent supernatural healing in the third and into the fourth centuries (2662–70).

20. Brown, "Saint as Exemplar."

21. Drijvers, "Saint as Symbol," 151.

22. See Isaiah of Scetis, *Ascetic Discourses*, trans. Chryssavgis and Penkett, 43–45; E. A. W. Budge, trans., *Paradise or Garden of the Holy Fathers* (London: Chatto & Windus,

1907). I will return to the understanding of asceticism as a restoration of prelapsarian health, including the *Letters* and *Life of Antony* and the *Life of Paul of Thebes*, in Chapter 3. The theme is well discussed elsewhere, such as the excellent discussion (focused on diet rather than health) in Shaw, *Burden of the Flesh*, 161–219. On the reclamation of Paradise (and its ambiguities) in Syrian asceticism, see Harvey, "Embodiment in Time and Eternity," esp. 118–19. Also see Eliot, *Roads to Paradise*, to whose arguments I will return in Chapter 3. On the rather different ascetic interpretation of Gen. 2:15, Adam's tilling of the garden, see Bumazhnov, "Adam Alone in Paradise."

23. On the symbolic models of Jesus, Job, and Paul in early Christianity, see Garrett, "Paul's Thorn." Garrett's effective application of the anthropological concept of cognitive models will inform my analysis in later chapters, particularly Chapter 6.

24. Shemunkasho, *Healing*; Simon of Taibutheh, "Mystical Works."

25. Judge, "Earliest Known Use of *Monachos*"; Goehring and Boughner, "Egyptian Monasticism"; van Minnen, "Roots of Egyptian Christianity."

26. Alternatively spelled "Phathor," "Hathyr," and "Hathyrti"; see Kramer and Shelton, *Das Archiv des Nepheros*, 11. Hathor was located on the borders of the Herakleopolite and Upper Kynopolite nomes in Egypt, some 150–200 km south of modern Cairo; the precise location is unknown. See Bagnall, *Egypt in Late Antiquity*, 308; and Kramer and Shelton, *Archiv*, 11–14.

27. Goehring, "Melitian Monastic Organization."

28. The Melitian adherence of the monastery is widely accepted, although it is based largely on circumstantial evidence; see Williams, *Arius*, 32–41; Bagnall, *Egypt in Late Antiquity*, 308; Goehring, "Melitian Monastic Organization," 189, relying primarily on the Paieous archive; Hauben, "Melitian 'Church of the Martyrs'"; and Bell, *Jews and Christians*, 38–45. Samuel Rubenson disputes their Melitian affiliation and suggests that the archives could represent roughly contemporary monasteries called Hathor, each unknown from any other sources; see Rubenson, trans., *The Letters of St. Antony: Origenist Theology, Monastic Tradition, and the Making of a Saint*, Bibliotheca Historico-Ecclesiastica Lundensis 24 (Lund: Lund University Press, 1990), 121. Another skeptical critique, especially of the association of the Paphnutius archives with the Hathor Melitians, is in Barrett-Lennard, *Christian Healing after the New Testament*, 45–50. On the ambiguous boundaries between "Melitian" and "orthodox," see Goehring, "Monastic Diversity"; and Brakke, "Outside the Places, within the Truth," 468.

29. Goehring, "Melitian Monastic Organization," 193. See also Rousseau, *Pachomius*, 58–64.

30. Goehring, "Melitian Monastic Organization," 193–95. Regardless, Pachomius—or at least his biographer—was certainly familiar with the Melitian communities; see, for example, *V.Pach. SBo* 129; *V.Pach G1* 120.

31. The fragments are preserved in an eleventh-century Coptic miscellany. Pachomius's writings are edited in various places: Greek and Coptic texts are edited by Hans Quecke, *Die Briefe Pachoms: Griechischer Text der Handschrift W. 145 der Chester Beatty Library*, Textus Patristici et Liturgici 11 (Regensburg, 1975); Jerome's translations are found in Amand

Boon, *Pachomiana Latina*, Bureau de la Revue d'histoire ecclésiastique 7 (Louvain: Bureau de la Revue, 1932); for the Coptic fragments, see the edition of L.-Th. Lefort, *Oeuvres de s. Pachôme et de ses disciples*, CSCO 160 (Louvain: Durbecq, 1956), 26–30.

32. Joest, "Die Pachom-Briefe 1 und 2"; idem, "Die Geheimschrift Pachoms"; Wisse, "Language Mysticism." Barsanuphius, a subject of Chapter 6 in this volume, will continue the tradition of spiritual ciphers; see Bitton-Ashkelony and Kofsky, *Monastic School of Gaza*, 107–26, and the discussion of Pachomius at 110–11.

33. I use Coptic in this context as both a linguistic and a cultural category, thus comprising the Copto-Arabic tradition as well.

34. Rousseau, *Pachomius*, 43–45; Armand Veilleux, *Pachomian Koinonia*, CS 45 (Kalamazoo, Mich.: Cistercian Publications, 1980), 1:1–6. Veilleux has also further elaborated the stemma by positing two proto-lives, one of Pachomius and one of Theodore, later edited together to form the (now lost) source for the First Greek and Great Coptic *Lives*. This source-critical hypothesis is less certain. See, e.g., Rousseau, *Pachomius*, 41–42; and de Vogüé, "Saint Pachôme et son oeuvre."

35. Although there are certainly ways that one could do that in historically sensitive ways, as reflected in the important studies of Goehring, *Ascetics, Society and the Desert;* and Rousseau, *Pachomius.*

36. The textual transmission is covered in Rubenson, *Letters of St. Antony*, 15–34; see the stemma on 34. Rubenson's translation is appended to the Studies in Antiquity and Christianity reprint (Harrisburg, Pa.: Trinity Press International, 1995), 196–231. For the Georgian and Coptic critical edition, see Gérard Garitte, *Lettres de Saint Antoine: Version géorgienne et fragments coptes*, CSCO 148–49 (Louvain: L. Durbecq, 1955); and E. O. Winstedt, "The Original Text of One of St. Antony's Letters," *Journal of Theological Studies* 7 (1906): 540–45. One Syriac version, though not a critical or reliable one, is F. Nau, "La version syriaque de la première lettre de Saint Antoine," *Revue de l'Orient chrétien* 14 (1909): 282–97. I rely on Rubenson's translation of the Georgian.

37. The resurgence of interest in Antony's *Letters* owes much to Rubenson's important monograph on the subject, *Letters of St. Antony.* Drawing on his analysis, other scholars have incorporated Antony's *Letters* into more comparative and synthetic studies, notably David Brakke's recent work on demons, "Making of Monastic Demonology," at 23–32; and idem, *Demons*, 16–22.

38. An up-to-date survey of early Coptic literature in Byzantine Egypt can be found in Emmel, "Coptic Literature."

39. I accept the *Letters* as genuine. Some are still skeptical; cf. Harmless, *Desert Christians*, 81: "If these letters really come from Antony—and that is an important 'if'—then we need to adjust our picture of early monasticism and monastic literature." Harmless, however, does not give any further details on the reasons for his skepticism. Others at least have relied on a certain circularity of reasoning for dismissing the *Letters*; see Rubenson, *Letters of St. Antony*, 35–42. Rowan Williams questions their authenticity based on differences in tone and interest between Antony's *Letters* and those of Ammonas, by tradition his disciple, although allowing that there may be "an authentic underlay in the Antonian letters"; see

Williams, *Faith and Experience in Early Monasticism*, 31–34, at 34. Samuel Rubenson has argued that the two corpora are not so far apart as Williams contends; see Rubenson, "As Already Translated to the Kingdom," 271–89.

40. Rubenson, *Letters of St. Antony*, 42–46; idem, "St. Antony, 'The First Real Coptic Author,'" responding to Orlandi, "Coptic Literature," 64. On Coptic as the original language of the corpus, see Rubenson, *Letters of St. Antony*, 33–34.

41. See, for example, the discussion in Brakke, *Athanasius and the Politics of Asceticism*; Barnes, "Angel of Light or Mystic Initiate"; and Rousseau, "Antony as Teacher," 100–104. A succinct review of the arguments may be found in Urbano, "Read It Also to the Gentiles," 893–94n53. Harmless, *Desert Christians*, 112–13, provides a longer overview with a bibliography.

42. It is worth noting that many of the similarities between the *Life* and Athanasius's theology reflect Alexandrian theological tradition more generally and not uniquely Athanasian elements; see Rousseau, "Antony as Teacher," 101–2.

43. See, e.g., Perkins, *Suffering Self*, 200.

44. Kannengiesser, "Athanasius of Alexandria," esp. 490–91; Williams, "*Life of Antony*," 23; Brakke, *Demons*, 23. On the development of the biography as genre and difficulties in locating it generically, see Miller, *Biography in Late Antiquity*.

45. Tim Vivian, trans., *Histories of the Monks of Upper Egypt and the Life of Onnophrius, by Paphnutius*, CS 140 (Kalamazoo, Mich.: Cistercian Publications, 1993), 42–50.

46. A fuller bibliography of the versional evidence is in Voytenko, "Paradise Regained or Paradise Lost," 635n1.

47. British Museum Ms. Or. 7027, ed. E. A. Wallis Budge, *Coptic Martyrdoms Etc. in the Dialect of Upper Egypt*, Coptic Texts, vol. 4 (London: British Museum, 1914), 205–24. Tim Vivian has published a second translation of the *Life of Onnophrius* based on an unpublished manuscript in the Pierpont Morgan Library, New York, Codex M. 580, ff. 1V–19V, in Vivian, *Journeying into God: Seven Early Monastic Lives* (Minneapolis: Fortress Press, 1996), 166–87, published in an earlier form as "The Life of Onnophrius: A New Translation," *Coptic Church Review* 102 (1991): 99–111. While I have consulted Vivian's translation of this unpublished manuscript, I have not collated the original, and my Coptic readings are based exclusively on the London manuscript as published by Budge. At times I adopt Vivian's translation, which I sometimes alter (noted), but in some passages I offer my own.

48. Bibliographical information on these (more minor) sources is located in the relevant discussions in the chapters.

49. The Greek text is published in the Migne edition of Athanasius, *PG* 28.1487–1558; I have consulted the English translations by Elizabeth A. Castelli, "Pseudo-Athanasius: The Life and Activity of the Holy and Blessed Teacher Syncletica," in *Ascetic Behavior*, ed. Wimbush, 265–311; and Elizabeth Bryson Bongie, *The Life & Regimen of the Blessed & Holy Teacher Syncletica*, Peregrina Translation Series 21, Akathist Series 3, corrected edition (Toronto: Peregrina Publishing, 1996). I have usually preferred Bongie's translation, but other times I have provided my own translation where necessary. I use the shorthand *Life of Syncletica*. Other manuscripts attribute the *Life* to a certain Polycarp or to an Arsenius of Pegades; see Bongie, *Life & Regimen*, 5.

50. Silvas, *Asketikon of St. Basil*

51. Palladius, *HL* 38.2.

52. On intellectual connections between the Cappadocians and Evagrius, see Clark, *Origenist Controversy*, 60–61. See also Corrigan, *Evagrius and Gregory*.

53. The complicated textual transmission of Evagrius's literary corpus is presented by Claire Guillaumont, in *Évagre le pontique: Traité pratique ou le moine*, ed. Antoine Guillaumont and Claire Guillaumont, SC 170 (Paris: Cerf, 1971), 1:127–337.

54. See, e.g., Bloomfeld, *Seven Deadly Sins*, esp. 57–67. On Evagrius's ascetic theology, see Robert E. Sinkewicz, *Evagrius of Pontus: The Greek Ascetic Corpus*, Oxford Early Christian Studies (Oxford: Oxford University Press, 2003), xxi–xxxvii; and John Eudes Bamberger, *Evagrius Ponticus: The Praktikos, Chapters on Prayer*, CS 4 (Kalamazoo, Mich.: Cistercian Publications, 1970), lxxxi–xciv. A number of recent studies of Evagrius's spiritual teachings have appeared, including David Brakke's introduction to his new translation of Evagrius of Pontus, *Talking Back: A Monastic Handbook for Combating Demons*, CS 229 (Kalamazoo, Mich.: Cistercian Publications, 2009), 1–40; and Konstantinovsky, *Evagrius Ponticus*.

55. E.g., Konstantinovsky, *Evagrius Ponticus*, 22.

56. The *Letters* have not had the prominence among historians of late ancient asceticism that other hagiographic and gnomic sources have, to a large extent because of the inaccessibility of editions (even noncritical ones), a difficulty noted a generation ago by Chitty, *Desert a City*, 132–33; and Hevelone-Harper, *Disciples of the Desert*, 18. Now with the publication of a complete critical edition, interest in the monks from Gaza has grown considerably. For the critical edition with French translation, see Barsanuphius and Jean de Gaza, *Correspondance*, ed. François Neyt and Paula Angelis-Noah, trans. L. Regnault, SC 426–27, 450–51 (Paris: Cerf, 1997–2001). They have been translated into English by John Chryssavgis, *Barsanuphius and John: Letters*, 2 vols., Fathers of the Church (Washington, D.C.: Catholic University of America Press, 2007). Recent monographic treatments include Bitton-Ashkelony and Kofsky, *Monastic School of Gaza*; and Hevelone-Harper, *Disciples of the Desert*. The former is especially useful as an introduction to the literature and history of Gaza monasticism, as are also the introductory chapters of Neyt and Angelis-Noah, *Correspondance*, 1.1:11–155. Also of note are the earlier remarks of Chitty, *Desert a City*, 132–40; and Chitty's only partially completed critical edition and English translation, *Barsanuphius and John: Questions and Responses*, PO 31.3 (Paris: Firmin Didot, 1966).

57. Cf. Hevelone-Harper, *Disciples of the Desert*, 154n43.

58. A list of important topics is in Bitton-Ashkelony and Kofsky, *Monastic School of Gaza*, 84–85.

59. Hevelone-Harper, *Disciples of the Desert*, 76–77.

60. I treat the three archives connected with Hathor collectively.

61. For example, Larchet, *Theology of Illness*, trans. Breck and Breck; and Dörnemann, *Krankheit und Heilung*. The scholarly literature surveyed and ancient sources in Dörnemann are extensive.

62. To note just two examples, Peregrine Horden touches on a number of these issues in an interesting essay, "Death of Ascetics"; and Anne Elizabeth Merideth's dissertation,

"Illness and Healing in the Early Christian East," touches on some of the issues that interest me.

CHAPTER I

1. NHCI,2, 3.25–34, trans. Francis E. Williams, altered considerably, *Nag Hammadi Codex I (The Jung Codex)*, ed. Harold W. Attridge, Nag Hammadi Studies 22 (Leiden: Brill, 1985). Dating the composition of the Greek original is, typical of so many texts from Nag Hammadi, quite difficult; see Williams, *Nag Hammadi Codex I*, 27.

2. See discussion in Dankward Kirchner, *Epistula Jacobi Apocrypha: Die zweite Schrift aus Nag-Hammadi-Codex I* (Berlin: Akademie, 1989), 92; Michel Malinine et al., *Epistula Iacobi Apocrypha* (Zurich and Stuttgart: Rascher Verlag, 1968), 45; and Jan Helderman, *Die Anapausis im Evangelium Veritatis*, Nag Hammadi Studies 18 (Leiden: Brill, 1985).

3. *Lausiac History* 12.2, trans. Robert T. Meyer, *Palladius: The Lausiac History*, ACW 34 (New York: Paulist Press, 1964); Dom Cuthbert Butler, ed., *The Lausiac History of Palladius*, Texts and Studies 6.I–II (Cambridge: Cambridge University Press, 1898), 2:35. While *nosos* and *astheneia* are more common terms for illness, late ancient Christian writers came to use *pathos* also to refer to bodily illness, while previously it would have more commonly signified emotions or passions. See Lampe, *Patristic Greek Lexicon*, s.v. *pathos*; and Foucault, *History of Sexuality*, 54–55.

4. *Lausiac History* 12.3, trans. Meyer. A brief survey of dropsy is in *OED*, s.v.

5. Papias, Fragment 18, trans. Michael W. Holmes, *The Apostolic Fathers*, 3rd ed., ed. Michael W. Holmes (Grand Rapids, Mich.: Baker Book House, 2006), 316.

6. On the diverse explanations of the death of Judas more generally, see Harris, "Did Judas Really Commit Suicide?"

7. *Lausiac History* 12.3, trans. Meyer, altered. Meyer translates *xenizōmetha* as "surprised," but "puzzled" or "unable to comprehend" (LSJ⁹ s.v. *xenizō* II) captures the meaning more exactly; the readers will not just be surprised (i.e., taken unaware), but more fundamentally unable to make sense of the narrative.

8. *Lausiac History* 24.2, trans. Crislip [Cuthbert, 78]. Meyer dutifully omits the precise location of the ulcers in his translation but includes the Greek in an endnote, without translation; see LSJ⁹, s.v. *balanos*.

9. Papias, Fragment 18, trans. Holmes.

10. Also censored by the modern translator, *Lausiac History* 26.4, trans. Crislip [Cuthbert, 82].

11. See LeGoff, *Birth of Purgatory*, trans. Goldhammer, 50.

12. *Lausiac History* 24.2, trans. Meyer.

13. *Lausiac History* 24.3, trans. Meyer, altered [Cuthbert, 78].

14. *Lausiac History* 24.3, trans. Meyer [Cuthbert, 78].

15. Burrus, *Saving Shame*, 86. Merideth has also noted Palladius's interesting perspective on Benjamin and Stephen; see Merideth, "Illness and Healing," 50–53.

16. Burrus, *Saving Shame*, 85. Palladius's discussion of shame and humiliation is discussed on 86–95.

17. Rosenwein, *Emotional Communities*.

18. Burrus, *Saving Shame*, 85.

19. Cross and Livingstone, eds., *Oxford Dictionary of the Christian Church*, s.v. Chrysostom, St. John. Palladius too, I may note, had to abandon the ascetic life due to poor health (dropsy, like Benjamin) caused, he claimed, by ascetic practice; see *Lausiac History* 35.11–12.

20. *Hom. de statuis* 1.5–7, according to the NPNF numbering; *PG* 49.15–34.

21. *Hom. de statuis* 1.14ff.; *PG* 49.23–34. Cf. the hagiographer's description of Syncletica's physiology, discussed in Chapter 4.

22. *Hom. 16 de Tim.*, trans. NPNF 13, *PG* 62.585–90, at 587. Given Palladius's connections to Chrysostom, having even composed an apology for him, the *Dialogue on the Life of John Chrysostom*, it is possible that Palladius's own reactions to the tales of Benjamin and Stephen could have been influenced by Chrysostom's reflections on 1 Timothy 5:23.

23. *Hom. 26 de 2 Cor.*, trans. Chambers, NPNF; *PG* 61.575–84, at 577. On approaches to Paul's thorn, see Amundsen and Ferngren, "Perception of Disease," 2847; Price, "Illness Theodicies," 315; and Garrett, "Paul's Thorn."

24. John Cassian, *Conferences* 6.1.1, trans. Boniface Ramsey, *John Cassian: The Conferences*, ACW 57 (New York: Paulist Press, 1997); Jean Cassien, *Conférences I–VII*, ed. Dom Eugène Pichery, SC 42bis (Paris: Cerf, 2008), 368–415, at 370, 372.

25. Gregory of Nazianzus, *On His Sister Gorgonia* 15.

26. *Conferences* 6.3.2–6.3.6, 6.9.5, 6.9.7, 6.14.2. It is also worth noting that in the ancient context the distinctions between wounds and disease may be elided; the modern, biomedical distinction between wound and disease had not yet been drawn in ancient medical theory and practice. So Hippocrates or his imitator observes, "The wound, I believe, is a disease (*nousēma*)," *Diseases IV.50*, ed. Émile Littré, *Oeuvres completes d'Hippocrate*, vol. 7 (repr., Amsterdam: Hakkert, 1979), 582; trans. Guido Majno, *The Healing Hand: Man and Wound in the Ancient World* (Cambridge, Mass.: Harvard University Press, 1975), 183; also see the longer discussion 176–83.

27. *Conferences* 2.1, trans. Ramsey [Pichery, 372].

28. *Conferences* 6.3.5, trans. Ramsey [Pichery, 378].

29. Ibid.

30. Hadot, *Philosophy as a Way of Life*; Foucault, "Technologies of the Self."

31. Foucault, "Technologies of the Self," 18–19, 24–25.

32. Kleinman, *Illness Narratives*, 9.

33. *Iliad* 1.43–317; *Works and Days* 69–105.

34. Sophocles, *Philoctetes* 446–52.

35. Miseries roam the world, "bearing evils to mortals in silence, since the counselor Zeus took their voice away," in *Works and Days* 103–5, trans. Glenn W. Most, *Hesiod: Theogony, Works and Days, Testimonia,* Loeb Classical Library (Cambridge, Mass.: Harvard University Press, 2006).

36. It may be worth noting that contemporary medical anthropology and "medical

humanities" more generally—which to some extent informs the present study—are decidedly eclectic in the sources from which they draw; we see this in the frequently cited studies of Frank, *Wounded Storyteller*, and Hawkins, *Reconstructing Illness*.

37. Kleinberg, *Flesh Made Word*, 119.

38. This latter trend is described by Burrus, *Saving Shame*, 84–107, as part of the Christian and ascetic refashioning of shame.

39. Malina, "Pain, Power, and Personhood"; Frank, *Wounded Storyteller*, 33–35.

40. See Glucklich's phenomenologically informed study of religious hurting, *Sacred Pain*; and idem, "Self and Sacrifice." Also, for a view from contemporary social psychology, see Baumeister, *Escaping the Self*, on which Malina, "Pain, Power, and Personhood," draws for his observations on early Christian asceticism.

41. Sontag, *Illness as Metaphor*, 3.

42. A variety of approaches to the ancient self is seen in David Brakke, Michael L. Satlow, and Steven Weitzman, eds., *Religion and the Self in Antiquity* (Bloomington: Indiana University Press, 2005). Helpful as orientation (from the same volume) is Miller, "Shifting Selves in Late Antiquity."

43. Good, *Medicine, Rationality, and Experience*, 116.

44. Harvey, "Embodiment in Time and Eternity," 106.

45. Good, *Medicine, Rationality, and Experience*, 124, based on Schutz, "On Multiple Realities."

46. Good, *Medicine, Rationality, and Experience*, 124.

47. Ibid.

48. Palladius, *Lausiac History* 2.2, trans. Meyer.

49. Good quoting Schutz, in Good, *Medicine, Rationality, and Experience*, 125.

50. Good, *Medicine, Rationality, and Experience*, 125. See also Frank, *Wounded Storyteller*, 35–37.

51. Kleinman, *Illness Narratives*, 182.

52. *V.Ant.* 19, trans. Gregg [Bartelink, 186]. Hadot discusses the common ancient interest in this sort of advice in *Philosophy as a Way of Life*, 131–33.

53. Good, *Medicine, Rationality, and Experience*, 126.

54. As Brody documents in some detail in *Stories of Sickness*, 115–20.

55. Hadot, *Philosophy as a Way of Life*, 212, 217–37.

56. Gorovitz, *Doctors' Dilemmas*, 60–62; discussed in Brody, *Stories of Sickness*, 122.

57. Good's term in *Medicine, Rationality, and Experience*, 125.

58. Overviews of approaches to asceticism may be found in Freiberger, ed., *Asceticism and Its Critics*, 2–5; and Crislip, "Asceticism."

59. Valantasis, "Constructions of Power," 797; idem, "Is the Gospel of Thomas Ascetical"; idem, "Theory of the Social Function of Asceticism."

60. Valantasis, "Constructions of Power," 798.

61. See Hadot, *La philosophie comme manière de vivre*, 144; cited in Bitton-Ashkelony and Kofsky, *Monastic School of Gaza*, 158. See further Hadot, *Philosophy as a Way of Life*, 81–213.

62. *Enkrateia* is Basil of Caesarea's usual term for asceticism in his ascetic writings, for example, as we will see in Chapter 4.

63. Frank, *Wounded Storyteller*, 30–32; idem, *At the Will of the Body*.

64. Cioran, *Fall into Time*, trans. Howard, 126, 127; italics Cioran's.

65. Frank, *Wounded Storyteller*, 30–32. Of course, as Frank notes, such stigma is not automatic, as sufferers still have the ability to transform such meanings, for which in the ancient context see the remarks of Burrus, *Saving Shame*.

66. Barash, "Who Are We?"

67. Demonic etiology is found (but is not exclusive) in the New Testament; see Price, "Illness Theodicies," 309. The prevalence of demonic etiologies for disease in later periods is somewhat contentious. A widespread and even increasing focus on demons is widely accepted by scholars, but against which (with useful bibliography), see Ferngren, *Medicine and Health Care*, 53–55.

68. See Kleinman, *Illness Narratives*, 18–30; and Turner, *Body and Society*.

69. Kleinman, *Illness Narratives*, 8.

70. *OED*, s.v., citing L. Hutcheon, *Canad. Postmodern* iv. 66, or "The imposition of a narrative or narrative-like elements on real experiences or events; presentation or interpretation in terms of a story or narrative."

71. Kleinman, *Illness Narratives*, 27.

72. Frank prefers master narratives in *Wounded Storyteller*; Garrett uses cognitive or cultural models in "Paul's Thorn," which I find more appropriate to the study of early Christian sources.

73. For the latter, see Holland and Quinn, eds., *Cultural Models*, in particular Laurie Price, "Ecuadorian Illness Stories: Cultural Knowledge in Natural Discourse," in ibid. 313–42.

74. On the identification of the thorn, see discussion in Amundsen and Ferngren, "Disease and Disease Causality," 2947; and the bibliography in Garrett, "Paul's Thorn," 83nn4–5.

75. Adela Yarbro Collins, "Paul's Disability: The Thorn in His Flesh," in *Disability*, ed. Moss and Schipper, 165–83, surveys exegetical approaches to Paul's thorn from antiquity to the present, arguing for a diagnosis of epilepsy/Sacred Disease. My thanks to Candida Moss for generously providing a copy of the chapter in proofs.

76. See Jouanna, *Hippocrates*, 182–85.

77. Garrett, "Paul's Thorn," 84.

78. Ibid., 87–96.

79. Ibid., 85.

80. See Vlahogiannis, "'Curing' Disability," 183. Vlahogiannis focuses on "disability" but notes that disability is a modern category and for the ancients was "equated with disease" (181).

81. Evidence is collected in Rose, *Staff of Oedipus*.

82. Vlahogiannis, "'Curing' Disability," 183–84, includes a range of such texts.

83. See Rubenson, "Argument and Authority."

84. For the latter, see Clark, "Health of the Spiritual Athlete."

85. Avalos, *Illness and Health Care*, 241–46.

86. See Amundsen and Ferngren, "Disease and Disease Causality," 2945; they list examples as Num. 12; 2 Sam. 12:15–18; 2 Kings 5:21–27; and 2 Chron. 21:12, 26:16–21. Parts of this earlier article have been incorporated into Ferngren, *Medicine and Health Care*; I nonetheless have preferred the earlier and more detailed discussion for my purposes here. I use Old Testament advisedly since my concern is limited to the texts' influence on Christianity.

87. Avalos, *Illness and Health Care*, 243.

88. See Amundsen and Ferngren, "Disease and Disease Causality," 2945; they list examples as 2 Kings 13:14, 20:1–11 (cf. 2 Chron. 32:24–26 and Is. 38), Ps. 73:14 (cf. 73:4), Ps. 88, Dan. 8:27, and of course Job.

89. It is worth noting that ancients read the character of Job differently than moderns do. Garrett, "Paul's Thorn," 87–91, helpfully contrasts ancient interpretation of Job as a cultural model of affliction with modern approaches.

90. E.g., Luke 13:1–5 and John 9:3, discussed in Price, "Illness Theodicies," 311.

91. As Amundsen and Ferngren point out in "Disease and Disease Causality," 2949–50. The common assumption of the New Testament's overwhelming focus on demons may be seen in Böcher, *Christus Exorcista*; and also Price, "Illness Theodicies."

92. Amundsen and Ferngren, "Disease and Disease Causality," 2952, although I disagree with their contention that this atheological perspective necessarily implies a belief in "natural" causation rather than demonic.

93. For example, James O'Donnell, *Augustine: A New Biography* (New York: Ecco, 2005), 108, notes that Augustine did not find in illness a major source for anthropological or theological reflection.

94. Cf. Gilman, *Disease and Representation*. On the denigration of the deformed and "disabled" in antiquity, cf. Garland, *Eye of the Beholder*, 73–104.

95. Cioran, *Fall into Time*, 130.

CHAPTER 2

1. Norman Russell, *Lives of the Desert Fathers*, CS 34 (Kalamazoo, Mich.: Cistercian Publications, 1980), 134, citing Butler, *Lausiac History*, 2:185n7.

2. It should be noted that these are "ideal types." Monasteries existed on a continuum of solitary to communal, sometimes incorporating more than one lifestyle under their aegis.

3. *Hist. mon.* 17.1–2, trans. Russell, ed. André-Jean Festugière, *Historia Monachorum in Aegypto*, Subsidia Hagiographica 53 (Brussels: Société des Bollandistes, 1971), 113.

4. The dialectic in composition and transmission of late ancient pilgrimage narratives has been sensitively described by Frank, *Memory of the Eyes*, 35–78; and idem, "Miracles, Monks, and Monuments, 483–505.

5. Frank, *Memory of the Eyes*, 38.

6. *Hist. mon.* 17.3, trans. Russell; ed. Festugière, *Historia Monachorum in Aegypto*, 114.

7. For which see Frank, *Memory of the Eyes*, 45–49.

8. *V.Pauli* 8, trans. Paul B. Harvey, Jr., "Jerome, Life of Paul, the First Hermit," in *Ascetic Behavior in Greco-Roman Antiquity*, ed. Wimbush, 357–69.

9. Thus attracting the disdain of some modern interpreters; see discussion in Frank, *Memory of the Eyes*, 44.

10. *Hist. mon.*, Epilogue 1, trans. Russell.

11. Such wonders of the far south of Egypt are described in the contemporary *Histories of the Monks of Upper Egypt* and the *Life of Onnophrius* by Paphnutius, the latter of which is discussed in Chapter 3.

12. *Hist. mon.* 1.17.

13. *Hist. mon.* 2.1 ; trans. Russell, 7.1.

14. *Hist. mon.* 8.2, 10.1. On fecal onomastics in Egypt, see the anthropologically informed approach of Hobson, "Naming Practices in Roman Egypt," discussed in Bagnall, *Reading Papyri*, 99–101.

15. *Hist. mon.* 20.13.

16. *Hist. mon.* 13.7–8, trans. Russell, corrected; ed. Festugière, *Historia Monachorum in Aegypto*, 100. Such miraculous healing through harsh asceticism is also described for Piammonas; see *Hist. mon.* 25.3.

17. The "other" physiology of the saint may be found also in the description of Amma Syncletica's relationship with food in the *Life and Teachings*, discussed in Chapter 4.

18. Miller, *Corporeal Imagination*, 122. Miller cites Harpham's generalization that in Christian asceticism "the disfigured was figured as desirable"; see Harpham, *Ascetic Imperative*, 27.

19. *Hist. mon.* 1.12, 1.16, 2.6, 6.1, 7.2, 7.7, 9.11, 10.1, 13.8–9, 20.12 (trampling on snakes and scorpions), 21.17, 26.

20. *Hist. mon.* 10.24.

21. "Good" deaths: *Hist. mon.* 1.65, 10.15, 10.19, 11.4, 11.8. The exception in the *History* is unnamed monks who skipped the Synaxis (or mass); in this story attributed to Piammonas the presiding angel erased their name from the book of life, and they all died thirteen days later; see 25.3.

22. Brown, *Body and Society*, 220–24. A useful perspective on this same phenomenon informed by ancient physiognomy is Shaw, "*Askesis* and the Appearance of Holiness."

23. Clark, "Health of the Spiritual Athlete."

24. Other early sources are exclusively documentary, such as the archive of another Melitian monk Paieous (published by H. I. Bell in *P.Lond*. VI) dated to the 330s and the rare mention of a *monakhos* in other documentary papyri, e.g., in the well-known letter discussed by Judge, "Earliest Known Use"; and idem, "Fourth-Century Monasticism in the Papyri." No doubt the list could be expanded. Papyri are cited in accordance with Oates et al., *Checklist of Greek, Latin, Demotic and Coptic Papyri, Ostraca and Tablets*, http://scriptorium.lib.duke.edu/papyrus/texts/clist.html (last accessed April 2004).

25. The archives of Paieous and Paphnutius are published in Bell, *Jews and Christians* (*P.Lond*. VI 1913–21 [Paieous] and 1923–29 [Paphnutius]). The archive of Nepheros is

published in Kramer and Shelton, *Das Archiv des Nepheros*, 35–83 (*P.Neph.*). The Melitian affiliation of Hathor in the time of Paieous is clear from his archive, while the Melitian affiliation of Nepheros is argued circumstantially by Kramer and Shelton, *Das Archiv des Nepheros*, 11–14, which Goehring, "Melitian Monastic Organization," 189, has said may be used "cautiously" as a supplement to the early archives. The Paphnutius archive, which was partially included in the same "lot" of papyri as the Paieous, probably comes from the same community. Bagnall, *Egypt in Late Antiquity*, 308, concludes that the three archives should be understood as representative of the same monastery and of the Melitian church, as does Goehring in a later comment in the introduction to his collection of papers, *Ascetics, Society, and the Desert*, 7. In the discussion here I follow the general consensus that the three archives are connected to the same monastery over the course of several decades. Yet their provenance from a single community is not central to my argument. For more discussion, see Goehring, "Monastic Diversity," 201–3. Earlier editors were more circumspect about the relationship of Paphnutius to the Melitians; cf. the editio princeps of Bell, *Jews and Christians*, 100–103.

26. Goehring, "Through a Glass Darkly."

27. As Roger Bagnall emphasizes, while papyri were preserved and discovered by chance, the data they provide are by no means randomized; rather they depend on a host of conditions, not least of which are the relative infrequency of literacy and the environmental factors that allow for the preservation of written artifacts in certain locales while precluding their preservation in others; see Bagnall, *Egypt in Late Antiquity*, 4–6; and idem, *Reading Papyri*, 22–29.

28. Brown, *Authority and the Sacred*; idem, "Rise and Function of the Holy Man in Late Antiquity"; idem, "Town, Village and Holy Man"; Brakke, *Athanasius and Asceticism*, 201–65; and Goehring, *Ascetics, Society, and the Desert*.

29. *P.Lond.* VI 1916.30, 1921.30; *P.Neph.* 4.29–30, 9.17–22, 12.21–22. Here and elsewhere in transcriptions of Greek words I have not preserved the papyrological notations for the few letters in lacunae in the papyri and unsure letters, i.e., letters in brackets or dotted in the editio princeps. The editions of Bell, *Jews and Christians*; and Kramer and Shelton, *Das Archive des Nepheros,* are readily available for those interested.

30. *P.Neph.* 1.30–31, 2.10–12, 5.23–25, 7.12–13; *P.Lond.* VI 1923.19–21, 1925.23–24, 1928.8–11.

31. *P.Lond.* VI 1928.8–11, 1929.19–21; *P.Neph.* 1.30–31, 5.23–25, 7.12–13, 12.21–22, 13.16–19, 14.8–10.

32. *P.Lond.* VI 1928.8–11. Also *P.Lond.* VI 1929.19–21.

33. *P.Lond.* VI 1928, trans. Robert Boughner, in *Ascetic Behavior in Greco-Roman Antiquity*, ed. Wimbush, 458–63. The oil in question is holy oil, blessed by the monk and then sent to the person in need; it was apparently believed efficacious even far from the holy man. On such use of oil in healing in late ancient Egypt, see Barrett-Lennard, *Christian Healing*, 62–66; and idem, "Request for Prayer for Healing."

34. Bagnall, *Egypt in Late Antiquity*, 186, 247–48; Barrett-Lennard, "Request for Prayer for Healing"; Förster, "Christlicher Trostbrief."

35. Bagnall, *Egypt in Late Antiquity*, 182; cf. the quantitative analysis in Bagnall and Frier, *Demography of Roman Egypt*.

36. Bagnall, *Egypt in Late Antiquity*, 185.

37. Rosenwein, *Emotional Communities*, 28–29. Tonio Sebastian Richter touches on a similar issue of the relative "functional" and "psychological truth" of emotional expression in Coptic letters; to wit the "performative mode" of expression that we see in the Hathor letters, much like Rosenwein's analysis, reveals a "functional" truth. My thanks to Dr. Richter for sharing his unpublished paper ". . . Jealously We Looked at All the Sound Children Who Are Their Parents' Comfort. . . .: Pleasant and Unpleasant Emotions in Coptic Legal Documents" (paper presented at the 26th International Congress of Papyrology, Geneva, Switzerland, August 16–21, 2010).

38. Rosenwein, *Emotional Communities*, 29.

39. Bagnall, *Egypt in Late Antiquity*, 185.

40. Goehring, "Melitian Monastic Organization," 193; also Rousseau, *Pachomius*, 58–64. Whether Pachomius influenced the formation of such Melitian coenobia as that of Hathor or was influenced by them (or whether the systems developed independently) remains an open question; see Goehring, "Melitian Monastic Organization," 193–95.

41. Seen, for example, in *V.Pach. SBo* 129=*V.Pach. G1* 120.

42. *V.Pach. SBo* 28; *V.Pach. G1* 30, 31; cf. Goehring, "Pachomius's Vision of Heresy."

43. E.g., *Praecepta* 56, 57, 63, 64, 84, 86, 118.

44. *V.Pach. G1* 83, 122; Rousseau, *Pachomius*, 74–75.

45. Rousseau, *Pachomius*, 65–67, 98–99, 101–2.

46. *Letter* 5.11, citing Gal. 6:2.

47. *Letter* 5.2, trans. Veilleux.

48. *Letter* 5.2, citing 1 Tim. 5:8, trans. Veilleux.

49. Rousseau, *Pachomius*, 66.

50. Krawiec, *Shenoute*, 20–27; idem, "From the Womb of the Church."

51. *Praecepta* 129.

52. It is additionally possible that the coenobitic offices of nurses or infirmarians— attested in later Pachomian and otherwise coenobitic sources—had not yet fully developed. On nurses and other "ministers for the sick," see Crislip, *From Monastery to Hospital*, 14–18.

53. *Letter* 5.11, trans. Veilleux, 66, quoting Gal. 6:2, Is. 53:4, Matt. 8:17.

54. Discussed in Chapter 1. For Paul's use of Christ crucified as a model for sickness behavior, see Garrett, "Paul's Thorn."

55. Clark, *Origenist Controversy*, 43–84.

56. E.g., from Brakke, "Making of Monastic Demonology"; idem, *Demons and the Making of the Monk*.

57. My summary is drawn from and indebted to the longer discussion in Rubenson, *Letters of St. Antony*, 59–88.

58. See Rubenson, *Letters of St. Antony*, 141–42, 167.

59. I depend here on Rubenson's analysis in *Letters of St. Antony*, 51–58.

60. Rubenson, *Letters of St. Antony*, 48, 54.

61. Antony, *Letters* 2.1, 3.3, 5.1, 6.1, trans. Rubenson. In all passages that follow I cite Rubenson's translation.

62. Such as his Origenism and his thought on demons. Healing and illness are not dealt with in Rubenson's foundational monograph on the *Letters*; see Rubenson, *Letters of St. Antony*.

63. Harnack, *Mission*, 103–4.

64. For a full bibliography on the use of Christus medicus imagery as well as detailed discussion on its application in Shenoute's homilies, which I do not discuss in this book, see Crislip, "Shenoute of Atripe."

65. Dörnemann's survey *Krankheit und Heilung* is a useful gateway to early Alexandrian medical Christology.

66. The theme is documented most fully by Fernández, *Cristo medico según Orígenes*.

67. Rubenson, *Letters of St. Antony*, 59–69.

68. Ibid., 74n3.

69. Antony, *Letter* 2.4–5, trans. Rubenson. Also see *Letter* 3.10–11: "But through much weakness, the heaviness of the body and the concern for evil the law of promise has grown cold and the faculties of the mind have been worn out. Thus they have not been able to discover themselves as they were created, namely as an eternal substance, which is not dissolved with the body but still cannot be freed through its own righteousness," trans. Rubenson, corrected.

70. Wound is probably the Greek-Coptic *plēgē*; cf. the similar wording in *Letter* 4.10, for which the Coptic is preserved, the "unhealable wound" (*ouplēgē nattalco*), Garitte, *Lettres d'Antoine*, 46.

71. On the *pathē* in Antony's *Letters*, see Rubenson, *Letters of St. Antony*, 67.

72. See the discussion in Hankinson, "Actions and Passions," esp. 187–88.

73. *Letter* 6.30–42. See Rubenson's comments on passions and "movements," *pathē* and *kinēseis*, in Antony's thought (Rubenson, *Letters of St. Antony*, 66–67). Antony's Coptic original refers to *pathos* in *Letter* 7.8 (Garitte's numeration): *šantncmcom erjoeis ejnpathos nim*, "until we are able to restrain all passions," trans. Rubenson. We may also note that demons urge monks to attempt what they are unable to do in the *Life of Antony* 25.

74. *Letter* 3.9, trans. Rubenson.

75. *Letter* 3.10–12, trans. Rubenson, corrected.

76. *Letter* 3.15–16, trans. Rubenson. Also cf. *Letters* 2.9–10, 5.17–19, 6.8–9.

77. *Letter* 2.11–12, trans. Rubenson; cf. 5.17–19.

78. *Letters* 3.15, 3.21, 6.11.

79. Jer. 8:22 and 51:9 [28:9 LXX], trans. per Rubenson.

80. Antony speaks regularly of the *gnōsis* from Christ or the Holy Spirit, i.e., "Those who had come close, by being taught by the Holy Spirit, came to know themselves in their spiritual essence" [4.10]; cf. "He who knows himself knows God, he who knows God must worship him as is proper" [4.15], or "Truly, my beloved, it is great for you to attempt to understand the spiritual essence, in which there is neither man nor woman; rather it is an immortal essence, which has a beginning but no end. You ought to know how it is utterly

fallen into this humiliation and great confusion, which has come upon all of us" (6.5–6, trans. Rubenson).

81. For Origen's use of *archiatros* and related terminology, see Dörnemann, *Krankheit und Heilung*, 146–48.

82. *Letters* 3.16, 3.21, 6.11, trans. Rubenson.

83. The evidence from early Christian papyri, including the Hathor archives, is discussed in Barrett-Lennard, *Christian Healing after the New Testament*.

84. *Letters* 2.23 (also see 5.28), 3.25, trans. Rubenson.

85. *Letter* 2.23, cf. 3.25, trans. Rubenson.

86. E.g., "I lament over those who speak in the name of Jesus but act according to the will of their own hearts and bodies. Over those who have considered the lengthy time, their hearts failing them, and who have laid off the habit of godliness and become like beasts, I cry" (*Letter* 3.35–36, trans. Rubenson). Of Arius, Antony writes, "That man has begun a great task, an unhealable wound" (*Letter* 4.18, trans. Rubenson). Here the Coptic text is extant from the Naples codex, *prōme oun etmmau afhitootf eounoc nkaiphalaion, ouplēgē nattalco* (Garitte, *Lettres d'Antoine*, 45–46).

87. *Letter* 5.11–14, trans. Rubenson.

88. *Letter* 7.46, trans. Rubenson, altered.

89. *Letter* 1.1–17, trans. Rubenson.

90. *Letter* 1.20–22, trans. Rubenson.

91. *Letter* 1.23–24, trans. Rubenson.

92. *Letter* 1.77–78, trans. Rubenson.

93. *Letter* 1.29, trans. Rubenson.

94. *Letters* 1.30, 1.32, citing 1 Cor. 9:27, trans. Rubenson.

95. *Letter* 1.35–42; see Brakke, "Making of Monastic Demonology," 23–32.

96. *Letter* 1.47–49, trans. Rubenson, corrected.

97. *Letter* 1.72, trans. Rubenson.

98. *Letter* 1.49–73, trans. Rubenson.

99. The motif of sick humanity refusing to accept the cure of Christ the physician is reflected elsewhere in Egyptian monasticism, such as in the writings of Shenoute of Atripe; see Crislip, "Shenoute of Atripe."

CHAPTER 3

1. Perkins, *Suffering Self*, 200.

2. Kannengiesser, "Athanasius of Alexandria," esp. 490–91.

3. See discussion in Rousseau, "Antony as Teacher," 104–6, not specifically about the issue of prelapsarian health. He notes, "My own suggestion is that the differences [between the portrayals of Antony as teacher in the *Life* and *Letters*] are not, in any case, so great" (105).

4. *V.Ant.* 10.

5. *V.Ant.* 7 [Bartelink, 152]; LSJ⁹, s.v. *tonos.* Also see Sandbach, *Stoics,* 78; and Graver, *Stoicism and Emotion,* 18–20. On other possible Stoic parallels to Athanasius's characterization of Antony, see Brakke, *Demons,* 39–40.

6. Bartelink in his critical edition *Vie d'Antoine,* 153n2, accepts *noun* (mind) over the reading of *tonon* in most manuscripts, as *tēs psykhēs ho nous* is a phrase used by Athanasius elsewhere. I prefer the reading of *tonon,* which I think has an equal claim as the *lectio difficilior.* I acknowledge, however, that my comments might, if Bartelink is correct, refer more properly to a later stage in the manuscript transmission rather than the author of the *Life* himself.

7. *V.Ant.* 8.

8. Antony is "[s]truck and wounded" (*mastizomenos kai kentoumenos*) (*V.Ant.* 9, trans. Gregg [Bartelink, 160]).

9. *V.Ant.* 10, trans. Gregg [Bartelink, 162].

10. *V.Ant.* 10, trans. Gregg [Bartelink, 164].

11. *V.Ant.* Introduction, trans. Gregg [Bartelink, 126].

12. *V.Ant.* Introduction, trans. Gregg [Bartelink, 128].

13. *Zēlōsai tēn ekeinou prothesin, V.Ant.* Introduction, trans. Gregg [Bartelink, 126].

14. *V.Ant.* Introduction, trans. Gregg [Bartelink, 126].

15. *V.Ant.* 94, trans. Gregg [Bartelink, 376].

16. Gregory of Nazianzus, *Oration* 21.5.6–7.

17. Pseudo-Athanasius, *De virginitate* 5, 6, 7, ed. Eduard Freiherrn Von der Goltz, *Logos Sōtērias pros tēn Parthenon (De virginitate), Eine echte Schrift des Athanasius, TU* 14 (1905), 38, 39–40, 41. Von der Goltz argued for the treatise's authenticity, but see the current negative consensus as summarized in Johannes Quasten, *Patrology,* vol. 3 (Westminster, Md.: Newman Press, 1950), 45.

18. Martin, *Corinthian Body,* 3–37, esp. 7–15; P. N. Singer, trans., *Galen: Selected Works,* Oxford World's Classics (Oxford: Oxford University Press, 1997), xxxvi–xxxix.

19. Martin, *Corinthian Body,* 8.

20. Singer, trans., *Galen,* 154; Galen, *Opera omnia,* ed. K. G. Kühn, 22 vols. (Leipzig, 1821–33; repr., Hildesheim: G. Olms, 1964–65), 4:776–77. See, for example, the discussion in White, "Moral Pathology," 295.

21. Fruitful expositions of the significant intersections between Greco-Roman moral and medical discourse and Christian asceticism in the times of Paul and in late antiquity may be found in Martin, *Corinthian Body,* e.g., 3–37, 106–36; and Shaw, *Burden of the Flesh,* 27–124.

22. This is especially prevalent in the wake of Galen's influential reinterpretation of Hippocratic medicine; see Singer's introduction to *Galen,* xxxvi–xlii; and Galen, *Affections and Errors of the Soul; The Soul's Dependence on the Body,* in *Galen,* trans. Singer. Also cf. Foucault, *History of Sexuality,* 105–44.

23. Such descriptions are also rooted in the related practice of physiognomy. See especially Shaw, *Burden of the Flesh,* 39–40, which discusses the appearance of Socrates and Diogenes. Also see idem, "*Askesis* and the Appearance of Holiness"; and (for pagan

"athletes") Clark, "Health of the Spiritual Athlete." On the "most handsome and godlike" appearance of Pythagoras, see Iamblichus, *On the Pythagorean Life* 10, trans. John Dillon and Jackson Hershbell, *On the Pythagorean Way of Life*, Texts and Translations 29, Graeco-Roman Religion Series 11 (Atlanta: Scholars Press, 1990). Connections between the *Lives* of Antony and Iamblichus are surveyed in George, "Tugenden im Vergleich"; and for the extraordinary health of ascetic Egyptian priests, see Porphyry, *On Abstinence* 4:6–8, trans. Anitra Bingham Kolenkow, "Chaeremon the Stoic on Egyptian Temple Askesis," in *Ascetic Behavior*, ed. Wimbush, 389–92.

24. Temkin, *Hippocrates*, 154.

25. E.g., Plutarch, *De sanitate tuenda*; see Shaw, *Burden of the Flesh*, 44.

26. *Aphorisms* 1.4, trans. Chadwick and Mann, in *Hippocratic Writings*, ed. Lloyd; *Hippocrates*, ed. Jones.

27. Although sexual abstinence, unlike teetotalism and avoidance of bathing, was seen as healthful by certain physicians, such as the Roman "methodist" (a rival medical school to that of Galen) Soranus of Ephesus in his *Gynecology*, trans. Temkin, 27–30.

28. Fragment A, 4, trans. Brakke, *Athanasius*, 311; ed. Franz Diekamp, *Analecta Patristica*, Orientalia Lovaniensia Analecta 117 (Rome: Pont. Institutum Orientalium Studiorum, 1938), 5–8.

29. Brakke, *Athanasius*, 243–44.

30. *V.Ant.* 14, trans. Gregg [Bartelink, 172].

31. Brakke, *Athanasius*, 239–44; idem, *Demons*, 33.

32. Brakke, *Athanasius*, 243.

33. *V.Ant.* 93, trans. Gregg [Bartelink, 372, 374].

34. Deut. 34:7 (NRSV). It also concords nicely with the moral valuations of sickness and health in the Old Testament; see Amundsen and Ferngren, "Perception of Disease," esp. 2945.

35. *V.Ant.* 93, trans. Gregg [Bartelink, 374].

36. Kannengiesser, "Athanasius of Alexandria," 486.

37. On "collective biography," see Miller, "Strategies of Representations."

38. *V.Pauli* 1, trans. Paul B. Harvey, "Jerome, *Life of Paul, the First Hermit*," in *Ascetic Behavior*, ed. Wimbush, 357–69, at 360. Harvey gives the date of composition for the Latin *Life* as 377, at 358; *PL* 23:17–30. On the educated, monastic audience of the *Life*, see Davis, "Jerome's *Life of Paul*," 26–28.

39. See the summary in Harvey, "Jerome, *Life of Paul*," 358–59; and discussion in Davis, "Jerome's *Life of Paul*," 30.

40. *V.Pauli* 4, 5, trans. Harvey. The Edenic symbolism of the cave is also seen in the contemporary (also fourth-century) *Cave of Treasures*, preserved in Syriac, which describes the home of Adam and Eve after their expulsion as a cave at the edge of Eden.

41. Jerome places his first withdrawal to his country estate around the age of 16, his flight to the desert shortly thereafter, and his death at the age of 113.

42. *V.Pauli* 9, 16.

43. In Eliot, *Roads to Paradise*, 131–67, in the chapter titled "The Ascent: Paradise

Regained," the elements are described as food, sex, and the peaceable kingdom. Issues of paradisiacal health are absent from the study, so also see the table of themes and motifs (which mentions the dead saint's uncorrupted body) (215), and the index (237–44). Nor does it figure in the more recent Weingarten, *Saint's Saints*, 17–80, which is more concerned with showing an alleged influence of Rabbinic *aggadah* on Jerome's compositions.

44. Jerome's relationship with Paul of Concordia is discussed in Kelly, *Jerome*, 33, 60, 62. The evidence (epigraphic and otherwise) for the life of Paul of Concordia is assembled in Zovatto, "Paolo da Concordia," 165, 80; Rebenich, "Inventing an Ascetic Hero," 20–22; and Davis, "Jerome's *Life of Paul*," 27.

45. On Jerome's use of medical language, see Pease, "Medical Allusions."

46. Jerome, *Letter* 10.2., trans. W. H. Fremantle, G. Lewis, and W. G. Martley, NPNF, 2nd series, vol. 6, ed. Philip Schaff and Henry Wace (Buffalo, N.Y.: Christian Literature Publishing Co., 1893); Sancti Eusebii Hieronymi, *Epistulae*, ed. Isidorus Hilberg, CSEL 54 (Vienna: Österreichischen Akademie der Wissenschaften, 1996), 37.

47. Jerome, *Letter* 10.1.

48. Jerome, *Letter* 10.3.

49. *V.Pauli* 7.

50. *V.Pauli* 15, trans. Harvey.

51. *Vita Hilarionis 46*.

52. *V.Pauli* 13, 12, trans. Harvey, *PL* 23:26.

53. Voytenko, "Paradise Regained or Paradise Lost," 635–36.

54. Any direct relationship is tenuous. Eliot hypothetically posited Jerome's dependence on Paphnutius based on Émile Amelineau's dating of the *Life of Onnophrius* to the mid-fourth century, which is surely wrong; see Eliot, *Roads to Paradise*, e.g., 58, 164, 204. See the discussion in Weingarten, *Saint's Saints*, 27–28, which is more concerned to deny the influence of Paphnutius on Jerome than vice versa. Yet the two hagiographies share a number of motifs: Paphnutius discovers a dead monk still kneeling in prayer, as Antony finds Paul (2); the hermits Timothy and Onnophrius are both described as clothed simply with their own hair (3, 10); Timothy's desert retreat is the same as Paul's, a cave with a spring and a date palm inside (7); Elijah and John the Baptist are adduced as precursors to monasticism (11); Onnophrius heads to the desert with the same motivation as Antony (11); Onnophrius sends away Paphnutius before his death much as Paul dispatches Antony (21); birds feed Timothy and his companions four loaves daily, except when Paphnutius visits and they bring a fifth (25). Here and elsewhere paragraph numbers are according to Vivian's translation.

55. *V.Onn.* 2, fol. 1b [Budge, 206].

56. *V.Onn.* 3, fol. 2a [Budge, 206].

57. *V.Onn.* 6, fol. 3b [Budge, 207]. See also Crislip, "Envy and Anger," esp. 294–96.

58. "The air provides me a temperate climate," *erepaēr ti nai noukrasis esšēš* (*V.Onn.* 7, fol. 4b [Budge, 208]).

59. *V.Onn.* 8, fol. 4b [Budge, 208], trans. Vivian, altered.

60. *V.Ant.* 9, trans. Gregg, altered [Bartelink, 160].

61. *V.Ant.* 10, trans. Gregg [Bartelink, 162–64]. On the Athanasian theological context of the beam of light, see Gregg, *Life of Antony*, 136n24; and *V.Onn.* 8, trans. Vivian, fol. 4b [Budge, 208]. "A man radiant with glory" could be translated more simply as "a very glorious man."

62. Although Timothy does refer to the "attacks of the demons" later, there is no indication that his particular health complaints in the following episode are in any way connected to the demons; see *V.Onn.* 9, trans. Vivian, fol. 5b [Budge, 209].

63. *V.Onn.* 8, trans. Vivian, altered, fol. 5a–b [Budge, 208–9]. I have diverged in a number of passages from Vivian's translation.

64. *V.Onn.* 9, 10, fol. 6a [Budge, 209].

65. *V.Onn.* 10, fol. 6b [Budge, 210], trans. Vivian, which I have altered significantly.

66. *V.Onn.* 11, fols. 7b–8a [Budge, 211].

67. *V.Onn.* 12, fols. 8a–9a [Budge, 211–12], trans. Vivian, altered.

68. *V.Onn.* 17, fol. 12a [Budge, 215], trans. Vivian.

69. *V.Onn.* 16, fol. 10b [Budge, 213], trans. Vivian, altered.

70. *V.Onn.* 16, fols. 10b–11a [Budge, 213–14], trans. Vivian, altered.

71. *V.Onn.* 17, fols. 11b–12a [Budge, 214–25], trans. Vivian, altered.

72. *V.Onn.* 18, fol. 12a [Budge, 215], trans. Vivian.

73. The contrast between natural (*physikē*) and nonnatural (*mē physikē*) illness in another monastic context is discussed in Crislip, "Sin of Sloth."

74. A point ignored by Vivian, *Journeying into God*, 166–72; as in Eliot, *Roads to Paradise*.

75. Voytenko, "Paradise Regained or Paradise Lost."

76. *V.Onn.* 24, fol. 15a–15b [Budge, 217–18].

77. *V.Onn.* 27, fol. 16b [Budge, 218–19], trans. Vivian.

78. *V.Onn.* 34, fol. 20a–20b [Budge, 222], trans. Vivian.

79. *V.Onn.* 35, fol. 21a [Budge, 222].

80. *V.Ant.* Introduction [Bartelink 1994, 124], *V.Ant.* Introduction [trans. Gregg 1980, 29], *V.Ant.* 94 [trans. Gregg 1980, 99], Gregory of Nazianzus, *Oration* 21.5.6–7. See discussion above.

81. Augustine, *Confessions* 8.6; see discussion in Kannengiesser, "Athanasius of Alexandria," 485–86. The few references to the *monasterium Mediolanii* are discussed by James J. O'Donnell in Augustine, *Confessions*, vol. 3 (Oxford: Clarendon Press, 1992), 40.

82. Augustine, *Confessions* 8.6, trans. Pine-Coffin.

83. Pace Horden, who argues that "it is time we ceased marveling aimlessly at the physical stamina and frequent longevity of the great Byzantine ascetics." But his point appears not to question the ideological or literary basis of these depictions rather than to accept them as a sort of positivist evidence: "I do not suggest that being a Stylite was merely a way of working off surplus flab. But I do urge that we scrutinize the anthropology of asceticism—from which we may well learn that once an ascetic has absolutely conquered his body the illnesses he contracts are often comparatively minor and readily endured" (Horden, "Death of Ascetics," 50). The primary evidence for this claim is early ethnography of Indian asceticism; see 50n.

CHAPTER 4

1. An earlier version of portions of this chapter was published as Crislip, "I Have Chosen Sickness," in *Asceticism and Its Critics,* ed. Freiberger, 179–209. The present chapter is significantly revised and augmented from the earlier version.

2. Jerome, *Letter* 24.3, trans. W. H. Fremantle, G. Lewis, and W. G. Martley, NPNF, 2nd ser., vol. 6, ed. Philip Schaff and Henry Wace (Buffalo, N.Y.: Christian Literature Publishing, 1893), S. Hieronymi, *Epistulae,* CSEL 54, 214–17. For more context, see Cain, *Letters of Jerome,* 71–74.

3. Jerome, *Letter* 24.3, trans. Fremantle et al. Note that this description of ascetic diet differs from that of the *Life* of Syncletica, who even from a young age is comforted by ascetic diet but falls ill when she takes richer foods. See *V.Syn.* 10, noted by Crislip, "I Have Chosen Sickness," 193; also see Burrus, *Saving Shame,* 103.

4. Jerome, *Letter* 24.4, trans. Fremantle et al. [Hilberg, 216].

5. See discussion in Garrett, "Paul's Thorn."

6. Jerome, *Letter* 38.2, trans. Fremantle et al.

7. Jerome, *Letter* 39.2, trans. Fremantle et al.

8. Ibid.

9. Cain, *Letters of Jerome,* 99–128.

10. Jerome, *Letter* 39.6, trans. Fremantle et al., altered [Hilberg, 306]. This episode has been studied (with different interests) also by Cooper, *Virgin and the Bride,* 92–115; Cain, *Letters of Jerome,* 74–76, 101–5; and Shaw, *Burden of the Flesh,* 106–7.

11. There are many excellent introductions to the lifestyles in these communities. See, e.g., Regnault, *La vie quotidienne.* The collections, however, include sayings attributed to later and non-Egyptian fathers as well.

12. Greek collections of *Apophthegmata patrum* include Alphabetical, *PG* 65.71–440; Anonymous, ed. F. Nau, "Histoires des solitaires égyptiens," *Revue de l'Orient Chrétien* 13 (1908): 47–57, 14 (1909): 357–79, 17 (1912): 204–11, 18 (1913): 137–46; and Jean-Claude Guy, *Recherches sur la tradition grecque des Apophthegmata patrum,* Subsidia Hagiographica 36 (Brussels: Société des Bollandistes, 1962). Gould, *Desert Fathers,* 5–25, provides a useful overview of the textual transmission of the *Apophthegmata patrum.* The *Apophthegmata* were also transmitted in numerous collections in other languages, e.g., Latin, Coptic, and Syriac; see Bousset, *Apophthegmata,* 1–208. For the few apophthegmata cited in this study, I use the numeration in the convenient translation by Benedicta Ward, *The Sayings of the Desert Fathers,* CS 59 (Kalamazoo, Mich.: Cistercian Publications, 1975).

13. *Apoph. pat.* (alph.) Joseph of Thebes (*PG* 65.241).

14. Including the characteristic list of three virtues; cf. *Apoph. pat.* (alph.) Poemen 150.

15. For the variety of ways that monks achieved withdrawal (*anakhōrēsis*) and renunciation (*apotaxis*), see Goehring, "Withdrawing from the Desert"; and idem, "Through a Glass Darkly."

16. *Lausiac History* 2.2, trans. Meyer.

17. Caused by *Mycobacterium leprae* and to be distinguished from the many other

dermatological ailments described as "leprosy" (Greek *lepra leukē, alphos*) in antiquity; see Grmek, *Diseases*, 152–76.

18. *Lausiac History* 18.4, trans. Meyer.

19. For an overview and analysis, see Doran, *The Lives of Simeon Sylites*, 36–66. For a comparison of the three narratives of an episode, see Harvey, "Sense of a Stylite." The Greek Lives of Theodoret and Antony are critically edited in Lietzmann, *Das Leben des Heiligen Symeon Stylites*, 1–78; and Canivet and Leroy-Molinghen, eds., *Théodoret de Cyr: Histoire des Moines de Syrie*.

20. Theodoret, *HR* 26.5, trans. Doran.

21. *HR* 26.5, trans Doran [Lietzmann, 4].

22. On the heightened hagiographical character of the Simeon narrative in the *Historia religiosa*, see Harvey, "Sense of a Stylite," 378. On conflict over the propriety of Simeon's behavior in a coenobitic context, see Crislip, *From Monastery to Hospital*, 96–98; and Urbainczyk, *Theodoret of Cyrrhus*, 95–102.

23. Antonius's *Life of Simeon* 5–8. In the Syriac *Life* 21, which Harvey, "Sense of a Stylite," 381, has characterized as perhaps "the official or 'authorized' story of Simeon," the episode is greatly condensed,. See the comparison in Doran, trans., *Lives of Simeon Stylites*, 63–65.

24. Jacob of Serug (c. 449–521), *Homily on Simeon the Stylite*, in *Ascetic Behavior*, ed. Wimbush, 20–25; see discussion in Harvey, *Scenting Salvation*, 216–17.

25. For Basil's influence on the charitable activities of the church (and Basilian monasticism's prominent role in providing such charities), see Karayannopoulos, "St. Basil's Social Activity"; and Crislip, *From Monastery to Hospital*, 100–142.

26. Benoît Gain includes an appendix listing by date all of the references to Basil's own illnesses in his correspondence in *L'Église de Cappadoce*, 397–98. In his ordering the references span A.D. 357 to late 378, with the vast majority from 373 to 378. Perkins, *Suffering Self*, 173–89, offers a thoughtful take on Aelius Aristides.

27. *Letters* 1, 9, 27, 30, 94, 112, 138, 136, 137, 162, 200, 163, 201, 193, 202, 143, listed in order of date as given by Gain, *L'Église de Cappadoce*, 397–98.

28. Rousseau, *Basil of Caesarea*, 156.

29. Basil of Caesaria, *Letter* 232, trans. Blomfield Jackson, NPNF, 2nd ser., vol. 8, ed. Philip Schaff and Henry Wace (Buffalo, N.Y.: Christian Literature Publishing, 1895); ed. Roy J. Deferrari, *Saint Basil: The Letters*, vol. 3, Loeb Classical Library (Cambridge, Mass.: Harvard University Press, 1962), 364.

30. The full list of such comparisons, explicit and implicit, drawn from Gain's list is *Letters* 30, 140, 141, 136, 200, 256, 232, 237, 267.

31. "Fools say in their hearts, 'There is no God,'" Ps. 14 [LXX 13]:1 (NRSV).

32. Larchet, *Theology of Illness*, 26–39, synthesizes early Christian and Byzantine comments on illness and original sin.

33. Basil of Caesaria, *Quod Deus non est auctor malorum* [*PG* 31:329–54] 8, *PG* 31:348, trans. Harrison.

34. Basil of Caesaria, *Quod Deus non est auctor malorum* 6, *PG* 31:344, trans. Harrison.

35. Basil of Caesaria, *Quod Deus non est auctor malorum* 8, *PG* 31:348.

36. See, for example, the far-reaching discussion in Avalos, *Illness and Health Care*, 233–405.

37. Basil of Caesaria, *Quod Deus non est auctor malorum* 4, *PG* 31:336, trans. Harrison.

38. Basil of Caesaria, *Quod Deus non est auctor malorum* 3, *PG* 31:332, trans. Harrison.

39. Dörnemann, *Krankheit und Heilung*, 124–59, which covers the gamut of medical metaphors in Origen.

40. Basil of Caesaria, *Quod Deus non est auctor malorum* 3, *PG* 31:333, trans. Harrison, altered.

41. Cf. Martial 1.47, noted in Flemming, *Medicine*, 54. On the sometimes hostile and at least conflicted attitude of Romans toward professional medicine, see Nutton, *Ancient Medicine*, 161–70.

42. Basil of Caesaria, *Quod Deus non est auctor malorum* 3, *PG* 31:333, trans. Harrison.

43. Basil of Caesaria, *Quod Deus non est auctor malorum* 5, *PG* 31:337, trans. Harrison.

44. Basil of Caesaria, *Quod Deus non est auctor malorum* 3, *PG* 31:333.

45. Basil of Caesaria, *Quod Deus non est auctor malorum* 9, *PG* 31:349, trans. Harrison.

46. *Reg. fus.* 55, *PG* 31:1044, trans. Clarke; the at times controversial use of secular medicine in monasteries is covered in Crislip, *From Monastery to Hospital*, 18–38.

47. It was a problem that he would turn to more than once as he developed his ascetic philosophy, according to Silvas, *Asketikon of St. Basil*, 264n459.

48. *Reg. fus.* 55, *PG* 31:1044, trans. Silvas. Medicine was commonly referred to as "the art," as in the Hippocratic treatise *The Art*; see Jouanna, *Hippocrates*, 377–78.

49. *Reg. fus.* 55, *PG* 31:1044–45, trans. Clarke.

50. *Reg. fus.* 55, *PG* 31:1044. Trans. mine and Silvas's. The late ancient Christian preoccupation with the passions and the cure of souls is covered by Sorabji, *Emotion and Peace of Mind*, 343–71.

51. *Reg. fus.* 55, *PG* 31:1044. The latter trans. by Silvas, *Asketikon of St. Basil*, 265n461.

52. *Reg. fus.* 55, *PG* 31:1045, trans. Clarke.

53. *Reg. fus.* 55, *PG* 31.1048, trans. Silvas.

54. Ibid.

55. *Reg. fus.* 55, *PG* 31.1048–49, trans. Silvas.

56. *Reg. fus.* 55, *PG* 31.1049, trans. Silvas.

57. *Reg. fus.* 55, *PG* 31.1052, trans. Silvas. On the Christian adoption of Hippocratic doctrines more generally, see Temkin, *Hippocrates*, 149–80, 213–56.

58. *Reg. fus.* 55, *PG* 31.1052, trans. Silvas.

59. Cf. Galen, *De sanitate tuenda*, trans. Robert Montraville Green, *A Translation of Galen's Hygiene* (Springfield, Ill.: Thomas, 1951).

60. *Reg. fus.* 55, *PG* 31.1052, trans. Silvas.

61. See the introduction by Yarbrough, "Canons from the Council of Gangra," in *Ascetic Behavior*, ed. Wimbush, 448–55; and Silvas, *Asketikon of St. Basil*, 19–20, 53–56. No doubt Eustathius's connections to the controversial "homoiousians" also played a role in the negative attention he garnered.

62. In support of the 340 dating, see Silvas, *Asketikon of St. Basil*, 486, which gives an overview of the various approaches to the dating.

63. Canons 2, 18, 19, Yarbrough, "Canons," 451, 453.

64. On the importance of the Council of Gangra and Eustathian asceticism in the development of Basil's own ascetic thought, see Silvas, *Asketikon of St. Basil*, 19–20, 53–60.

65. *Reg. brev.* 128, *PG* 31.1168, trans. Clarke.

66. Ibid.; the passage is quoted according to the text of the *Small Asceticon* published in *PG*; the *Great Asceticon* prefaces the quote by "resulting in the severity to the body (Col. 2:23) condemned by the Apostle," trans. Silvas. The redaction history of the *Small Asceticon* and the *Great Asceticon* is addressed throughout in Silvas, *Asketikon of St. Basil*, but is not directly relevant to the passages discussed here.

67. *Reg. brev.* 129, *PG* 31.1169.

68. *Reg. brev.* 129, *PG* 31.1170, trans. Clarke.

69. Ibid.

70. *Reg. brev.* 137, *PG* 31.1173, trans. Clarke.

71. *Reg. brev.* 138, 139, *PG* 31.1173, 1175.

72. *Reg. brev.* 137, *PG* 31.1173, trans. Clarke.

73. *Reg. brev.* 138, *PG* 31.1173, trans. Silvas. He continues, "[I]f any man thinks he needs more, whether in fasting or watching or from any other cause, let him reveal his reason for needing more to those who are entrusted with the common care, and abide by their decisions. For it will often be necessary to satisfy his needs in some other way" (*Reg. brev.* 138, *PG* 31.1173, trans. Clarke).

74. *Reg. brev.* 139, *PG* 31.1175.

75. *Reg. brev.* 139, *PG* 31.1175, trans. Clarke.

76. *Reg. fus.* 16, *PG* 31.960, trans. Silvas.

77. Ibid.

78. Compare *Reg. fus.* 17, 18, and 19.

79. See Guillaumont, *Les "Kephalaia gnostica"*; and Evagrius of Pontus, *Kephalaia gnostica*.

80. Palladius, *Lausiac History,* trans. Vivian, *Four Desert Fathers*, 46–52; the Bohairic Coptic version is edited in Amélineau, *De Historia Lausiaca*, 104–24. I refer to this Coptic version of Palladius's text as the *Life of Evagrius*. In his translation of the Coptic version, Vivian has set out the various options for explaining their relationship. He makes a plausible case that the Coptic fragments represent an earlier Palladian version, which was later expurgated in the throes of the ongoing Origenist controversies of the fifth and sixth centuries.

81. *Life of Evagrius* 2, trans. Vivian. The passage is not in the Greek version of the *Lausiac History*, which may, Vivian suggests, reflect an expurgation of the Greek (Vivian, *Four Desert Fathers*, 30). I am inclined to agree. It is certainly more difficult to explain the insertion of such devotion to an alleged heretic in later centuries.

82. *Lausiac History* 38.11, trans. Meyer. The episodes are placed later in the Coptic *Life of Evagrius* 22–23.

83. *Lausiac History* 38.11–13.

84. *Lausiac History* 38.13, trans. Meyer.

85. Emended following Voguë and Vivian, *Four Coptic Lives*, 81n71. On the problems of identifying the precise body part paining Evagrius, whether it is the bladder, anus, or both, see ibid. Rather than wade too deeply into the bladder/anus debate, I adopt the suggested translation apud this very passage of "anus, rectum (?)" by Crum, *Coptic Dictionary*, 263b. A definitive answer would depend on a more comprehensive examination of Coptic bodily idioms, a desideratum too complex for the present study.

86. *Life of Evagrius* 13, trans. my own; Amélineau, *De Historia Lausiaca*, 112.

87. *V.Ant.* 19, trans. Gregg, and discussed in Introduction.

88. This saying draws on Paul's 1 Cor. 15:31: "I die daily." On the title of the *Praktikos*, see Evagrius of Pontus, *Praktikos,* ed. Guillaumont and Guillaumont, *Évagre le pontique: Traité pratique,* 399–409.

89. Evagrius of Pontus, *Praktikos* 29, trans. Robert E. Sinkewicz, *Evagrius of Pontus,* emphasis added. The Greek text is cited according to the critical edition of Guillaumont and Guillaumont, eds., *Évagre le pontique: Traité pratique,* in which the editors discuss the identification of Macarius the Great in their commentary, 566–67.

90. The allusion to *V.Ant.* 29 is noted by Guillaumont and Guillaumont, eds., *Évagre le pontique: Traité pratique,* 568.

91. See the discussion of the *Sermo asceticus* in Clarke, *St. Basil the Great,* 77–78. He suggests that it is spurious but perhaps written after Basil's death in one of the communities following his rules. See Crislip, "I Have Chosen Illness," 187–88.

92. Evagrius of Pontus, *Praktikos* 15, trans. Sinkewicz, *Evagrius of Pontus.*

93. Evagrius of Pontus, *Praktikos* 29.

94. See the recent introduction to Evagrius's theory of thought by David Brakke. *Talking Back: A Handbook for Combating Demons,* CS 229 (Kalamazoo, Mich.: Cistercian Publications, 2009), 1–40.

95. Evagrius of Pontus, *Praktikos* 40, trans. Sinkewicz.

96. Ibid.

97. Ibid.

98. Evagrius of Pontus, *On Thoughts* 35, trans. Sinkewicz, *Evagrius of Pontus.* I rely on the Greek text in Géhin, Guillaumont, and Guillaumont, eds., *Évagre le pontique: Sur les pensées,* and the translation by Sinkewicz, *Evagrius of Pontus.* Evagrius notes that the demon of *akēdia* can act similarly to gluttony. The pseudo-Basilian *Sermo asceticus* argues that the effects of excessive eating (gluttony) and excessive fasting are the same: "The same injury to the soul, indeed, results from both types of excess: when the flesh is not brought under subjection, natural vigor makes us rush headlong in the wake of our shameful impulses; on the other hand, when the body is relaxed, enfeebled and torpid, it is under constraint from pain. With the body in such a condition, the soul is not free to raise its glance upward, weighed down as it is in companionship with the body's malady, but is, perforce, wholly occupied with the sensation of pain and intent upon itself" (Pseudo-Basil, *Sermo asceticus* 3, trans. M. Monica Wagner, *Saint Basil: Ascetical Works,* Fathers of the Church 9 [New York: Fathers of the Church, 1950], 207–15, *PG* 31.870–82).

99. *V.Ant.* 25.

100. *V.Ant.* prologue 3, trans. Gregg, mine, respectively [Bartelink, 126]. Bartelink, *Vie d'Antoine*, 127n3, notes a number of other passages that present the saints' *Lives* as models for others.

101. Evagrius of Pontus, *On Thoughts* 35, trans. Sinkewicz [Géhin, 274, 276].

102. John is also depicted as imitating a scriptural exemplar, Elijah (cf. 2 Kings 1:8). Cf. Jerome, *Letter* 38.3, 5, in which Jerome specifically defends the ascetic imitation of John the Baptist, in response to critics of his protégés' ascetic intensity.

103. Evagrius of Pontus, *On Thoughts* 35, trans. Sinkewicz [Géhin, 272, 274].

104. Evagrius of Pontus, *On Thoughts* 35, trans. Sinkewicz [Géhin, 276].

105. On the *Life of Antony* and the other influences on the *Life of Syncletica*, see Brakke, *Demons*, 188.

106. *V.Syn.* 5, 7.

107. *V.Syn.* 6, 10.

108. *V.Syn.* 11ff.

109. *V.Syn.* 10, *PG* 28.1492.

110. *V.Syn.* 17, *PG* 28.1496. In her own teachings (preserved in the *Life* and the *Sayings*), Syncletica promotes an asceticism of suffering, which she describes as "painful asceticism and pure prayer [*askēseōs epiponou kai katharas proseukhēs*]" (*V. Syn.* 29). Specifically, however, the sufferings promoted in Syncletica's teachings are rather commonplace and not necessarily injurious: "fasting, sleeping on the ground [*khameunia*], and others," such as "the rejection of property" (*V.Syn.* 31).

111. *V.Syn.* 98.

112. *V.Syn.* 104–5, *PG* 28.1552.

113. *V.Syn.* 111, trans. Castelli.

114. Brakke, *Demons*, 192.

115. Ibid., 192–93; Harvey, *Scenting Salvation*, 217; *V.Syn.* 111, 112, *PG* 28.1556.

116. Harvey, *Scenting Salvation*, 217.

117. *V.Syn.* 111. On the potential ambivalence toward the monastic use of medicine in later sources, cf. Harvey, "Physicians and Ascetics"; and Horden, "Death of Ascetics."

118. *V.Syn.* 112, trans. Castelli.

119. Burrus, *Saving Shame*, 100–107; Brakke, *Demons*, 188–93; Harvey, *Scenting Salvation*, 217; Castelli, "Mortifying the Body."

120. Burrus, *Saving Shame*, 101–2.

121. *V.Syn.* 100, *PG* 28.1549, trans. Bongie.

122. Ibid.

123. Ibid.

124. *V.Syn.* 49, *PG* 28.1516, trans. Bongie.

125. *V.Syn.* 49, *PG* 28.1517, trans. Bongie. The gendering implications of such language are teased out by Brakke, *Demons*, 191–93.

126. *V.Syn.* 49, *PG* 28.1517, trans. Bongie.

127. *V.Syn.* 100, *PG* 28.1549, trans. Bongie. Cf. *Apoph. pat.* (alph.) Evagrius 6.

128. *V.Syn.* 100, *PG* 28.1549, trans. Bongie, altered.

129. *V.Syn.* 50, *PG* 28.1517; *Apoph. pat.* (alph.) Syncletica 16, *PG* 65.425, 428. Similar sentiments are preserved in *V.Syn.* 100.

130. In contemporary rules from Egyptian coenobia (for men and women), one meal a day was the standard allowance, which could be supplemented by limited snacks. In the monastic systems of Pachomius and Shenoute, for example, only children, the elderly, and the sick were allowed two meals a day. Cf. Evagrius of Pontus, who counsels monastics to eat once a day, *On Thoughts* 35. For a detailed case study of diet in Shenoute's monastic system (fourth and fifth century), see Layton, "Social Structure and Food Consumption."

131. *V.Syn.* 50, *PG 28.1517*, trans. Bongie. Syncletica refers to this as a *nosos*, disease or illness, in *V.Syn.* 51.

132. *V.Syn.* 50, *PG 28.1517*, trans. Bongie, altered.

133. *V.Syn.* 51, 49, 50, *PG 28.1517*, trans. mine.

134. Cf. Castelli, "Mortifying the Body."

135. *V.Syn.* 99, *PG* 28.1548, trans. mine.

136. *V.Syn.* 99, *PG* 28.1548, trans. Bongie, altered.

137. Ibid.

138. *Apoph. pat.* (alph.) Syncletica 8, *PG* 65.424, trans. Ward.

139. *V.Syn.* 99, *PG* 28.1548, trans. Bongie, altered.

140. *V.Syn.* 99, *PG* 28.1548–49, trans. Bongie.

141. This is perhaps with Evagrius's famous "strategy of driving out a nail with a nail" in mind; see, e.g., Brakke, *Demons*, 68.

142. *V.Syn.* 99, *PG* 28.1548–49.

143. See discussion in Chapter 1.

CHAPTER 5

1. As Bagnall, *Egypt in the Byzantine World*, 8, points out in the case of Coptic textiles.

2. Rousseau, *Pachomius*, 183–84. This episode will be discussed later in this chapter.

3. Chadwick, "Pachomios."

4. Bacht, *Das Vermächtnis des Ursprungs*, 30–31.

5. Burrows, "Visibility of God," 28, 27.

6. Brown, "Saint as Exemplar," 16.

7. Translations of the Great Coptic *Life* are mine unless otherwise noted, which mainly comprise those passages for which only the Arabic version has been preserved, as here. I have consulted and profited from Veilleux's translation. There will no doubt be some instances in which Veilleux and I inevitably share the same wording. For the few quotations of the Greek *Vita Prima*, I use Veilleux's translation.

8. *V.Pach. SBo* 1, trans. Veilleux, altered. The opening pages of the Sahidic and Bohairic manuscripts are missing; this passage is translated from the Vatican Arabic manuscript. See

the useful discussion of martyrdom and monastic self-understanding in Gaddis, *There Is No Crime*, 169–70.

9. *V.Pach. SBo* 7. The parallel in *V.Pach. G1* 4–5 does not specify which "tyrant" Constantine opposes.

10. *V.Ant.* 3 [Bartelink, 136], although unlike Antony, Pachomius does not learn from other ascetics at this point in the narrative.

11. *V.Pach. SBo* 8 [*VB*, 6]. Coptic texts are cited according to L.-T. Lefort, *S. Pachomii vita bohairice scripta* [*VB*], CSCO 89 (Paris: E Typographeo Reipublicae, 1925); and idem, *S. Pachomii vitae sahidice scriptae* [*VS*], CSCO 99–100 (Louvain: Institut Orientaliste, 1933–34).

12. *V.Pach. SBo* 8 [*VB*, 6]. On "progress" as a component of asceticism, see the *Correspondence* of Barsanuphius and John of Gaza, discussed in the next chapter.

13. *V.Pach. SBo* 8 [*VB*, 5–6].

14. *V.Pach. SBo* 8 [*VB*, 6].

15. *V.Pach. SBo* 9 [*VB*, 7].

16. *V.Pach. G1* 6, trans. Veilleux.

17. *V.Pach. SBo* 8 [*VB*, 6]. The Coptic vision is rendered a bit more forcefully, given the Abrahamic references that begin the *Life*: "[The honeycomb] fell upon the earth and spread out over the face of the entire earth."

18. *V.Pach. SBo* 9–10 [*VB*, 7].

19. It is worth noting that the hostility toward the care of the sick from outside the community is reflected elsewhere in coenobitic literature, such as in the writings of Shenoute of Atripe. See Crislip, "Care for the Sick."

20. See Goehring, "First Sahidic *Life of Pachomius*," 22.

21. *V.Pach. SBo* 7 [*VB*, 4].

22. *V.Pach. G1* 4.

23. Crum, *Coptic Dictionary*, 784b–85a. We may remember that most literary Coptic is translated from Greek originals.

24. Brakke, *Demons*, 192–93; *V.Syn.* 112, 80; Brakke, "The Lady Appears," 27. See discussion in Chapter 4.

25. Cobb, *Dying to Be Men*. See also Castelli, *Martyrdom and Memory*, 62–63, on the dissolution of gender in martyrdom (which generally defaults to masculinizing).

26. *V.Pach. SBo* 74 [*VB*, 78], restoration in lacuna by Lefort; and the story of Cornelius at *V.Pach. SBo* 59 [*VB*, 59]. I have transliterated the Bohairic "barred hori" as ḥ.

27. Kuefler, *Manly Eunuch*, 111. He cites Cyprian's *Ad Demetrianum* as an example of this orientation.

28. Rousseau, *Pachomius*, 109–12.

29. Such values are explored in detail in Shaw, "Body/Power/Identity."

30. *V.Pach. SBo* 10, trans. Veilleux. The passage falls at the end of a two-page lacuna in the Bohairic (see *VB*, 10) for which Veilleux substitutes the Arabic. Veilleux's notation of the incipit of f. 136 of the Bohairic version is incorrect; see Armand Veilleux, trans., *Pachomian Koinonia*, vol. 1, CS 45 (Kalamazoo, Mich.: Cistercian Publications, 1980), 32, 267.

31. *V.Pach. SBo* 10 [*VB*, 10].

32. Veilleux, trans., *Pachomian Koinonia*, 32. The Greek verb *enkakein* probably echoes Luke 18:1 and thus might call for the slightly more general rendering "to grow weary"; cf. Luke 18:1: "Then Jesus told them a parable about their need to pray always and not to lose heart (*mē enkakein*)" (NRSV).

33. *V.Pach. SBo* 16 [*VB*, 17]; *saḥ nsēini* might render the Greek *arkhiatros*.

34. *V.Pach. SBo* 16 [*VB*, 17–18], cf. *V.Pach. G1* 13a. "To be sick," Coptic *erjōb*=Greek *asthenein* (Crum, *Coptic Dictionary*, 805b).

35. *V.Pach. G1* 13, trans. Veilleux, altered; cf. *V.Pach. G1* 13a.

36. "So courageously giving himself to *askēsis*, he fell ill after a month. Pachomius was visiting him from Tabennesi. Sitting at his side, he tended his father as was appropriate until God visited him" (*V.Pach. G1* 13, trans. Veilleux, altered).

37. *V.Pach. SBo* 16 [*VB*, 18].

38. *V.Pach. SBo* 18=*V.Pach. S3* [*VS*, 102, a231–a233].

39. *V.Pach. SBo* 17 [*VB*, 18].

40. For more on the "peaceable kingdom," see Eliot, *Roads to Paradise*, 144–67. Rousseau, *Pachomius*, 58, 66, describes the foundation of the Koinonia and its significance.

41. *V.Pach. SBo* 19 [*VS*, 105, a26].

42. Though after riding the crocodile Apa Helle goes on to curse the crocodile for the people it has killed, and it promptly dies (*Hist. mon.* 12.7).

43. Pachomian care for the sick is covered in Crislip, *From Monastery to Hospital*, 9–38, 68–99. For the evidence from Shenoute's monastic federation, in the Pachomian tradition, cf. also idem, "Care for the Sick."

44. *V.Pach. SBo* 36 [*VB*, 38]. The parallel in *V.Pach. G1* 90 is significantly different, framing Pachomius's response more closely to certain sayings in the apophthegmata tradition, such as that attributed to Joseph of Thebes or Syncletica: "But the one who lies sick can be struggling far more than the one in good health in strength of soul and patience. Then such a man has a double crown" (trans. Veilleux).

45. *V.Pach. SBo* 42.

46. *V.Pach. SBo* 41 [*VB*, 44].

47. *V.Pach. SBo* 44.

48. *V.Pach. SBo* 46 [*VB*, 48].

49. *V.Pach. SBo* 47 [*VB*, 49].

50. *V.Pach. SBo* 47 [*VB*, 49–50].

51. I argue that this account is quite similar to other, particularly Greek, monastic descriptions of demonically induced illness more generally and the monastic condition of *akēdia* more specifically; see Crislip, "Sin of Sloth."

52. *V.Pach. G1* 52, trans. Veilleux, altered from "physical" to "natural." See François Halkin, ed., *Sancti Pachomii Vitae Graece*, Subsidia Hagiographica 19 (Brussels: Société Bollandistes, 1932), 34.

53. *V.Pach. SBo* 16 [*VB*, 17]; *V.Pach. SBo* 48 [*VB*, 50].

54. See Layton, "Food Consumption and Social Structure."

55. *V.Pach. SBo* 48 [*VB*, 51].

56. *V.Pach. SBo* 61 [*VB*, 60].

57. *VB*, 235; LSJ⁹, s.v.; *garelaion* is mentioned by the doctor Galen, K 6.716. More details are in *Der Neue Pauly*, s.v. "Fischspeisen."

58. See Crislip, *From Monastery to Hospital*, 30; and Layton, "Food Consumption and Social Structure," table 3.

59. *V.Pach. SBo* 61 [*VB*, 60].

60. *V.Pach. SBo* 11.

61. *V.Pach. SBo* 10.

62. *V.Pach. SBo* 94 [*VB*, 109].

63. *V.Pach. SBo* 73.

64. *V.Pach. SBo* 94 [*VB*, 110].

65. The precise sin is named by Theodore at the end of the story, as he leaves Pachomius's monastery (*V.Pach. SBo* 95 [*VB*, 120]). *V.Pach. SBo* 94 [*VB*, 110–111].

66. For this episode, limited to *V.Pach. SBo* 114 in Veilleux's paragraph numeration, the Bohairic translation is lost, but the parallel text is preserved in a Sahidic manuscript, BM Or. 4719(a) fol. 3 verso ff. (Lefort's *S2*), in *VS*, 17ff.

67. *V.Pach. SBo* 114 [*VS*, 17].

68. *V.Pach. SBo* 114 [*VS*, 18].

69. *V.Pach. SBo* 114 [*VS*, 18–19].

70. *V.Pach. SBo* 114 [*VS*, 19–20]. The biblical quotations are 2 Cor. 12:2 and 4.

71. Pachomius's vision of paradise is lengthy, perhaps drawing on commonplaces from the types of apocalyptic literature that circulated in fourth-century Egypt, but the specifics of his vision do not appear to be a direct borrowing from prominent apocalyptic texts; cf. *Apocalypse of Paul*, in *New Testament Apocrypha*, ed. Wilhelm Schneemelcher and Edgar Hennecke, Eng. ed., Robert McL. Wilson, vol. 2 (Philadelphia: Westminster, 1963–66), 720–30. Notable, and unique in my readings in apocalyptic literature, is Pachomius's assertion in the *Life* that "there was a great, deep darkness (*ounoc nkake efhtmtōm*) surrounding that realm (*paiōn*), filled with subtle creatures (*nthērion e[u]šoome*), so that no one can go there unless led there by an angel of god." Precisely what these "fine" or "subtle creatures" are is unclear, as I have not found the phrase *nthērion e[u]šoome* (or similar) used elsewhere in Coptic literature. Lefort translates it as "bestioles très fines," while Veilleux renders it a bit more loosely—if more vividly—as "tiny insects"; see L.-Th. Lefort, trans., *Les Vies coptes de saint Pachôme*, Bibliothèque du *Muséon* 16 (Louvain: Institut Orientaliste, 1943), 30; *V.Pach. SBo* 114 [*VS*, 23].

72. It is worth noting that Pachomius's trial for heresy—because of his clairvoyance—at a synod in Latopolis, which could conceivably have been characterized as a type of martyrdom, is not included in the Great Coptic *Life*, as it is in the Greek *Vita Prima*, *V.Pach. G1* 112.

73. *SBo* 117 [*VS*, 87]. Note the *Life*'s description of Pachomius's *tfmntjōōrei ettajrēu*, literally, "firm strength," an interesting contrast to his general weakness. But what kind of strength is this, as he falls on his face? Veilleux renders the phrase as "his strong will," which I think must be the implication. I have rendered it as "his determination." However we render this "firm strength," it is a very different strength from Antony's.

74. *V.Pach. SBo* 117 [*VS*, 87].

75. *V.Pach. SBo* 119 [*VS*, 91].

76. Yanney, "Illness and Death of Saint Pachomius."

77. Ibid., 56. He also sees a clear reference to malaria in the *Life*'s description of another monk who fell ill every three days (*V.Pach. SBo* 112).

78. *V.Pach. SBo* 118 [*VS*, 88].

79. Ibid.

80. *V.Pach. SBo* 194 [*VB*, 184]; cf. *Liber Orsiesii* 50 and the description of Pachomius and Palamon discussed previously; also *S1* 111. Cf. *V.Pach. SBo* 139.

81. *V.Pach. SBo* 118 [*VS*, 90–91].

82. *V.Pach. SBo* 118 [*VS*, 91].

83. *V.Pach. SBo* 121.

84. *V.Pach. SBo* 123 [*VS*, 94]. For his *martyrion, V.Pach. SBo* 122.

85. *V.Pach. SBo* 146 [*VS*, 192].

86. Veilleux, trans., *Pachomian Koinonia*, 287, 466, citing also Chitty, *Desert a City*; this more reliable dating is based on the *Letter of Ammon* and other sources.

87. Crislip, *From Monastery to Hospital*, 68–99.

88. *V.Pach. SBo* 107; cf. Crislip, "Sin of Sloth."

89. *V.Pach. SBo* 82 [*VS*, 91–92].

90. *V.Pach. SBo* 82 [*VB*, 92–93].

91. On the dating of Pachomius's death, see note 86.

92. For the ancient evidence for Shenoute's rather implausible longevity, see Emmel, *Shenoute's Literary Corpus*, 6–14. This is disputed by Lusier, "Chénouté, Victor." We may also note the close connection between Shenoute's White Monastery and the successors to Pachomius. After the turmoil of the post-Chalcedonian schisms in Egypt, it is in Shenoute's federation that Pachomius's memory and his Lives (especially the Sahidic versions) would be transmitted; see Goehring, "Remembering Abraham of Farshut."

93. *V.Pach. SBo* 123 [*VS*, 96], trans. Veilleux.

94. Veilleux, trans., *Pachomian Koinonia*, 287.

95. As explained by ibid., 287–88.

96. *V.Pach. SBo* 126 [*VS*, 177].

97. *V.Pach. SBo* 126 [*VS*, 177].

98. *V.Pach. SBo* 128 [*VS*, 179].

99. *V.Pach. SBo* 127.

100. *V.Pach. SBo* 129.

101. Veilleux, trans., *Pachomian Koinonia*, 288.

CHAPTER 6

1. Basil's *Rules* may be a slightly different case if we take Irénée Hausherr's definition of spiritual direction as between one director and one disciple, as opposed to between a director and a community; see Hausherr, *Spiritual Direction*, 1–2.

2. The *Letters* have not had the prominence among historians of late ancient asceticism that other hagiographic and gnomic sources have, to a large extent because of the inaccessibility of editions (even noncritical ones), a difficulty noted by Chitty, *Desert a City*, 132–33; and Hevelone-Harper, *Disciples of the Desert*, 18. Now with the publication of a complete critical edition, interest in the monks from Gaza has grown considerably. For the critical edition with French translation, see Barsanuphius and John of Gaza, *Correspondance*, ed. François Neyt and Paula Angelis-Noah, trans. L. Regnault, SC 426–27, 450–51 (Paris: Cerf, 1997–2001). They have been translated into English by John Chryssavgis, *Barsanuphius and John: Letters*, 2 vols., Fathers of the Church (Washington, D.C.: Catholic University of America Press, 2007). Recent monographic treatments include Bitton-Ashkelony and Kofsky, *Monastic School of Gaza*; and Hevelone-Harper, *Disciples of the Desert*. The former is especially useful as an introduction to the literature and history of Gaza monasticism, as is also the introductory chapters of Neyt and Angelis-Noah, eds., *Correspondance*, I.I:11–155. Also of note are the earlier remarks of Chitty, *Desert a City*, 132–40; and his only partially completed critical edition and English translation, *Barsanuphius and John*.

3. See the outline of the *Letters*' contents in Neyt and Angelis-Noah, eds., *Correspondance*, I.I:48–49.

4. See Hevelone-Harper, *Disciples of the Desert*, 20–21. It is no surprise in a text as well attested as the *Letters* that there is some variation of order and preservation of the letters among the various manuscript recensions. The variations in attestation and order, including some among the letters that I discuss here, are presented in Neyt and Angelis-Noah, eds., *Correspondance*, I.I.:137–55. In any case I have not found that the vagaries of the manuscript transmission impact my reading.

5. On sickness and healing directed to lay followers, see Hevelone-Harper, *Disciples of the Desert*, 84–89; and on their attitude toward medicine, see Bitton-Ashkelony and Kofsky, *Monastic School of Gaza*, 190–93. Dorotheus's career is discussed in Hevelone-Harper, *Disciples of the Desert*, 61–78.

6. Sometimes Barsanuphius's letters are prefaced with "Response by the same Great Old Man to the same person," *Letters* 115, 116 (trans. Chryssavgis), which may mean that it was not responding to a new letter; it might also mean that the editor simply declined to summarize one of Andrew's letters.

7. On dialectic as a component of ancient psychological healing, see Jackson, *Care of the Psyche*, 24.

8. Exceptions to the rule include Aelius Aristides's narrative of his travails and healing at the hands of Asclepius, *P. Aelii Aristidis Opera Quae Extant Omnia*, ed. C. A. Behr (Leiden: Brill, 1976); and *P. Aelius Aristides: The Complete Works*, trans. C. A. Behr (Leiden: Brill, 1981–86), 205–93. Aelius Aristides is discussed by Perkins, *Suffering Self*, 73–89, which

also adduces other voices of suffering, a category construed far more broadly than illness. We also might include the correspondence between Marcus Aurelius and his tutor Fronto, e.g., *The Correspondence of Marcus Cornelius Fronto*, ed. C. R. Haines, Loeb Classical Library (Cambridge, Mass: Harvard University Press, 1962), 1:186–203, also discussed in Perkins, *Suffering Self*, 197–99.

9. Even in the study of modern medicine, it is only in the past generation that doctors and medical anthropologists have criticized the overweening subjective orientation of modern medicine toward the doctor and argued for a greater sensitivity to the voices and concerns of patients, for which see Kleinman, *Illness Narratives*; and Frank, *Wounded Storyteller*.

10. I follow the numeration of Neyt's and de Angelis-Noah's critical edition and John Chryssavgis's translation. Chitty's earlier critical edition of the letters has a slightly different numeration for Andrew's correspondence.

11. The origin mutatis mutandis of the modern terms "psychotherapeutics" and "psychotherapy," probably from the French *psychothérapie* in the late nineteenth century, *OED*, s.v. psychotherapy. Yet, of course, the ancient phenomenon is quite its own thing, as argued (perhaps a bit pedantically) by Gill, "Ancient Psychotherapy." A useful introduction from the perspective of the history of psychiatry is in Jackson, *Care of the Psyche*, 16–33.

12. In Galen, *Selected Works*, 100–149; and Cicero, *Tusculan Disputations*, trans. J. E. King, Loeb Classical Library (Cambridge, Mass.: Harvard University Press, 1945).

13. Surveyed enthusiastically and sympathetically in Hausherr, *Spiritual Direction*.

14. Seen, for example, in ibid., 53–67.

15. Lucien Regnault, in idem, Philippe Lemaire, and Bernard Outtier, trans., *Barsanuphe et Jean de Gaza: Correspondance* (Sablé-sur-Sarthe: Solesmes, 1972), 6, cited per Brown, *Body and Society*, 233; and Bitton-Ashkelony and Kofsky, *Monastic School of Gaza*, 129.

16. Discussion of Gazan monasticism along with the Christological battles of the fifth and sixth centuries may be found in Hevelone-Harper, *Disciples of the Desert*, 10–60; Bitton-Ashkelony and Kofsky, *Monastic School of Gaza*, 6–81; and Horn, *Asceticism*. Isaiah wrote in the tradition of Antony's *Letters* on the monastic reclamation of paradise by controlling the passions in his *Discourse* 2; see discussion below.

17. Bitton-Ashkelony and Kofsky, *Monastic School of Gaza*, 21.

18. Ibid., 36–40; and Hevelone-Harper, *Disciples of the Desert*, 33–36, provide information on the evidence for the built environment of Thavatha.

19. Hevelone-Harper, *Disciples of the Desert*, 45.

20. The persistence of this trope is chronicled in McNeill, *History of the Cure of Souls*.

21. See Kleinman, *Patients and Healers*, 82.

22. The distinctions between disease and illness are usefully presented in ibid., 72–80.

23. Ibid., 82; Pilch, *Healing in the New Testament*, 155.

24. Pilch, *Healing in the New Testament*, 156.

25. See, for example, Kleinman's lengthy exposition of the "consensus model" in his *Rethinking Psychiatry*, 108–41.

26. Dow, "Universal Aspects of Symbolic Healing," 56. Kleinman, *Rethinking Psychiatry*,

131–34, gives a different version of the fourfold structure (which he calls "structural processes"), but for various reasons I prefer Dow's earlier version. On the continuing relevance of the "meaning response" and symbolic healing in the anthropology of medicine, see Moerman, *Meaning, Medicine, and the "Placebo Effect,"* esp. 89–99.

27. For more recent important work on illness narratives in a contemporary anthropological context, in addition to Kleinman, *Illness Narratives*, see Mattingly and Garro, eds., *Narrative and the Cultural Construction of Illness and Healing*; and Mattingly, *Healing Dramas and Clinical Plots*.

28. Barsanuphius and John of Gaza, *Letter* 72, trans. Chryssavgis [Neyt and Angelis-Noah, 346].

29. Barsanuphius and John frequently received such requests from nonmonastic followers, and yet they rarely heal bodily afflictions; see Hevelone-Harper, *Disciples of the Desert*, 84–89.

30. *Letter* 72, trans. Chryssavgis [Neyt and Angelis-Noah, 346].

31. Ibid.

32. Gal. 6:2, "Bear one another's burdens, and in this way you will fulfill the law of Christ" (trans. NRSV). See Bitton-Ashkelony and Kofsky, *Monastic School of Gaza*, 150–51. On empathy in ancient psychological healing, see Jackson, *Care of the Psyche*, 43, 44; and Hausherr, *Spiritual Direction*, 141–48.

33. Pentony, *Models of Influence*, 134; Hausherr, *Spiritual Direction*, 68. This is seen in the epistolary spiritual direction of Evagrius of Pontus, on whose paradoxical strategy of "pos[ing] as a fool" while giving spiritual advice, see Young, "Cannibalism and Other Family Woes," 130–39.

34. *Letter* 72, trans. Chryssavgis [Neyt and Angelis-Noah, 348].

35. This might also reflect a common cross-cultural element of symbolic healing, that the healer himself must also be healed. See Dow, "Universal Aspects," 57.

36. In a letter to another sick monk Barsanuphius refers to past illness, though how distant in the past is not clear; see *Letter* 512.

37. *Letter* 72, trans. Chryssavgis [Neyt and Angelis-Noah, 348]. Burrus, *Saving Shame*, 3, argues that shame is an ambiguous affect that in early Christianity could be transformed into "a poignant, even defiant, acceptance of human finitude and vulnerability."

38. *dēlōson moi ti esti tauta*, *Letter* 88, trans. Chryssavgis [Neyt and Angelis-Noah, 378].

39. Kleinman, *Rethinking Psychiatry*, 133.

40. In *Wounded Storyteller* the sociologist Arthur Frank argues that contemporary North Americans tell their stories of illness through three narrative types. The master narratives of postmodernity are not the same—I should underscore—as those of late antiquity.

41. E.g., Mattingly and Garro, eds., *Narrative and the Cultural Construction*; Mattingly, *Healing Dramas*; Holland and Quinn, eds., *Cultural Models*; and D'Andrade and Strauss, eds., *Human Motives*.

42. The term is of Garrett, "Paul's Thorn."

43. *Letter* 74, trans. Chryssavgis [Neyt and Angelis-Noah, 350, 352].

44. *Letter* 74, trans. Chryssavgis [Neyt and Angelis-Noah, 352].

45. *Letter* 78, trans. Chryssavgis, altered [Neyt and Angelis-Noah, 362].

46. *Letter* 78, trans. Chryssavgis [Neyt and Angelis-Noah, 362]; Garrett, "Paul's Thorn."

47. *Letter* 78, trans. Chryssavgis [Neyt and Angelis-Noah, 362].

48. *Letter* 78, trans. Chryssavgis, altered [Neyt and Angelis-Noah, 362, 364]. Cf. *Letter* 511, trans. Chryssavgis, to another sick monk, in which Barsanuphius distinguishes between "bodily illness" and "demonic hindrance."

49. *Letter* 88, my translation [Neyt and Angelis-Noah, 378, 380].

50. *Letter* 88, trans. Chryssavgis [Neyt and Angelis-Noah, 380].

51. See Crislip, "Sin of Sloth"; cf. for example, Evagrius of Pontus, *Praktikos* 12.

52. *Letter* 88, trans. Chryssavgis [Neyt and Angelis-Noah, 380].

53. Trans. Chryssavgis [Neyt and Angelis-Noah, 378].

54. *Letter* 102, trans. Chryssavgis [Neyt and Angelis-Noah, 418].

55. Hadot, *Philosophy as a Way of Life*, 20; Foucault, "Technologies of the Self"; *Letter* 102, trans. Chryssavgis, altered [Neyt and Angelis-Noah, 418].

56. *Letter* 102, trans. Chryssavgis. On self-knowledge in ancient spiritual exercises, see Hadot, *Philosophy as a Way of Life*, 20, 90.

57. Bitton-Ashkelony and Kofsky, *Monastic School of Gaza*, 7, 20–24. As with Barsanuphius and John, in Isaiah's *Logoi* "[a]llegories and Evagrian language are accepted without qualms. But there is little if any cosmic or theological speculation" (Chitty, *Desert a City*, 75).

58. Isaiah of Scetis, *Ascetic Discourses*, trans. Chryssavgis and Penkett, 35. On Isaiah's career and dossier, see Chitty, *Desert a City*, 73–76.

59. This is numbered *Discourse* 2 in the translation of Chryssavgis and Penkett, which I quote here, and *Logos* 9 in the critical edition of the fully extant Syriac version, Draguet, ed., *Les cinq recensions de l'Ascéticon syriaque d'Abba Isaïe*. The list of parallel texts is in vol. 289, 97; French translation, vol. 293, 118–23.

60. *Logos* 9=*Discourse* 2, trans. Chryssavgis and Penkett [Draguet, 98].

61. *Logos* 9=*Discourse* 2, trans. Chryssavgis and Penkett [Draguet, 102]. On the precept to take care of oneself, see Foucault, "Technologies of the Self," 19–22. Cf. the discussion of Antony in Chapter 2.

62. *Logos* 9=*Discourse* 2, trans. Chryssavgis and Penkett [Draguet, 102].

63. *Logos* 9=*Discourse* 2 [Draguet, 99].

64. See further discussion in Ware, "Meaning of 'Pathos.'"

65. Bitton-Ashkelony and Kofsky, *Monastic School of Gaza*, 127–29, 158–64 passim; Hevelone-Harper, *Disciples of the Desert*, 24–25.

66. The incongruity between Evagrius's own teachings and those attributed to him by critics in the sixth century is discussed in Konstantinovsky, *Evagrius Ponticus*, 170–76.

67. It may be worth noting that *athumia* had long been recognized as disastrous to the sick. It is the same term that Thucydides uses in his influential description of the plague of Athens in 431 B.C. For Thucydides, *athumia* or despair was "the most dreadful thing" (*deinotaton*) about the plague, for those infected simply gave up hope" (Thucydides, *History*

of the Peloponnesian War 2.51, trans. Charles Forster Smith, Loeb Classical Library [Cambridge, Mass.: Harvard University Press, 1962]).

68. *Letter* 106, trans. Chryssavgis [Neyt and Angelis-Noah, 428].

69. *mē oun lupētheis, Letter* 106 [Neyt and Angelis-Noah, 428].

70. *Letters* 81, 82 [Neyt and Angelis-Noah, 368, 370].

71. *Letter* 82, trans. Chryssavgis [Neyt and Angelis-Noah, 370].

72. *Letter* 85, trans. Chryssavgis [Neyt and Angelis-Noah, 372].I cannot answer why Andrew is asking such basic questions now, when he is a senior monk (*gerōn*) in charge of his own disciple. Perhaps it is only through his illness that he has begun corresponding with the Great Old Men. We need not presume that most monks of the community corresponded with them regularly.

73. Recent discussion of *apatheia* in its pagan and Christian adaptations may be found throughout the wide-ranging investigations of Sorabji, *Emotion and Peace of Mind*; Knuuttila, *Emotions in Ancient and Medieval Philosophy*; and Graver, *Stoicism and Emotion*, 210–11. Bitton-Ashkelony and Kofsky discuss *apatheia* in the *Letters* of the Great Old Men in *Monastic School of Gaza*, 174–75. *Letter* 87 [Neyt and Angelis-Noah, 377].

74. While Evagrius is famous for structuring the evil thoughts in a group of eight in some of his treatises (such as the *Praktikos*), his octad is not in use by Barsanuphius and John. Their lists of passions or thoughts to avoid nonetheless echo Evagrian orientations: fornication (*porneia*), gluttony (*gastrimargia*), hate (*misos*), anger (*orgē*), envy (*phthonos*), vainglory (*kenodoxia*), and sadness (*lupē*, or grief).

75. *Letter* 83, trans. Chryssavgis [Neyt and Angelis-Noah, 370].

76. *Letters* 83 and 84, trans. Chryssavgis [Neyt and Angelis-Noah, 372]. For recent approaches to demonic envy in Christian antiquity, see Blowers, "Envy's Narrative Scripts"; and Crislip, "Envy and Anger ."

77. On the evil eye, see Rakoczy, *Böser Blick*, esp. 216–26, which surveys Christian authors; and Wazana, "Case of the Evil Eye."

78. *Letter* 78 [Neyt and Angelis-Noah, 362].

79. Cf. Harvey, "Embodiment in Time and Eternity," 106, discussed in the Introduction.

80. Valantasis, "Constructions of Power in Asceticism," 797. Also see idem, "Theory of the Social Function of Asceticism"; and idem, "Is the Gospel of Thomas Ascetical?"

81. As described in Good, *Medicine, Rationality, and Experience*, 116–34, and discussed in Chapter 1.

82. A phenomenon well studied among medical anthropologists and sociologists. See Frank, *Wounded Storyteller*; Hawkins, *Reconstructing Illness*; Kleinman, *Illness Narratives*; and Brody, *Stories of Sickness*.

83. *Letter* 74, trans. Chryssavgis [Neyt and Angelis-Noah, 352].

84. *Letter* 74 [Neyt and Angelis-Noah, 352, 354].

85. In a similar story from John Moschus, *Spiritual Meadow*, trans. John Whortley, CS 139 (Kalamazoo, Mich.: Cistercian Publications, 1992), 201 (a Palestinian collection slightly later than Barsanuphius and John), a woman laments that god has ceased to visit her with illness.

86. *Letter* 77, trans. Chryssavgis, altered [Neyt and Angelis-Noah, 356]. Despair of one's hope for salvation is typical of the thought of sadness in monastic psychology; see Evagrius of Pontus, *Antirrhetikos*, Book 4, trans. Brakke, *Talking Back*.

87. *Letter* 77, trans. Chryssavgis [Neyt and Angelis-Noah, 358].

88. *Letter* 77, trans. Chryssavgis, altered [Neyt and Angelis-Noah, 358].

89. *Letter* 77, trans. Chryssavgis [Neyt and Angelis-Noah, 360]. The perfect saints are thus "freed from all the faults and passions and sins of this life."

90. *Letter* 78 [Neyt and Angelis-Noah, 362]. I presume that this does not refer to being compelled to eat by his neighbors, as monks prone to self-destructive fasting are to be treated in the *Life of Syncletica*.

91. *Letter* 78, trans. Chryssavgis [Neyt and Angelis-Noah, 362].

92. *Letter* 78, trans. Chryssavgis [Neyt and Angelis-Noah, 362, 364].

93. Dow, "Universal Aspects," 56.

94. *Letter* 118 [Neyt and Angelis-Noah, 448, 450].

95. *Letter* 119, trans. Chryssavgis [Neyt and Angelis-Noah, 450–52].

96. *Letter* 119, trans. Chryssavgis [Neyt and Angelis-Noah, 454].

97. Kleinman, *Rethinking Psychiatry*, 121–22; also cf. idem, *Illness Narratives*, 185–86.

98. *Letter* 79, trans. Chryssavgis [Neyt and Angelis-Noah, 364].

99. *Letter* 79, trans. Chryssavgis [Neyt and Angelis-Noah, 366].

100. E.g., Crislip, *From Monastery to Hospital*, 87–90.

101. *Letter* 90, trans. Chryssavgis [Neyt and Angelis-Noah, 382].

102. *Letter* 90, trans. Chryssavgis [Neyt and Angelis-Noah, 386].

103. The summary of Andrew's letter in *Letter* 76 does not specify that he has been continuously ill but provides the content of Andrew's letter without reference to the letters that precede or follow: "The same old man lived with a certain brother, and both of them fell ill." I think it unlikely that he had experienced a recovery and fallen ill again, since when he recovers later in the *Correspondence* it is the source both of much joy and of much anxiety, as discussed above. I think it is more likely that it is a function of the editor's summarizing, interested less in creating a narrative out of the correspondence (as I am) and more in facilitating the use of discrete letters as sources of spiritual direction.

104. Bitton-Ashkelony and Kofsky, *Monastic School of Gaza*, 202–3; e.g., in *Letters* 233, 251, 503, 504.

105. *Letter* 92, trans. Chryssavgis.

106. *Letter* 92, trans. Chryssavgis [Neyt and Angelis-Noah, 390].

107. Described in Hadot, *Philosophy as a Way of Life*, 130–36.

108. *Letter* 92, trans. Chryssavgis [Neyt and Angelis-Noah, 392]. See Hausherr, *Spiritual Direction*, 89, and for *antirrhēsis* in Barsanuphius, 3.

109. Evagrius of Pontus, *Talking Back* 5.9–11, trans. Brakke, corrected.

110. *Letter* 93, trans. Chryssavgis [Neyt and Angelis-Noah, 392].

111. This may be because the letters are to Andrew. If we had a simultaneous letter to the other brother, blame might fall very differently.

112. *Letter* 93, trans. Chryssavgis [Neyt and Angelis-Noah, 394].

113. Ibid.

114. *Letter* 94, trans. Chryssavgis [Neyt and Angelis-Noah, 396, 398].

115. *Letter* 94 and *Letter* 92, trans. Chryssavgis [Neyt and Angelis-Noah, 398, 388].

116. *Letter* 96, trans. Chryssavgis [Neyt and Angelis-Noah, 404].

117. *Letter* 98, trans. Chryssavgis [Neyt and Angelis-Noah, 408].

118. *Letter* 98, trans. Chryssavgis [Neyt and Angelis-Noah, 410].

119. *Letter* 109, trans. Chryssavgis [Neyt and Angelis-Noah, 432–34].

120. *Letter* 122, trans. Chryssavgis [Neyt and Angelis-Noah, 456].

121. *Letter* 122, trans. Chryssavgis [Neyt and Angelis-Noah, 458].

122. *Letter* 123, trans. Chryssavgis, altered [Neyt and Angelis-Noah, 458, 460].

123. *Letter* 73, trans. Chryssavgis [Neyt and Angelis-Noah, 350].

CONCLUSION

1. Krueger, *Writing and Holiness*; idem, "Writing as Devotion."

2. On the fame of his narrative of Simeon, see Krueger, *Writing and Holiness*, 17. Theodoret refers to these narratives as *diēgēmata* (16).

3. Jacob's illness is discussed in Urbainczyck, *Theodoret of Cyrrhus*, 125–26, with different emphases; but the narrative of Jacob's illness is not discussed in Canivet, *Le Monachisme syrien selon de Cyr.*

4. Theodoret, *Historia religiosa* 21.5, trans. Price [Canivet and Leroy-Molinghen, 76, 78]; the title, organization, and context of Theodoret's *History* is covered in Krueger, *Writing and Holiness*, 15–17.

5. Theodoret, *Historia religiosa* 21.8, trans. Price [Canivet and Leroy-Molinghen, 80, 82].

6. Theodoret, *Historia religiosa* 21.11, trans. Price [Canivet and Leroy-Molinghen, 84, 86].

Works Cited

ANCIENT SOURCES

Aelius Aristides. *Sacred Tales.* Edited by C. A. Behr. *P. Aelii Aristidis Opera Quae Extant Omnia.* Leiden: Brill, 1976. Translated by C. A. Behr. *P. Aelius Aristides: The Complete Works.* Leiden: Brill, 1981–86.

Antony. *Letters.* Edited by Gérard Garitte. *Lettres de Saint Antoine: Version géorgienne et fragments coptes.* CSCO 148–49. Louvain: L. Durbecq, 1955. E. O. Winstedt. "The Original Text of One of St. Antony's Letters." *Journal of Theological Studies* 7 (1906): 540–45. (Syriac) F. Nau. "La version syriaque de la première lettre de Saint Antoine." *Revue de l'Orient Chrétien* 14 (1909): 282–97. Translated by Samuel Rubenson. *The Letters of St. Antony: Origenist Theology, Monastic Tradition, and the Making of a Saint.* Reprint, Harrisburg, Pa.: Trinity Press International, 1995.

Apocalypse of Paul. Translated in *New Testament Apocrypha.* Edited by Wilhelm Schneemelcher and Edgar Hennecke. English edition by Robert McL. Wilson. Vol. 2. Philadelphia: Westminster, 1963–66.

Apophthegmata patrum. Alphabetical series. *PG* 65.71–440. Anonymous series. Edited by F. Nau. "Histoires des solitaires égyptiens." *Revue de l'Orient Chrétien* 12–14 (1907–9); 17–18 (1912–13). Translated by Jean-Claude Guy. *Recherches sur la tradition grecque des Apophthegmata Patrum.* Subsidia Hagiographica 36. Brussels: Société des Bollandistes, 1962. Benedicta Ward. *The Sayings of the Desert Fathers.* CS 59. Kalamazoo, Mich.: Cistercian Publications, 1975.

Athanasius. *Life of Antony.* Edited by G. J. M. Bartelink. *Athanase d'Alexandrie, Vie d'Antoine.* SC 400. Paris: Cerf, 1994. Translated by Robert C. Gregg. *Athanasius: The Life of Antony and the Letter to Marcellinus.* Classics of Western Spirituality. Mahwah, N.J.: Paulist Press, 1980.

———. "On Sickness and Health." Edited by Franz Diekamp. *Analecta Patristica.* Orientalia lovaniensa analecta 117. Rome: Pont. Institutum Orientalium Studiorum, 1938.

Augustine. *Confessions.* Translated by R. S. Pine-Coffin. London: Penguin, 1961.

Barsanuphius and John of Gaza. *Letters.* Edited by François Neyt and Paula Angelis-Noah. Translated by Lucien Regnault. *Barsanuphius et Jean de Gaza: Correspondance.* SC 426–27, 450–51. Paris: Cerf, 1997–2001. Edited by Derwas V. Chitty. *Barsanuphius and John: Questions and Responses. PO* 31.3. Paris: Firmin Didot, 1966. Translated by John Chryssavgis. *Barsanuphius and John: Letters.* 2 vols. Fathers of the Church 113–14. Washington, D.C.: Catholic University of America Press, 2007. Translated by Philippe Lemaire and Bernard Outtier. *Barsanuphe et Jean de Gaza: Correspondance.* Sablé-sur-Sarthe: Solesmes, 1972.

Basil of Caesaria. *Letters.* Edited and translated by Roy J. Deferrari. *Saint Basil: The Letters.* Loeb Classical Library. Cambridge, Mass.: Harvard University Press, 1962. Translated by Blomfield Jackson. NPNF. 2nd series, vol. 8. Peabody, Mass.: Hendrickson Publishers, 1994.

———. *Quod Deus non est auctor malorum. PG* 31:329–54. Translated by Nonna Verna Harrison. *St. Basil the Great: On the Human Condition.* Popular Patristics Series. Crestwood, N.Y.: St. Vladimir's Seminary Press, 2005.

———. *Regulae brevius tractatae. PG* 31.1080–1305. Translated by W. L. K. Clarke. *The Ascetic Works of Saint Basil.* London: SPCK, 1925. Anna M. Silvas. *The Asketikon of St. Basil the Great.* Oxford Early Christian Studies. Oxford: Oxford University Press, 2005.

———. *Regulae fusius tractatae. PG* 31.889–1052. Translated by W. L. K. Clarke. *The Ascetic Works of Saint Basil.* London: SPCK, 1925. Anna M. Silvas. *The Asketikon of St. Basil the Great.* Oxford Early Christian Studies. Oxford: Oxford University Press, 2005.

Cicero. *Tusculan Disputations.* Translated by J. E. King. Loeb Classical Library. Cambridge, Mass.: Harvard University Press, 1945.

Evagrius of Pontus. *Antirrhetikos.* Translated by David Brakke. *Talking Back: A Handbook for Combating Demons.* CS 229. Kalamazoo, Mich.: Cistercian Publications, 2009.

———. *Kephalaia gnostica.* Edited by Antoine Guillaumont. *Les six centuries des "Kephalaia gnostica" d'Évagre le Pontique. PO* 28.1. Paris: Firmin-Didot, 1958.

———. *On Thoughts.* Edited by Antoine Guillaumont, Claire Guillaumont, and Paul Géhin. *Évagre le pontique: Sur les Pensées. SC* 356. Paris: Cerf, 1989. Translated by Robert E. Sinkewicz. *Evagrius of Pontus: The Greek Ascetic Corpus.* Oxford Early Christian Studies. Oxford: Oxford University Press, 2003.

———. *Praktikos.* Edited by Antoine Guillaumont and Claire Guillaumont. *Évagre le pontique: Traité pratique ou le moine.* 2 vols. SC 170–71. Paris: Cerf, 1971. Translated by Robert E. Sinkewicz. *Evagrius of Pontus.* John Eudes Bamberger. *Evagrius Ponticus: The Praktikos, Chapters on Prayer.* CS 4. Kalamazoo, Mich.: Cistercian Publications, 1970.

Fronto. *The Correspondence of Marcus Cornelius Fronto.* Edited by C. R. Haines. Loeb Classical Library. Cambridge, Mass.: Harvard University Press, 1962.

Galen. *De sanitate tuenda.* Translated by Robert Montraville Green. *A Translation of Galen's Hygiene (De sanitate tuenda).* Springfield, Ill.: Thomas, 1951.

———. *Opera omnia.* Edited by K. G. Kühn. 22 vols. Leipzig, 1821–33. Reprint, Hildesheim: G. Olms, 1964–65.

———. *Selected Works.* Translated by P. N. Singer. Oxford World's Classics. Oxford: Oxford University Press, 1997.

Gregory of Nazianzus. *On His Sister Gorgonia. PG* 35.789–818.

———. *Oration 21. PG* 35.1081–1121.

Hesiod. *Theogony* and *Works and Days*. Translated by Glenn W. Most. *Hesiod: Theogony, Works and Days, Testimonia*. Loeb Classical Library. Cambridge, Mass.: Harvard University Press, 2006.

Hippocrates. Edited by W. H. S. Jones. Vol. 4. Loeb Classical Library. Cambridge, Mass.: Harvard University Press, 1959.

Hippocrates. *Diseases IV*. Edited by Émile Littré. *Oeuvres completes d'Hippocrate*. Vol. 7. Amsterdam: Hakkert, 1979.

Hippocratic Writings. Translated by J. Chadwick and W. N. Mann. Edited by G. E. R. Lloyd. London: Penguin, 1978.

Historia monachorum in Aegypto (*History of the Monks in Egypt*). Edited by André-Jean Festugière. *Historia monachorum in Aegypto*. Subsidia Hagiographica 53. Brussels: Société des Bollandistes, 1971. Translated by Norman Russell. *Lives of the Desert Fathers*. CS 34. Kalamazoo, Mich.: Cistercian Publications, 1980.

Homer. *Iliad*. Translated by A. T. Murray. 2nd ed. Cambridge, Mass.: Harvard University Press, 1999.

Iamblichus. *On the Pythagorean Life*. Translated by John Dillon and Jackson Hershbell. *On the Pythagorean Way of Life*. Texts and Translations 29. Graeco-Roman Religion Series 11. Atlanta: Scholars Press, 1990.

Isaiah of Scetis. *Ascetic Discourses*. Edited by René Draguet. *Les cinq recensions de l'Ascéticon syriaque d'Abba Isaïe*. CSCO 289, 293. Louvain: Secrétariat du CSCO, 1968. Translated by John Chryssavgis and Pachomios (Robert) Penkett. CS 150. Kalamazoo, Mich.: Cistercian Publications, 2002.

Jacob of Serug. *Homily on Simeon the Stylite*. Translated by Susan Ashbrook Harvey. In *Ascetic Behavior in Greco-Roman Antiquity*, edited by Vincent L. Wimbush, 15–28. Studies in Antiquity and Christianity. Minneapolis: Fortress Press, 1990.

Jerome. *Letters*. Translated by W. H. Fremantle, G. Lewis, and W. G. Martley. NPNF. 2nd series, vol. 6. Peabody, Mass.: Hendrickson, 1994. Edited by Isidorus Hilberg. *Sancti Eusebii Hieronymi. Epistulae*. CSEL 54. Vienna: Österreichischen Akademie der Wissenschaften, 1996.

———. *Life of Paul. PL* 23:17–30. Translated by Paul B. Harvey. "Jerome, *Life of Paul, the First Hermit*." In *Ascetic Behavior*, edited by Wimbush, 357–69.

———. *Vita Hilarionis. PL* 23.29–53.

John Cassian. *Conferences*. Edited by Dom Eugène Pichery. *Jean Cassien: Conférences I-VII*. SC 42bis. Paris: Cerf, 2008. Translated by Boniface Ramsey. *John Cassian: The Conferences*. ACW 57. New York: Paulist, 1997.

John Chrysostom. *Hom. de statuis 1. PG* 49.15–34. NPNF. 1st series, vol. 9.

———. *Hom. 16 de Tim. PG* 62.585–90. NPNF. 1st series, vol. 13.

———. *Hom. 26 de 2 Cor. PG* 61.575–84. Translated by Talbot W. Chambers. NPNF. 1st series, vol. 12.

Liber Orsiesii. Edited by L.-Th. Lefort. *Oeuvres de. S.Pachôme et de ses disciples*. CSCO 159–60. Louvain: L. Durbecq, 1956.

Life of Adam and Eve. Translated by M. D. Johnson. In *The Old Testament Pseudepigrapha,* edited by James H. Charlesworth, 2:249–95. Anchor Bible Reference Library. New York: Doubleday, 1985. Edited by Johannes Tromp. *The Life of Adam and Eve in Greek: A Critical Edition.* Pseudepigrapha Veteris Testamenti Graece 16. Leiden: Brill, 2005. Edited by Gary A. Anderson and Michael E. Stone. *A Synopsis of the Books of Adam and Eve.* SBL Early Judaism and Its Literature 5. Atlanta: Scholars Press, 1994.

Lives of Pachomius. Edited by L.-T. Lefort. *S. Pachomii vita bohairice scripta.* CSCO 89. Paris: E Typographeo Reipublicae, 1925. Idem. *S. Pachomii vitae sahidice scriptae.* CSCO 99–100. Louvain: Institut Orientaliste, 1933–34. Edited by François Halkin. *Sancti Pachomii Vitae Graece.* Subsidia Hagiographica 19. Brussels: Société Bollandistes, 1932. Translated by Armand Veilleux. *Pachomian Koinonia.* Vol. 1. CS 45. Kalamazoo, Mich.: Cistercian Publications, 1980. Translated by L.-Th. Lefort. *Les Vies coptes de saint Pachôme.* Bibliothèque du *Muséon* 16. Louvain: Institut Orientaliste, 1943.

Lives of Simeon Stylites. Edited by Hans Lietzmann. *Das Leben des Heiligen Symeon Stylites.* TU 32. Leipzig: Hinrichs, 1908. Translated by Robert Doran. *The Lives of Simeon Stylites.* CS 112. Kalamazoo, Mich.: Cistercian Publications, 1992.

Pachomius. *Letters.* Edited by Hans Quecke. *Die Briefe Pachoms: Griechischer Text der Handschrift W. 145 der Chester Beatty Library.* Textus Patristici et Liturgici 11. Regensburg, 1975. Translated by Armand Veilleux. *Pachomian Koinonia.* Vol. 3. CS 47. Kalamazoo, Mich.: Cistercian Publications, 1982.

———. *Praecepta.* Translated by Armand Veilleux. *Pachomian Koinonia.* Vol. 2. CS 46. Kalamazoo, Mich.: Cistercian Publications, 1981.

———. *Rules.* Edited by Amand Boon. *Pachomiana Latina.* Bibliothèque de la Revue d'histoire ecclésiastique 7. Louvain: Bureau de la Revue, 1932. (Coptic) L.-Th. Lefort. *Oeuvres de s. Pachôme et de ses disciples.* CSCO 160. Louvain: Durbecq, 1956.

Palladius. *Lausiac History.* Edited by Dom Cuthbert Butler. *The Lausiac History of Palladius.* Texts and Studies 6.I–II. Cambridge: Cambridge University Press, 1898. Translated by Robert T. Meyer. *Palladius: The Lausiac History.* ACW 34. New York: Paulist, 1964. Coptic fragments edited by Émile Amélineau. *De Historia Lausiaca, quaenam sit huius ad Monachorum Aegyptiorum historiam scribendam utilitas.* Paris: Leroux, 1887. Translated by Tim Vivian. *Four Desert Fathers: Pambo, Evagrius, Macarius of Egypt, and Macarius of Alexandria, Coptic Texts Relating to the* Lausiac History *of Palladius.* Popular Patristics Series. Crestwood, N.Y.: St. Vladimir's Seminary Press, 2005.

Paphnutius. *Histories of the Monks of Upper Egypt and the Life of Onnophrius, by Paphnutius.* Edited by E. A. Wallis Budge. *Coptic Martyrdoms Etc. in the Dialect of Upper Egypt.* Coptic Texts. Vol. 4, 205–24. London: British Museum, 1914. Translated by Tim Vivian. CS 140. Kalamazoo, Mich.: Cistercian Publications, 1993. Alternate translation by Tim Vivian. *Journeying into God: Seven Early Monastic Lives,* 166–87. Minneapolis: Fortress Press, 1996. Revised from "The Life of Onnophrius: A New Translation." *Coptic Church Review* 102 (1991): 99–111.

Papias. Translated and edited by Michael W. Holmes. *The Apostolic Fathers.* 3rd ed. Grand Rapids, Mich.: Baker Academic, 2006.

Paradise or Garden of the Holy Fathers. Translated by E. A. W. Budge. London: Chatto & Windus, 1907.

Porphyry. *On Abstinence.* Translated by Anitra Bingham Kolenkow. "Chaeremon the Stoic on Egyptian Temple Askesis." In *Ascetic Behavior*, edited by Wimbush, 389–92.

Pseudo-Athanasius. *De virginitate.* Edited by Eduard Freiherrn Von der Goltz. *Logos Sōtērias pros tēn Parthenon (De virginitate), Eine echte Schrift des Athanasius. TU* 14 (1905).

———. *Life and Regimen of the Blessed and Holy Teacher Syncletica. PG* 28.1487–1558. Translated by Elizabeth Bryson Bongie. *The Life & Regimen of the Blessed & Holy Teacher, Syncletica.* Peregrina Translation Series 21, Akathist Series 3. Corrected edition. Toronto: Peregrina Publishing, 1996. Elizabeth A. Castelli. "Pseudo-Athanasius: The Life and Activity of the Holy and Blessed Teacher Syncletica." In *Ascetic Behavior*, edited by Wimbush, 265–311.

Pseudo-Basil. *Sermo asceticus. PG* 31.870–82. Translated by M. Monica Wagner. *Saint Basil: Ascetical Works.* Fathers of the Church 9. New York: Fathers of the Church, 1950.

Simon of Taibutheh. "Mystical Works of Simon of Taibutheh." Edited and translated by Alphonse Mingana. *Woodbrooke-Studies* 7. *Early Christian Mystics*, 1–69, 201–30. Cambridge: Heffer and Sons, 1934.

Sophocles. *Philoctetes.* Translated by Hugh Lloyd-Jones. Loeb Classical Library. Cambridge, Mass.: Harvard University Press, 1994.

Soranus of Ephesus. *Gynecology.* Translated by Owsei Temkin. Baltimore: Johns Hopkins University Press, 1956.

Theodoret of Cyrrhus. *History of the Monks of Syria (Historia religiosa).* Translated by R. M. Price. CS 88. Kalamazoo, Mich.: Cistercian Publications, 1985. Edited by Pierre Canivet and Alice Leroy-Molinghen. SC 234, 257. Paris: Cerf, 1977–79.

Thucydides. *History of the Peloponnesian War.* Translated by Charles Forster Smith. Loeb Classical Library. Cambridge, Mass.: Harvard University Press, 1962.

MODERN SOURCES

Amundsen, Darrel W., and Gary B. Ferngren. "The Perception of Disease and Disease Causality in the New Testament." *ANRW* 37.3 (1996): 2934–56.

Avalos, Hector. *Illness and Health Care in the Ancient Near East: The Role of the Temple in Greece, Mesopotamia, and Israel.* Harvard Semitic Museum Monographs 54. Atlanta: Scholars Press, 1995.

Avalos, Hector, Sarah J. Melcher, and Jeremy Schipper, eds. *This Abled Body: Rethinking Disabilities in Biblical Studies.* SBL Semeia Studies. Atlanta: Scholars Press, 2007.

Bacht, Heinricht. *Das Vermächtnis des Ursprungs. Studien zum frühen Mönchtum II: Pachomius—Der Mann und sein Werk.* Münster: Echter Verlag, 1983.

Bagnall, Roger, ed. *Egypt in the Byzantine World (300–700).* Cambridge: Cambridge University Press, 2008.

———. *Egypt in Late Antiquity.* Princeton, N.J.: Princeton University Press, 1993.

———. *Reading Papyri, Writing Ancient History.* Approaching the Ancient World. New York: Routledge, 1995.

Bagnall, Roger S., and Bruce W. Frier. *The Demography of Roman Egypt.* Cambridge Studies in Population, Economy, and Society in Past Time 23. Cambridge: Cambridge University Press, 1994.

Barash, David P. "Who Are We?" *Chronicle of Higher Education.* November 7, 2008.

Barnes, Timothy D. "Angel of Light or Mystic Initiate? The Problem of the *Life of Antony.*" *Journal of Theological Studies* 37 (1986): 353–68.

Barrett-Lennard, R. *Christian Healing after the New Testament.* Lanham, Md.: University Press of America, 1994.

———. "Request for Prayer for Healing." In *New Documents Illustrating Early Christianity: A Review of Greek Inscriptions and Papyri Published in 1979,* edited by G. H. R. Horsley, 245–50. Sydney: Macquarie University, 1987.

Baumeister, Roy. *Escaping the Self: Alcoholism, Spirituality, Masochism, and Other Flights from the Burden of Selfhood.* New York: Basic Books, 1991.

Bell, H. Idris. *Jews and Christians in Egypt.* Oxford: Oxford University Press, 1924.

Bitton-Ashkelony, Brouria, and Aryeh Kofsky. *The Monastic School of Gaza.* Supplements to *Vigiliae Christianae* 78. Leiden: Brill, 2005.

Bloomfeld, Morton W. *The Seven Deadly Sins: An Introduction to the History of a Religious Concept, with Special Reference to Medieval English Literature.* [East Lansing, Mich.]: Michigan State College Press, 1952.

Blowers, Paul M. "Envy's Narrative Scripts: Cyprian, Basil, and the Monastic Sages on the Anatomy and Cure of the Invidious Emotions." *Modern Theology* 25 (2009): 21–43.

Böcher, Otto. *Christus Exorcista: Dämonismus und Taufe im Neuen Testament.* Stuttgart: W. Kohlhammer, 1972.

Bousset, Wilhelm. *Apophthegmata: Studien zur Geschichte des ältesten Mönchtums.* Tübingen: J. C. B. Mohr [P. Siebeck], 1923.

Brakke, David. *Athanasius and the Politics of Asceticism.* Oxford Early Christian Texts. Oxford: Oxford University Press, 1995. Reprint, *Athanasius and Asceticism.* Baltimore: Johns Hopkins University Press, 1998.

———. *Demons and the Making of the Monk: Spiritual Warfare in Early Christianity.* Cambridge, Mass.: Harvard University Press, 2005.

———. "The Lady Appears: Materializations of 'Woman' in Early Monastic Literature." In *The Cultural Turn in Late Ancient Studies: Gender, Asceticism, and Historiography,* edited by Dale B. Martin and Patricia Cox Miller, 25–39. Durham, N.C.: Duke University Press, 2005.

———. "The Making of Monastic Demonology: Three Ascetic Teachers on Withdrawal and Resistance." *Church History* 70 (2001): 19–48.

———. "'Outside the Places, within the Truth': Athanasius of Alexandria and the Localization of the Holy." In *Pilgrimage and Holy Space in Late Antique Egypt,* edited by David Frankfurter, 468–69. Religions in the Graeco-Roman World 134. Leiden: Brill, 1998.

Brody, Howard. *Stories of Sickness.* 2nd ed. New York: Oxford University Press, 2003.

Brown, Peter L. *Authority and the Sacred: Aspects of the Christianisation of the Roman World.* Cambridge: Cambridge University Press, 1995.

———. *The Body and Society: Men, Women, and Sexual Renunciation in Early Christianity.* Lectures in the History of Religions. New York: Columbia University Press, 1988.

———. "The Rise and Function of the Holy Man in Late Antiquity." In *Society and the Holy,* 103–52. Berkeley: University of California Press, 1982.

———. "The Saint as Exemplar in Late Antiquity." *Representations* 1.2 (1983): 1–25.

———. "Town, Village and Holy Man: The Case of Syria." In *Society and the Holy,* 153–65.

Bumazhnov, Dmitrij F. "Adam Alone in Paradise: A Jewish-Christian Exegesis and Its Implications for the History of Asceticism." In *The Exegetical Encounter between Jews and Christians in Late Antiquity,* edited by Emmanouela Grypeou and Helen Spurling, 31–41. Jewish and Christian Perspective Series 18. Leiden: Brill, 2009.

Burrows, Mark S. "The Visibility of God in the Holy Man: A Reconsideration of the Role of the Apa in the Pachomian Vitae." *Vigiliae Christianae* 41 (1987): 11–33.

Burrus, Virginia. *Saving Shame: Martyrs, Saints, and Other Abject Subjects.* Divinations: Rereading Late Ancient Religions. Philadelphia: University of Pennsylvania Press, 2008.

Cain, Andrew. *The Letters of Jerome: Asceticism, Biblical Exegesis, and the Construction of Christian Authority in Late Antiquity.* Oxford Early Christian Studies. Oxford: Oxford University Press, 2009.

Canivet, Pierre. *Le Monachisme syrien selon de Cyr.* Théologie historique 42. Paris: Beauchesne, 1997.

Castelli, Elizabeth A. *Martyrdom and Memory: Early Christian Culture Making.* Gender, Theory, and Religion. New York: Columbia University Press, 2004.

———. "Mortifying the Body, Curing the Soul: Beyond Ascetic Dualism in the Life of Saint Syncletica." *Differences* 4 (1992): 134–53.

Chadwick, Henry. "Pachomios and the Idea of Sanctity." In *The Byzantine Saint,* edited by Sergei Hackel, 11–24. London: Fellowship of St. Alban and St. Sergius, 1981. Reprint, Crestwood, N.Y.: St. Vladimir's Seminary Press, 2001.

Chitty, Derwas J. *The Desert a City.* Oxford: Blackwell, 1966. Reprint, Crestwood, N.Y.: St. Vladimir's Seminary Press, 1995.

Cioran, E. M. *The Fall into Time.* Translated by Richard Howard. Chicago: Quadrangle Books, 1970.

———. *Tears and Saints.* Translated by Ilinca Zarifopol-Johnston. Chicago: University of Chicago Press, 1995.

Clark, Elizabeth A. *The Origenist Controversy: The Cultural Construction of an Early Christian Debate.* Princeton, N.J.: Princeton University Press, 1992.

Clark, Gillian. "The Health of the Spiritual Athlete." In *Health in Antiquity,* edited by Helen King, 216–29. London: Routledge, 2005.

Clarke, W. K. Lowther. *St. Basil the Great: A Study in Monasticism.* Cambridge: Cambridge University Press, 1913.

Cobb, L. Stephanie. *Dying to Be Men: Gender and Language in Early Christian Martyr Texts.* Gender Theory and Religion. New York: Columbia University Press, 2008.

Cooper, Kate. *The Virgin and the Bride: Idealized Womanhood in Late Antiquity.* Cambridge, Mass.: Harvard University Press, 1996.

Corrigan, Kevin. *Evagrius and Gregory: Mind, Soul, and Body in the 4th Century.* Farnham, U.K.: Ashgate, 2009.

Crislip, Andrew. "Asceticism." In *The Cambridge Dictionary of Christian Theology,* edited by Ian A. McFarland et al. Cambridge: Cambridge University Press, 2011.

———. "Care for the Sick in Shenoute's Monasteries." In *Christianity and Monasticism in Upper Egypt,* edited by Gawdat Gabra and Hany Takla, 21–30. Vol. 1, *Akmim and Sohag.* Cairo: American University in Cairo Press, 2008.

———. "Envy and Anger at the World's Creation and Destruction in the Treatise without Title *On the Origin of the World* (NHC II,5)." *Vigiliae Christianae* 65 (2011): 285–310.

———. *From Monastery to Hospital: Christian Monasticism and the Transformation of Health Care in Late Antiquity.* Ann Arbor: University of Michigan Press, 2005.

———. "'I Have Chosen Sickness': The Controversial Function of Sickness in Early Christian Ascetic Practice." In *Asceticism and Its Critics: Historical Accounts and Comparative Perspectives,* edited by Oliver Freiberger, 179–209. AAR Cultural Criticism Series. New York: Oxford University Press, 2006.

———. "Shenoute of Atripe on Christ the Physician and the Cure of Souls." *Le Muséon* 122 (2009): 265–95.

———. "The Sin of Sloth or the Illness of the Demons? The Demon of Acedia in Early Christian Monasticism." *Harvard Theological Review* 98 (2005): 143–69.

Cross, F. L., and E. A. Livingstone, eds. *Oxford Dictionary of the Christian Church.* 2nd ed. Oxford: Oxford University Press, 1974.

Crum, W. E. *Coptic Dictionary.* Oxford: Clarendon Press, 1939.

D'Andrade, Roy G., and Claudia Strauss, eds. *Human Motives and Cultural Models.* Publications of the Society for Psychological Anthropology. Cambridge: Cambridge University Press, 1992.

Davis, Stephen J. "Jerome's *Life of Paul* and the Promotion of Egyptian Monasticism in the West." In *The Cave Church of Paul the Hermit at the Monastery of St. Paul, Egypt,* edited by William Lyster, 25–41. New Haven, Conn.: Yale University Press/American Research Center in Egypt, 2008.

Dörnemann, Michael. *Krankheit und Heilung in der Theologie der frühen Kirchenväter.* Studien und Texte zu Antike und Christentum 20. Tübingen: Mohr Siebeck, 2003.

Dörries, Hermann. "Die *Vita Antonii* als Geschichtsquelle." *Nachrichten der Akademie der Wissenschaften in Göttingen, Phil.-hist. Klasse* 14 (1949): 357–410.

Dow, James. "Universal Aspects of Symbolic Healing: A Theoretical Synthesis." *American Anthropologist* 88 (1986): 56–69.

Drijvers, H. J. W. "The Saint as Symbol: Conceptions of the Person in Late Antiquity and Early Christianity." In *Concepts of Person in Religion and Thought,* edited by Hans G.

Kippenberg, Ume B. Kuiper, and Andy F. Sanders, 137–57. Berlin and New York: Mouton de Gruyter, 1990.

Eldridge, Michael D. *Dying Adam and His Multiethnic Family.* Studia in Veteris Testamenti pseudepigrapha 16. Leiden: Brill, 2001.

Eliot, Alison Goddard. *Roads to Paradise: Reading the Lives of the Early Saints.* Hanover, N.H.: University Press of New England, 1987.

Emmel, Stephen. "Coptic Literature in the Byzantine and Early Islamic World." In *Egypt in the Byzantine World*, edited by Bagnall, 83–102.

———. *Shenoute's Literary Corpus.* CSCO 599–600. Louvain: Peeters, 2004.

Fernández, S. *Cristo medico según Orígenes: La actividad médica como metáfora de la acción divina.* Studia ephemeridis "Augustinianum" 64. Rome: Institutum patristicum Augustinianum, 1999.

Ferngren, Gary B. *Medicine and Health Care in Early Christianity.* Baltimore: Johns Hopkins University Press, 2009.

Ferngren, Gary B., and Darrel W. Amundsen. "Medicine and Christianity in the Roman Empire: Compatibilities and Tensions." *ANRW* 37.3 (1996): 2957–80.

Flemming, Rebecca. *Medicine and the Making of Roman Women.* Oxford: Oxford University Press, 2000.

Förster, Hans. "Christlicher Trostbrief." In *Wiener Papyri als Festgabe zum 60. Geburtstag von Hermann Harrauer (P.Harrauer)*, edited by P. Palme, 213–22. Vienna: Holhausen, 2001.

Foucault, Michel. *The History of Sexuality.* Vol. 3, *The Care of the Self.* Translated by Robert Hurley. New York: Vintage, 1990.

———. "Technologies of the Self." In *Technologies of the Self: A Seminar with Michel Foucault*, edited by Luther H. Martin, Huck Gutman, and Patrick H. Hutton, 16–49. Amherst: University of Massachusetts Press, 1988.

France, Anatole. *Thaïs.* Translated by Basis Gulati. Chicago: University of Chicago Press, 1976.

Frank, Arthur W. *At the Will of the Body: Reflections on Illness.* Boston: Houghton Mifflin, 1991.

———. *The Wounded Storyteller: Body, Illness, and Ethics.* Chicago: University of Chicago Press, 1995.

Frank, Georgia. *The Memory of the Eyes: Pilgrims to Living Saints in Christian Late Antiquity.* Transformation of the Classical Heritage 30. Berkeley: University of California Press, 2000.

———. "Miracles, Monks, and Monuments: The *Historia Monachorum in Aegypto* as Pilgrims' Tales." In *Pilgrimage and Holy Space in Late Antique Egypt*, edited by David Frankfurter, 483–505. Religions in the Graeco-Roman World 134. Leiden: Brill, 1998.

Freiberger, Oliver, ed. *Asceticism and Its Critics.* AAR Cultural Criticism Series. New York: Oxford University Press, 2006.

Gaddis, Michael. *There Is No Crime for Those Who Have Christ: Religious Violence in the*

Christian Roman Empire. Transformation of the Classical Heritage 39. Berkeley: University of California Press, 2005.

Gain, Benoît. *L'Église de Cappadoce au IVᵉ siècle d'après le correspondance de Basile de Césarée (330–379)*. Orientalia christiana analecta 225. Rome: Pontificium Institutum Orientale, 1985.

Garland, Robert. *The Eye of the Beholder: Deformity and Disability in the Graeco-Roman World*. Ithaca, N.Y.: Cornell University Press, 1995.

Garrett, Susan R. "Paul's Thorn and Cultural Models of Affliction." In *The Social World of the First Christians: Essays in Honor of Wayne A. Meeks*, edited by O. Larry Yarbrough and L. Michael White, 82–99. Minneapolis: Fortress Press, 1995.

———. "Sociology (Early Christianity)." In *Anchor Bible Dictionary*, edited by David Noel Freedman, 6:91–92. New York: Doubleday, 1992.

Garro, Linda C. "Cognitive Medical Anthropology." In *Encyclopedia of Medical Anthropology: Health and Illness in the World's Cultures*, edited by Carol R. Ember and Melvin Ember, 12–23. New York: Kluwer, 2004.

George, Martin. "Tugenden im Vergleich: Ihre soteriologische Funktion in Jamblichs *Vita Pythagorica* und in Athanasios' *Vita Antonii*." In *Jamblich: Pythagoras, Legende—Lehre—Lebensgestaltung*, edited by Michael von Albrecht et al., 303–22. Scripta Antiquitatis Posterioris ad Ethicam Religionque pertinentia 4. Darmstadt: Wissenschaftliche Buchgesellschaft, 2002.

Gill, Christopher. "Ancient Psychotherapy." *Journal of the History of Ideas* 46 (1985): 307–25.

Gilman, Sander L. *Disease and Representation: Images of Illness from Madness to AIDS*. Ithaca, N.Y.: Cornell University Press, 1988.

Glucklich, Ariel. *Sacred Pain: Hurting the Body for the Sake of the Soul*. New York: Oxford University Press, 2001.

———. "Self and Sacrifice: A Phenomenological Psychology of Sacred Pain." *Harvard Theological Review* 92 (1999): 479–506.

Goehring, James E. "The First Sahidic *Life of Pachomius*." In *Religions of Late Antiquity in Practice*, edited by Richard Valantasis, 19–33. Princeton Readings in Religion. Princeton, N.J.: Princeton University Press, 2000.

———. "Melitian Monastic Organization." In idem, *Ascetics, Society, and the Desert*, 189–95. Studies in Antiquity and Christianity. Harrisburg, Pa.: Trinity Press International, 1999. Reprint, *Studia Patristica* 25 (1993): 388–95.

———. "Monastic Diversity and Ideological Boundaries in Fourth-Century Christian Egypt." In idem, *Ascetics, Society, and the Desert*, 196–218. Reprint, *JECS* 5 (1997): 61–84.

———. "Pachomius's Vision of Heresy: The Development of a Pachomian Tradition." In idem, *Ascetics, Society, and the Desert*, 137–61. Reprint, *Le Muséon* 95 (1982): 241–62.

———. "Remembering Abraham of Farshut: History, Hagiography, and the Fate of the Pachomian Tradition." *JECS* 14 (2006): 1–26.

———. "Through a Glass Darkly: Diverse Images of the *Apotaktikoi(ai)* in Early Egyptian

Monasticism." In idem, *Ascetics, Society, and the Desert*, 53–72. Reprint, *Semeia* 58 (1992): 25–45.

———. "Withdrawing from the Desert: Pachomius and the Development of Village Monasticism in Upper Egypt." In idem, *Ascetics, Society, and the Desert*, 89–109. Reprint, *Harvard Theological Review* 89 (1996): 267–85.

Goehring, James E., and Robert F. Boughner. "Egyptian Monasticism (Selected Papyri)." In *Ascetic Behavior in Greco-Roman Antiquity*, edited by Vincent Wimbush, 456–63. Studies in Antiquity and Christianity. Minneapolis: Fortress Press, 1990.

Goffman, Erving. *Stigma: Notes on the Management of Spoiled Identity.* New York: Simon & Schuster, 1963.

Good, Byron J. *Medicine, Rationality, and Experience: An Anthropological Perspective.* Lewis Henry Morgan Lectures 1990. Cambridge: Cambridge University Press, 1994.

Gorovitz, Samuel. *Doctors' Dilemmas: Moral Conflict and Medical Care.* New York: Macmillan, 1982.

Gould, Graham. *The Desert Fathers on Monastic Community.* Oxford Early Christian Studies. Oxford: Clarendon Press, 1993.

Graver, Margaret R. *Stoicism and Emotion.* Chicago: University of Chicago Press, 2007.

Grmek, Mirko. *Diseases in the Ancient Greek World.* Translated by Mireille Muellner and Leonard Mueller. Baltimore: Johns Hopkins University Press, 1989.

Guillaumont, Antoine. *Les "Kephalaia gnostica" d'Évagre le Pontique et l'histoire de l'origénisme chez les Grecs et chez les Syriens.* Patristica Sorboniensia. Paris: Eds. du Seuil, 1962.

Hadot, Pierre. *La philosophie comme manière de vivre: Entretiens avec Jeannie Carlier et Arnold I. Davidson.* Paris: A. Michel, 2001.

———. *Philosophy as a Way of Life.* Edited and translated by Arnold I. Davidson. Oxford: Blackwell, 1995.

Hägg, Tomas, and Philip Rousseau, eds. *Greek Biography and Panegyric in Late Antiquity.* Transformation of the Classical Heritage 32. Berkeley: University of California Press, 2000.

Hankinson, James. "Actions and Passions: Affection, Emotion, and Moral Self-management in Galen's Philosophical Psychology." In *Passions & Perceptions: Studies in Hellenistic Philosophy of Mind, Proceedings of the Fifth Symposium Hellenisticum*, edited by Jacques Brunschwig and Martha C. Nussbaum, 184–222. Cambridge: Cambridge University Press, 1993.

Harmless, William. *Desert Christians: An Introduction to the Literature of Early Monasticism.* New York: Oxford University Press, 2004.

Harnack, Adolf. *The Mission and Expansion of Christianity in the First Three Centuries.* Translated by James Moffatt. New York: Harper & Brothers, 1961.

Harpham, Geoffrey Halt. *The Ascetic Imperative in Culture and Criticism.* Chicago: University of Chicago Press, 1987.

Harris, J. Rendel. "Did Judas Really Commit Suicide?" *American Journal of Theology* 4 (1900): 490–513.

Harvey, Susan Ashbrook. "Embodiment in Time and Eternity: A Syriac Perspective." *St. Vladimir's Theological Quarterly* 43 (1999): 105–30.

———. "Physicians and Ascetics in John of Ephesus: An Expedient Alliance." *Dumbarton Oaks Papers* 38 (1984): 87–93.

———. *Scenting Salvation: Ancient Christianity and the Olfactory Imagination.* Transformation of the Classical Heritage 42. Berkeley: University of California Press, 2006.

———. "The Sense of a Stylite: Perspectives on Simeon the Elder." *Vigiliae Christianae* 42 (1988): 376–94.

Hauben, H. "The Melitian 'Church of the Martyrs': Christian Dissenters in Ancient Egypt." In *Ancient History in a Modern University*, edited by T. W. Hillard et al. Vol. 2, 329–49. Sydney: Macquarie University Ancient History Documentary Research Center, 1998.

Hausherr, Irénée. *Spiritual Direction in the Early Christian East.* Translated by Antony P. Gythiel. CS 116. Kalamazoo, Mich.: Cistercian Publications, 1990.

Hawkins, Anne Hunsaker. *Reconstructing Illness: Studies in Pathography.* 2nd ed. West Lafayette, Ind.: Purdue University Press, 1999.

Hevelone-Harper, Jennifer L. *Disciples of the Desert: Monks, Laity, and Spiritual Authority in Sixth-Century Gaza.* Baltimore: Johns Hopkins University Press, 2005.

Hobson, D. W. "Naming Practices in Roman Egypt." *Bulletin of the American Society of Papyrologists* 26 (1989): 157–74.

Holland, Dorothy, and Naomi Quinn, eds. *Cultural Models in Language and Thought.* Cambridge: Cambridge University Press, 1987.

Horden, Peregrine. "The Death of Ascetics: Sickness and Monasticism in the Early Byzantine Middle East." In *Monks, Hermits and the Ascetic Tradition*, edited by W. J. Sheils, 41–52. Studies in Church History 22. Oxford: Blackwell, 1985.

Horn, Cornelia B. *Asceticism and the Christological Controversy in Fifth-Century Palestine: The Career of Peter the Iberian.* Oxford Early Christian Studies. Oxford: Oxford University Press, 2006.

Jackson, Stanley W. *Care of the Psyche: A History of Psychological Healing.* New Haven, Conn.: Yale University Press, 1999.

Joest, Christoph. "Die Geheimschrift Pachoms—Versuch einer Verschlüsselung." *Ostchristliche Studien* 45 (1996): 268–89.

———. "Die Pachom-Briefe 1 und 2: Auflösung der Geheimbuchstaben und Entdeckungen zu den Briefüberschriften." *Journal of Coptic Studies* 4 (2002): 25–98.

Jouanna, Jacques. *Hippocrates.* Translated by M. B. DeBevoise. Medicine & Culture. Baltimore: Johns Hopkins University Press, 1999.

Judge, E. A. "The Earliest Known Use of Monachos for 'Monk' (*P.Coll.Youtie* 77) and the Origins of Monasticism." *Jahrbuch für Antike und Christentum* 20 (1977): 72–89.

———. "Fourth-Century Monasticism in the Papyri." In *Proceedings of the Sixteenth International Congress of Papyrology*, edited by Roger Bagnall et al., 613–20. Chico, Calif.: Scholars Press, 1981.

Kannengiesser, Charles. "Athanasius of Alexandria and the Ascetic Movement of His

Time." In *Asceticism*, edited by Vincent Wimbush and Richard Valantasis, 479–92. New York: Oxford University Press, 1995.

Karayannopoulos, Ioannes. "St. Basil's Social Activity: Principles and Praxis." In *Basil of Caesarea: Christian, Humanist, Ascetic*, edited by Paul J. Fedwick, 375–91. Toronto: Pontifical Institute of Mediaeval Studies, 1981.

Kelly, J. N. D. *Jerome: His Life, Writings, and Controversies*. London: Duckworth, 1975.

King, Helen, ed. *Health in Antiquity*. London: Routledge, 2005.

Kleinberg, Aviad. *Flesh Made Word: Saints' Stories and the Western Imagination*. Cambridge, Mass.: Harvard University Press, 2008.

Kleinman, Arthur. *The Illness Narratives: Suffering, Healing, and the Human Condition*. New York: Basic Books, 1988.

———. *Patients and Healers in the Context of Culture: An Exploration of the Borderland between Anthropology, Medicine, and Psychiatry*. Comparative Studies of Health Systems and Medical Care. Berkeley: University of California Press, 1980.

———. *Rethinking Psychiatry: From Cultural Category to Personal Experience*. New York: Free Press, 1988.

Knuuttila, Simo. *Emotions in Ancient and Medieval Philosophy*. Oxford: Clarendon Press, 2004.

Konstantinovsky, Julia. *Evagrius Ponticus: The Making of a Gnostic*. Farnham, U.K.: Ashgate, 2009.

Kramer, Bärbel, and John C. Shelton. *Das Archiv des Nepheros und Verwandte Texte*. Aegyptiaca Treverensia 4. Mainz am Rhein: von Zabern, 1987.

Krawiec, Rebecca. "'From the Womb of the Church': Monastic Families." *JECS* 11 (2003): 283–307.

———. *Shenoute and the Women of the White Monastery*. New York: Oxford University Press, 2002.

Krueger, Derek. *Writing and Holiness: The Practice of Authorship in the Early Christian East*. Divinations: Rereading Late Ancient Religion. Philadelphia: University of Pennsylvania Press, 2004.

———. "Writing as Devotion: Hagiographical Composition and the Cult of Saints in Theodoret of Cyrrhus and Cyril of Scythopolis." *Church History* 66 (1997): 707–19.

Kuefler, Mathew. *The Manly Eunuch: Masculinity, Gender Ambiguity, and Christian Ideology in Late Antiquity*. Chicago: University of Chicago Press, 2001.

Lampe, G. W. H. *Patristic Greek Lexicon*. Oxford: Oxford University Press, 1961.

Larchet, Jean-Claude. *The Theology of Illness*. Translated by John Breck and Michael Breck. Crestwood, N.Y.: St. Vladimir's Seminary Press, 2002.

Layton, Bentley. "Social Structure and Food Consumption in an Early Christian Monastery: The Evidence of Shenoute's *Canons* and the White Monastery Federation, A.D. 385–465." *Le Muséon* 115 (2002): 25–55.

LeGoff, Jacques. *The Birth of Purgatory*. Translated by Arthur Goldhammer. Chicago: University of Chicago Press, 1984.

Loewe, Ron. "Illness Narratives." In *Encyclopedia of Medical Anthropology: Health and Illness in the World's Cultures*, edited by Carol R. Ember and Melvin Ember, 42–49. New York: Kluwer, 2004.

Lusier, Philippe. "Chénouté, Victor, Jean de Lycopolis et Nestorius: Quand l'archimandrite d'Atripé en Haute-Égypte est-il mort?" *Orientalia* 78 (2009): 258–81.

Majno, Guido. *The Healing Hand: Man and Wound in the Ancient World.* Cambridge, Mass.: Harvard University Press, 1975.

Malina, Bruce J. "Pain, Power, and Personhood: Ascetic Behavior in the Ancient Mediterranean." In *Asceticism*, edited by Wimbush and Valantasis, 162–77.

Martin, Dale B. *The Corinthian Body.* New Haven, Conn.: Yale University Press, 1995.

Mattingly, Cheryl. *Healing Dramas and Clinical Plots: The Narrative Structure of Experience.* Cambridge: Cambridge University Press, 1998.

Mattingly, Cheryl and Linda C. Garro, eds. *Narrative and the Cultural Construction of Illness and Healing.* Berkeley: University of California Press, 2000.

McNeill, John Thomas. *A History of the Cure of Souls.* New York: Harper, 1951.

Merideth, Anne Elizabeth. "Illness and Healing in the Early Christian East." Ph.D. dissertation, Princeton University, 1999.

Miller, Patricia Cox. *Biography in Late Antiquity: A Quest for the Holy Man.* Transformation of the Classical Heritage 5. Berkeley: University of California Press, 1983.

———. *The Corporeal Imagination: Signifying the Holy in Late Ancient Christianity.* Divinations: Rereading Late Ancient Religion. Philadelphia: University of Pennsylvania Press, 2009.

———. "Shifting Selves in Late Antiquity." In *Religion and the Self in Antiquity*, edited by David Brakke, Michael L. Satlow, and Steven Weitzman, 15–39. Bloomington: Indiana University Press, 2005.

———. "Strategies of Representations in Collective Biography: Constructing the Subject as Holy." In *Greek Biography*, edited by Hägg and Rousseau, 209–54.

Milobenski, Ernst. *Der Neid in der Griechischen Philosophie.* Klassisch-Philosophische Studien 29. Wiesbaden: Harrassowitz, 1964.

Moerman, Daniel. *Meaning, Medicine, and the "Placebo Effect."* Cambridge: Cambridge University Press, 2002.

Moss, Candida R. and Jeremy Schipper, eds. *Disability Studies and Biblical Literature.* New York: Palgrave Macmillan, 2011.

Der Neue Pauly. Stuttgart: J. B. Metzler, 1998,

Nietzsche, Friedrich. *The Genealogy of Morals.* Translated by Horace B. Samuel. New York: Modern Library, n.d.

Nutton, Vivian. *Ancient Medicine.* Sciences of Antiquity. New York and London: Routledge, 2004.

Oates, John F., Roger S. Bagnall, Sarah J. Clackson, Alexandra A. O'Brien, Joshua D. Sosin, Terry G. Wilfong, and Klaas A. Worp, eds. *Checklist of Greek, Latin, Demotic and Coptic Papyri, Ostraca and Tablets.* http://scriptorium.lib.duke.edu/papyrus/texts/clist.html. April 2004.

Orlandi, Tito. "Coptic Literature." In *The Roots of Egyptian Christianity*, edited by Birger

Pearson and James E. Goehring, 51–81. Studies in Antiquity and Christianity. Philadelphia: Fortress Press, 1986.

Pease, Arthur S. "Medical Allusions in the Works of St. Jerome." *Harvard Studies in Classical Philology* 25 (1914): 73–86.

Pentony, Patrick. *Models of Influence in Psychotherapy.* New York: Free Press, 1981.

Perkins, Judith. *The Suffering Self: Pain and Narrative Representation in the Early Christian Era.* London and New York: Routledge, 1995.

Pilch, John J. *Healing in the New Testament: Insights from Medical and Mediterranean Anthropology.* Minneapolis: Fortress Press, 2000.

Price, Robert M. "Illness Theodicies in the New Testament." *Journal of Religion and Health* 25 (1986): 309–15.

Quasten, Johannes. *Patrology.* 4 vols. Westminster, Md.: Newman Press, 1950.

Rakoczy, Thomas. *Böser Blick, Macht des Auges und Neid der Götter: Eine Untersuchung zur Kraft des Blickes in der griechischen Literatur.* Classica Monacensia 13. Tübingen: Narr, 1996.

Rebenich, Stefan. "Inventing an Ascetic Hero: Jerome's *Life of Paul the First Hermit.*" In *Jerome of Stridon: His Life, Writings, and Legacy,* edited by Andrew Cain and Josef Lössl, 13–27. Farnham, U.K.: Ashgate, 2009.

Regier, Willis G. "Cioran's Nietzsche." *French Forum* 30 (2005): 75–90.

Regnault, Lucien. *La vie quotidienne des Pères du désert en Égypte au IVᵉ siècle.* Paris: Hachette, 1990.

Richter, Tonio Sebastian. ". . . Jealously We Looked at All the Sound Children Who Are Their Parents' Comfort . . .": Pleasant and Unpleasant Emotions in Coptic Legal Documents." Paper presented at the 26th International Congress of Papyrology, Geneva, Switzerland, August 16–21, 2010.

Rose, Martha L. *The Staff of Oedipus: Transforming Disability in Ancient Greece.* Corporealities: Discourses of Disability. Ann Arbor: University of Michigan Press, 2003.

Rosenwein, Barbara H. *Emotional Communities in the Early Middle Ages.* Ithaca, N.Y.: Cornell University Press, 2006.

Rousseau, Philip. "Antony as Teacher in the Greek *Life.*" In *Greek Biography,* edited by Hägg and Rousseau, 89–109.

———. *Basil of Caesarea.* Transformation of the Classical Heritage 20. Berkeley: University of California Press, 1994.

———. *Pachomius: The Making of a Community in Fourth-Century Egypt.* Transformation of the Classical Heritage 8. Berkeley: University of California Press, 1985.

Rubenson, Samuel. "Argument and Authority in Early Monastic Correspondence." In *Foundations of Power and Conflicts of Authority in Late-Antique Monasticism,* edited by Alberto Camplani and Giovanni Filoramo, 75–87. Orientalia lovaniensia analecta 157. Leuven: Peeters, 2004.

———. "'As Already Translated to the Kingdom While Still in the Body': The Transformation of the Ascetic in Early Egyptian Monasticism." In *Metamorphoses: Resurrection, Body and Transformative Practices in Early Christianity,* edited by Turid Karlsen Seim and Jorunn Øklund, 271–89. Ekstasis: Religious Experience from Antiquity to the Middle Ages. Berlin: Walter de Gruyter, 2009.

————. *The Letters of St. Antony: Origenist Theology, Monastic Tradition, and the Making of a Saint.* Bibliotheca Historico-Ecclestiastica Lundensis 24. Lund: Lund University Press, 1990. Reprint, Harrisburg, Pa.: Trinity Press International, 1995.

————. "St. Antony, 'The First Real Coptic Author.'" In *Actes due IVe congrès international des études coptes, Louvain-la-Neuve, septembre 1988,* edited by M. Rassart-Debergh and J. Ries, 16–27. Publications de l'Institut Orientaliste Louvain 41. Louvain: Peeters, 1992.

Sandbach, F. H. *The Stoics.* 2nd ed. Indianapolis: Hackett Publishing, 1989.

Scarry, Elaine. *The Body in Pain: The Making and Unmaking of the World.* New York: Oxford University Press, 1985.

Schutz, Alfred. "On Multiple Realities." In *Collected Papers,* edited by Maurice Natanson, 1:207–59. Phaenomenologica 11. The Hague: Martinus Nijhoff, 1967.

Shaw, Brent D. "Body/Power/Identity: Passions of the Martyrs." *JECS* 4 (1996): 269–312.

Shaw, Teresa. "*Askesis* and the Appearance of Holiness." *JECS* 6 (1998): 485–99.

————. *The Burden of the Flesh: Fasting and Sexuality in Early Christianity.* Minneapolis: Fortress Press, 1998.

Shemunkasho, Aho. *Healing in the Theology of Saint Ephrem.* Piscataway, N.J.: Gorgias Press, 2002.

Silvas, Anna M. *The Asketikon of St. Basil the Great.* Oxford Early Christian Studies. Oxford: Oxford University Press, 2005.

Sontag, Susan. *Illness as Metaphor* and *AIDS and Its Metaphors.* New York: Picador/Farrar, Straus, Giroux, 1990.

Sorabji, Richard. *Emotion and Peace of Mind: From Stoic Agitation to Christian Temptation.* Gifford Lectures. Oxford: Oxford University Press, 2000.

Temkin, Owsei. *Hippocrates in a World of Pagans and Christians.* Baltimore: Johns Hopkins University Press, 1991.

Turner, Bryan S. *The Body and Society: Explorations in Social Theory.* 2nd ed. London: SAGE, 1996.

Urbainczyk, Theresa. *Theodoret of Cyrrhus: The Bishop and the Holy Man.* Ann Arbor: University of Michigan Press, 2002.

Urbano, Arthur, Jr. "'Read It Also to the Gentiles': The Displacement and Recasting of the Philosopher in the *Vita Antonii.*" *Church History* 77 (2008): 877–914.

Valantasis, Richard. "Constructions of Power in Asceticism." *JAAR* 63 (1995): 775–821.

————. "Is the Gospel of Thomas Ascetical? Revisiting an Old Problem with a New Theory." *JECS* 7 (1999): 55–81.

————. "A Theory of the Social Function of Asceticism." In *Asceticism,* edited by Wimbush and Valantasis, 544–52. New York: Oxford University Press, 1995.

van Minnen, Peter. "The Roots of Egyptian Christianity." *Archiv für Papyrusforschung* 40 (1994): 71–85.

van Unnik, Willem C. "Der Neid in der Paradiesgeschichte nach einigen Gnostischen

Texten." In *Essays on the Nag Hammadi Texts in Honour of Alexander Böhlig*, edited by M. Krause, 120–32. Nag Hammadi Studies 3. Leiden, 1972.

Veilleux, Armand. *La Liturgie dans le cénobitisme pachômien au quatrième siècle*. Studia Anselmiana 57. Rome: Libreria Herder, 1968.

Vlahogiannis, Nicholas. "'Curing' Disability." In *Health in Antiquity*, edited by Helen King, 180–91. London: Routledge, 2005.

de Vogüé, Adelbert. "Saint Pachôme et son oeuvre d'àpres plusieures etude récentes." *Revue d'histoire ecclésiastique* 69 (1974): 425–53.

Voytenko, Anton. "Paradise Regained or Paradise Lost: The Coptic (Sahidic) Life of St. Onnophrius and Egyptian Monasticism at the End of the Fourth Century." In *Actes du huitième Congrès international d'études coptes: Paris, 28 juin–3 juillet 2004*, edited by Nathalie Bosson and Anne Boud'hors, 635–44. Orientalia lovaniensia analecta 163. Louvain: Peeters Press, 2007.

Walcot, Peter. *Envy and the Greeks: A Study of Human Behavior*. Warminster: Aris and Philips, 1978.

Ware, Kallistos T. "The Meaning of 'Pathos' in Abba Isaias and Theodoret of Cyrus." *Studia Patristica* 20 (1989): 315–22.

Wazana, Nili. "A Case of the Evil Eye." *Journal of Biblical Literature* 126 (2007): 685–702.

Weingarten, Susan. *The Saint's Saints: Hagiography and Geography in Jerome*. Ancient Judaism & Early Christianity 58. Leiden: Brill, 2005.

White, L. Michael. "Moral Pathology: Passions, Progress, and Protreptic in Clement of Alexandria." In *Passions and Moral Progress in Greco-Roman Thought*, edited by John T. Fitzgerald, 284–321. London: Routledge, 2008.

Williams, Michael A. "The *Life of Antony* and the Domestication of Charismatic Wisdom." In *Charisma and Sacred Biography*, edited by Michael A. Williams, 23–45. *JAAR* Thematic Studies 48.3–4. Chambersburg, Pa.: AAR, 1982.

Williams, Rowan. *Arius: Heresy and Tradition*. Revised ed. Grand Rapids, Mich.: Eerdmans, 2001.

———. *Faith and Experience in Early Monasticism: New Perspectives on the Letters of Ammonas*. Akademische Reden und Kolloquien der Friedrich-Alexander-Universität Erlangen Nürnberg 20. Erlangen-Nürnberg, 2002.

Wimbush, Vincent L., ed. *Ascetic Behavior in Greco-Roman Antiquity*. Studies in Antiquity and Christianity. Minneapolis: Fortress Press, 1990.

Wimbush, Vincent, and Richard Valantasis, eds. *Asceticism*. New York: Oxford University Press, 1995.

Wisse, Frederik. "Language Mysticism in the Nag Hammadi Texts and in Early Christian Monasticism I: Cryptography." *Enchoria* 9 (1979): 101–20.

Yanney, Rodolph. "The Illness and Death of Saint Pachomius." *Coptic Church Review* 13 (1992): 55–58.

Yarbrough, O. Larry. "Canons from the Council of Gangra." In *Ascetic Behavior*, ed. Wimbush, 448–55.

Young, Robin Darling. "Cannibalism and Other Family Woes in Letter 55 of Evagrius of

Pontus." In *The World of Early Egyptian Christianity: Language, Literature, and Social Context. Essays in Honor of David W. Johnson*, edited by James E. Goehring and Janet A. Timbie, 130–39. CUA Studies in Early Christianity. Washington, D.C.: Catholic University of America Press, 2007.

Zovatto, Paolo. "Paolo da Concordia." In *Aquileia e l'Africa*, edited by Sergio Tavano, 165–80. Antichità altoadriatiche 5. Udine: Arti Grafiche Friulane, 1974.

Index

Abraham, 55, 111

abstinence, 63, 94, 96, 192 n.27; moderation in, 98–100

acedia, 98, 100, 132, 149

Adam, 3. See also *Life of Adam and Eve*

Ambrose, Bishop, 78

Ammonius, 18

Amundsen, Darrel W., 33–34

Andrew of Thavatha, 13–14, 139–40, 142, 170, 210 n.72; conflict with fellow monks, 158–63; illnesses of, 145–57, 163–65, 211 n.103

Antonius, 87

Antony, 1, 48–58, 115, 167; attempts to emulate, 104, 106; contrasted with Pachomius, 121; contrasted with Paul, 68–71; demons and, 99; described as feeble, 135–36; Eulogius and, 159; extreme asceticism of, 60–66, 100; good health of, 64–66, 110, 117; longevity of, 134; Origenist theology of, 48–49, 51; sayings of, 27; theology of illness, 51–54, 56–58. See also *Letters* of Antony; *Life of Antony*

apatheia, 150, 152, 210 n.73

Apocryphon of James, 15

Apophthegmata patrum, 6, 51, 85, 102, 105. See also *Sayings of the Desert Fathers*

Aristides, Aelius, 88

asceticism, 23–24, 156–57; of Antony, 60–64; Basil on, 94–95; definition of, 153; demons and, 103–6; excessive asceticism leading to illness, 86, 93, 95–100, 102–6, 118–19, 121–22, 124, 168–70; extraordinary health of ascetics, 4, 13, 37–41, 59–70, 76–80, 82, 101, 111, 154, 167–68, 194 n.83; goal of, 152; illness and, 1–2, 5, 13, 24, 27–30, 35, 81, 156, 164; illness as ascetic practice, 24–28, 88, 101–2, 106–8, 117, 120, 140, 155, 170; martyrdom and, 111; medical view of, 63;

of Pachomius, 112, 121–24, 131–32; spiritual direction and, 138; in Syncletica's teachings, 103–6; utility of illness in, 18, 21, 28–29, 92, 102

ascetic pendulum, 23–24, 39

Asella, 81–82, 84

Athanasius of Alexandria, 101; as author of *Life of Antony*, 1, 8–10, 13, 38, 59–67, 71; as author of *Life of Syncletica*, 10

athumia, 151, 209 n.67

Augustine of Hippo, 10, 78, 185 n.93

Avalos, Hector, 33

Bacht, Henrich, 110

Barash, David, 29

Barsanuphius of Thavatha, 13–14, 28, 139; correspondence with Andrew, 145–65; good health of, 154–55; life of, 141–42. See also *Letters* of Barsanuphius and John

Basil of Caesarea, 10–11, 13, 87–96, 102, 105–7, 132, 167–68; as spiritual director, 138

Benjamin, 16–19, 21, 31, 82

Bitton-Ashkelony, Brouria, 141

Blesilla, 81–85, 107

Brakke, David, 8, 101

Brown, Peter, 40, 110

Burrows, Mark, 110

Burrus, Virginia, 18

Burton, Robert, 171

Cassian, John, 11, 20–23, 79, 93

Chadwick, Henry, 110

Chrysostom, John, 19–23, 31, 79, 93

Cicero, 140

Cioran, E. M., 1–2, 5, 29

Clark, Gillian, 40

Clement of Alexandria, 50

Climacus, John. *See* John Climacus

Acknowledgments

I would like to thank the faculty, administration, and staff of the Department of History and College of Humanities and Sciences at Virginia Commonwealth University, my home for the period in which I wrote this book, including (but not exclusive to) Bernard Moitt, Catherine Ingrassia, Bill Blake, Kathleen Murphy, and Gail Bartee. The William E. and Miriam S. Blake Foundation in the History of Christianity at VCU has been an immensely important source of support for travel for research and conferences, as well as for underwriting the indexing and permissions for the current volume, as has VCU's Presidential Research Incentive Program. The interlibrary loan department at Cabell Library has been extremely helpful in acquiring materials. Selections from Tim Vivian, trans., *Paphnutius, Histories of the Monks of Upper Egypt and the Life of Onnophrius*, CS 140 (1993) are reprinted with permission, copyright by Cistercian Publications, published by Liturgical Press, Collegeville, Minn. Selections from Barsanuphius and John, *Letters, Volume 1*, trans. John Chryssavgis (Washington, D.C.: Catholic University of America Press, 2006) are reprinted with permission from the Catholic University of America Press. Early versions of what are parts of Chapters 2, 3, and 4 in the present volume are published in Oliver Freiberger, ed., *Asceticism and Its Critics: Historical Accounts and Comparative Perspectives* (New York: Oxford University Press, 2006), and the Festschrift for Frederik Wisse (*ARC: Journal of the Faculty of Religious Studies McGill University*, 2005). My earlier reflections have been wholly revised, corrected, augmented, and reconceived for the current versions. My earlier forays into the subject were completed during my tenure at the University of Hawaii, of which Helen Baroni, Robert Littman, Lee Siegel, and S. Cromwell Crawford are due my thanks for their encouragement and friendship over the years. Various components of the present work have been presented at the University of Texas, Holy Cross Greek Orthodox Seminary, the University of Hawaii, the Catholic University of America, Union Presbyterian Seminary, the North American Patristics Society, and the International Conference on Patristic Studies. Thanks to Jim Goehring, Philip

Rousseau, Janet Timbie, Oliver Freiberger, and David Brakke, who have listened to (and sometimes read) various portions of the work in progress for this book and offered helpful critiques or words of encouragement. Thanks also to Dale Martin, who offered some prescient criticisms and advice on a proposal for the book. Special thanks are due to the editors of the Divinations series at the University of Pennsylvania Press and to the Press's two external readers (who later revealed themselves as Peregrine Horden and Caroline Schroeder) for their perspicacious comments on the whole manuscript, to which I have tried to respond as far as my abilities and tastes allow. The book is surely much improved thanks to their generous readings. Thanks are due as well to Jerry Singerman, editor at Penn Press, and Erica Ginsburg, associate managing editor, for guiding the manuscript efficiently through the whole process. Any defects that remain are of course my own. Last, thanks to my family, my wife Heather, and my daughters, Grace and Renna. I began roughly to conceive the book in its current form shortly after Grace's birth in 2005; the period of writing the manuscript coincided with the first two years of Renna's life. I dedicate this volume to them in gratitude for the joy they have given me.